P9-CKX-711

YOUR TABLE
IS READY

YOUR TABLE IS READY

TALES OF A NEW YORK CITY MAÎTRE D'

MICHAEL CECCHI-AZZOLINA

ST. MARTIN'S PRESS

NEW YORK

This is for everyone who has ever worked in a restaurant.

First published in the United States by St. Martin's Press,
an imprint of St. Martin's Publishing Group

YOUR TABLE IS READY. Copyright © 2022 by Michael Cecchi-Azzolina.
All rights reserved. Printed in the United States of America. For information, address
St. Martin's Publishing Group, 120 Broadway, New York, NY 10271.

www.stmartins.com

Designed by Jonathan Bennett

Library of Congress Cataloging-in-Publication Data

Names: Cecchi-Azzolina, Michael, author.
Title: Your table is ready : tales of a New York City maître d' / Michael
    Cecchi-Azzolina.
Description: First edition. | New York : St. Martin's Press, [2022] |
Identifiers: LCCN 2022035063 | ISBN 9781250281982 (hardcover) |
    ISBN 9781250281999 (ebook)
Subjects: LCSH: Cecchi-Azzolina, Michael. | Restaurateurs—United
    States—Biography. | Restaurants—New York (State)—New York.
Classification: LCC TX910.5.C385 A3 2022 | DDC 647.95092 [B]—
    dc23/eng/20220810
LC record available at https://lccn.loc.gov/2022035063

Our books may be purchased in bulk for promotional, educational, or business use. Please
contact your local bookseller or the Macmillan Corporate and Premium Sales Department at
1-800-221-7945, extension 5442, or by email at MacmillanSpecialMarkets@macmillan.com.

First Edition: 2022

10 9 8 7 6 5 4 3

To "Uncle Rob" Dies. Without whose continued encouragement, support, and advice, this book would never have been written.

CONTENTS

YOUR TABLE
IS READY

Introduction

FROM THE MOMENT I trained as a waiter (we'd yet been neutered into *servers*), inexperienced, eager, excited, I fell in love with the restaurant business. Thirty-five years later I'm still at it. I haven't served a table in years, at least not all the way through, yet here I am, still toiling away, greeting guests, overseeing staff, and doing my best to create an environment of good food and great atmosphere and hopefully bring a bit of sustenance and joy to my guests. Restaurants have served as the family I never had. Nothing matches the feeling I get when I am in a packed dining room, the bar full, guests talking, laughing, having a cocktail or a glass of wine while waiting for a meal. I get comfort from the families who come, the couples, the dates, the music, the dim lights, the laughter, conversations, orders being taken, drinks poured, the clatter of plates, the clanging of silverware, glasses tapped together in toast, a bartender's shaker—the sound of the ice and liquor slamming against the top and sides of the tin (I still salivate at the sound)—the arguments, the nasty customers, it's all a grand symphony to me. It's why I love this sometimes-shitty business and why many others like me are drawn to it.

We restaurant workers are a band of misfits, many of us unable to work a "real" job, one in an office or a factory, or the millions of variants we call normal. Many in the business, especially the front of the house, are transient. I never met anyone who grew up wanting to be a server. Most are there because they needed work in college or something temporary because of a lost position, or they are pursuing other careers and take a restaurant job while they wait for something in their desired line of work. And there are those who do this every day and have made a career out of it. To all of you, I tip my hat.

Restaurant jobs are plentiful, and honestly, what does it take to write down *hamburger* on a piece of paper, walk to a machine, punch the order in, pick up the food when it's ready, bring it to the table, drop a check once the meal is finished, then collect the money. You don't need an advanced degree or to be highly intelligent (though many of those I've worked with over the years are incredibly so), though it does take a special sort of person to put up with the long hours, the demands of the customers, the multitasking, the sometimes awful ownership, the shit managerial staff, the abusive chefs and cooks—yet there's a beauty in all of it. A well-run dining room is an art, a ballet, a confluence of pieces that come together to bring a guest a meal.

Our guests come not just for sustenance, but to celebrate—birthdays, anniversaries, a wedding, a death, a date, friends getting together, the pursuit of sex, love, it's all happening on any given night, and on any given night most of my working life has been spent in this environment. I am just a piece in the show. For many years, restaurants enabled me artistically, socially, and sexually. I've met the loves of my life in restaurants, my greatest friends have worked alongside me, and many are still my friends even though the name above the door has changed numerous times for us. I've had trysts, got naked, fucked, laughed, drunk, drugged, puked, and shared the gamut of our human existence in restaurants. It's now time to share these experiences, the people, the food, the insanity of the places so many of us take for granted.

This industry is composed of misfits and losers, artists and drunks, unbelievable beauties, downtrodden addicts, and some of the greediest and most narcissistic people you will ever meet, all counterbalanced with the most generous, loving, hardworking, and creative people on the planet, those of us who create, inhabit, and give life to the hospitality industry. I've spent thirty-plus years working with or have been in the company of some of the best this industry has. Legends that turned American cuisine on its head: Larry Forgione, hailed as the Godfather of American Cuisine; Charlie Palmer, who made it elegant and insightful; David Burke, who built gravity-defying structures of food, turned things upside down, and reinvented what we thought was beautiful;

Rick Moonen; Buzzy O'Keeffe; the Raoul brothers; Keith and Brian McNally; Thomas Keller—the list goes on and on.

Do I love the industry? Yes. Do I hate it? Fuck yeah. This business helped pay the bills, kept me fueled in booze, drugs, and women. Has given me entrée to the richest, the most powerful, the most celebrated of actors, designers, politicians, heads of state, industrialists, stockbrokers, prostitutes, porn stars, alcoholics, millionaires, and billionaires. I've drunk and played with many of them, celebrated with them, fucked some, shared stories, and, most important, welcomed them as who they are—fellow humans with the same desires, drives, wants, and problems we all have. Who am I? I'm your neighborhood waiter, bartender, and maître d'hôtel. I'm the one you come to for a table, the right table, at any time, greeted with a hug and sometimes a kiss—always a smile, treating many of you as if you were my brother, sister, or lover. I love it because it's real, because I love the people who come to me every night. I want to be in their orbit, and because of my position, where I work and have worked, they want to be in mine. I am you. All of you, and you are all of me; we need to escape, celebrate, run, hide, and live. We give one another life.

What follows is my story. As best I can remember, since many of those days are recalled from when I was under a haze of alcohol and drugs. The restaurant industry is not just about truffles and sweetbreads, caviar and cream, a prime fillet of beef or a freshly caught Dover sole. It's also about sex, drugs, and an array of misbehaviors perpetrated by both staff and guests. It's a cutthroat, shitty business, the hours long, the work grueling, at times the only relief being the booze up at the front bar. Sometimes, if you get really lucky, maybe a chance to screw the closing hostess, though that presents its own set of problems. If you've ever dined in a restaurant, partaken of food in its all glories and abominations, if you are a foodie, chef, cook, server, busser, dishwasher, or hungry patron, you've experienced at least some of this, or, I guarantee, you have been in the proximity of it all. It goes hand in hand, from ours to yours. Those EMPLOYEES MUST WASH HANDS signs are no joke—our hands are dirty, very dirty. Will I offend here? I expect so. Most of this book takes place in a very different age from today. The restaurant industry, as many others, has been rocked by abuses of power, horrific sex scandals, and a complete disregard for women. #MeToo is here for a reason, and a very good one. What I chronicle in these pages was of a time, and I write about those times as they were. To edit what happened or to soften some of the details would not be true, nor would it be a representation of the times, which were both amazing and heartbreaking. This is the way it was for me and many of those I have worked with and for.

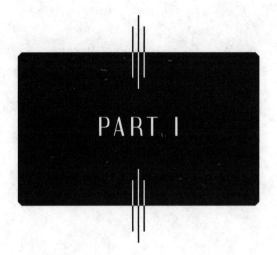

PART I

The James Beard Awards,
Civic Opera House, Chicago, May 1, 2017

THIS IS THE NIGHT the food industry salutes itself, it's our Oscars, our Tonys, and our Grammys. The night when the best of the best are celebrated. Hundreds of restaurant industry stars and professionals are hugging, kissing, glad-handing, or, in the words of the first great maître d'hôtel I worked with, giving each other "zee beeg blow job." Le Coucou restaurant, the creation of Stephen Starr and Daniel Rose, that heralded, new bastion of classic French cuisine in SoHo, New York City, is a finalist for the Best New Restaurant in America. Starr is up for Restaurateur of the Year. This is the seventh time he's been nominated. If he loses this one, he's destined to be the Susan Lucci of the restaurant world. Daniel Rose is the chef of Le Coucou. Me, I am the maître d' of Le Coucou. After thirty years in the business, with a failed acting career along the way, this is the closest to the Academy Awards I will ever get.

Paparazzi are everywhere, cameras clicking as the stars walk down the red carpet. Rachael Ray is leading the Food Network stars and is a presenter. The staff of Chicago's legendary Alinea, as well as those from Blue Hill at Stone Barns, Ken Friedman of Spotted Pig with his posse, unaware of the impending accusations against him, chef Jonathan Waxman, legendary Leah Chase of Dooky Chase's Restaurant in New Orleans, who is receiving the Lifetime Achievement Award—all are here, the biggest and best of the restaurant world. I walk the red carpet because Daniel Rose doesn't want to walk it alone. Rose, a kid from Chicago who left his home country for a failed attempt

3

at the French Foreign Legion, eventually ending up in cooking school, spent ten years honing his craft throughout France before opening up his legendary sixteen-seat Paris restaurant, Spring. While a genius of the sauce and a star in his dining room at Spring, he hates the adulation, the crowd. He'd rather be stirring a sauce in the beautiful movie set of a kitchen he helped create in the back of Le Coucou. Yet here he is, me by his side, flashbulbs popping, the smiles and handshakes, the incredible energy of walking the red carpet into the Civic Opera House. So this is what it's like. I like it. The attention, the acknowledgment. Even if it's not meant for me.

Once the carpet is walked, we enter the grand foyer of the opera house, whose thirty-six hundred seats are sold-out at the steep price of $500 each. Stephen Starr shelled out for at least twenty of them. We are ushered through the lobby and into the gilded and chandeliered auditorium, the space buzzing with the heightened energy of an awards evening. Tuxedoed and gowned, the crowd is befitting of such a grand space. The first inkling that it was going to be a long night was the roped-off lobby, behind which many local restaurants had set up booths to feed and water the crowd. Of the scores of booths, not one was open and nary a bar was in sight. There were rows of unopened bottles, all out of reach and all unavailable. Insanity? *Oui*, chef! The majority of us, we who each day shove copious amounts of food and booze down the throats of millions of Americans, have our tipple at the end of a shift, sometimes in the middle of the shift, and though some sip throughout the night, we professional enablers couldn't get a drop. I can't say I blame the folks at the Beard Awards. Who wants thirty-six hundred or so chefs, cooks, servers, managers, and all the other staff getting wasted? Most would be out in the lobby downing shots and champagne because this crowd never passes up a free drink. They'd only head into the auditorium to see if they'd won or lost. Most couldn't give a fuck about the others. The business is so fragile that, for many, it comes down to only fifty or so guests a week between you and Chapter 11. Win or lose, they'd just head back to the lobby to drink more, either in celebration of the gold medallion hanging from their necks or, as in Starr's case, in consolation for maybe losing once again. There's no in-between in the restaurant business. You're all in or nothing.

No booze for us. We are instead ushered into the great hall to our seats.

Most of the Starr retinue is already there. Two full rows of Starr's directors, managers, VIPs, and such. I needed something to stabilize the anxiety and suddenly remembered the flask handed to me at one of the pre-parties as a commemorative that I'd stuffed into my jacket. Already fueled by a half dozen glasses of bubbles, I didn't at the time have the need to see if the party favor was full. I reach into my tux, pull it out, and open it, and the sweet smell of bourbon fills my nostrils. Thank God. This was going to get me through the next couple of hours. Yes, I was anxious, I wanted this. To be here. To be celebrated. I wanted this, for me, for my team, for every single cook, server, manager, busser, dishwasher, and porter who works tirelessly, endlessly, every single day in restaurants throughout the world. Enduring the abuse, the ridiculously long hours, the constant training, the cooking, the serving, the screaming, the hugs, the kisses, sometimes a blow job in the bathroom or a fuck in the locker room. All after a fifteen-hour day and too many drinks at the end. The everything that goes into creating something that most everyone takes for granted: sitting in a restaurant and eating a meal. The something that has a 60 percent chance of failing the first year and of which 80 percent are closed after five years.

Insane? Probably. Addicting? Yes. For most of us here, this night was big. Every major restaurateur, chef, cookbook writer, manager, sommelier, you name it, was in attendance. This was the percent that had made it, and I wanted to be a part of it. I also wanted to give a big fuck-you to the doubters and naysayers. If we lost, there'd be the sniggers, told-you-sos. "All that money and publicity and they didn't win!" We did have the publicity. Three stars in *The New York Times*, the *New York Post* calling us one of the best restaurants of the century, all the magazine write-ups, it seemed endless. Le Coucou is a $5 million gem. A gorgeous restaurant incredibly lit and designed. Staffed with an army of all the necessary personnel it takes to put out an amazing meal at $150 a head. Minimum. Many restaurateurs are unable to do this. Stephen Starr has the firepower, the cash, the will, and the desire to do it and do it big. This creates a lot of resentment. Hence the seven nominations without a win.

In all fairness, this business is full of great people—those who love the business, the insanity of it, the desire to make people happy. In all my years of doing this, in some of the most heralded restaurants in NYC, I've never seen a response like that of our guests at Le Coucou: "Amazing! Incredible! Best dining experience ever," the giddiness of our guests as they savor classic French dishes, the *quenelle de brochette ris de veau à la tomate* and *tout le lapin*. I hear the accolades night after night. Some guests wait a year for a table and are not disappointed. Many of those in the audience this evening had been to Le Coucou. We were celebrated and singled out at the slew of pre-parties leading up to the awards. Many Chicago restaurant professionals had dined with us and had positive experiences. We'd hear, "Hey, there's the Coucou team! You guys are going to win!" and the like from many in the room. Am I contradicting myself? Nah. The ones who hate you always will.

Did I think we were going to win? Nope. Not a chance. I'm figuring there will be a backlash against our elegance, the millions Starr pumped into the restaurant, and the expat chef, famous in Paris, returning to the Big Apple. Stephen's street cred with the fine-restaurant folk was shit. He is known for big palaces, the Buddakans and Morimotos, his small restaurants in Philly, rip-offs of other people's ideas, but not fine dining. We had gotten so many words already, so much press, I figured there'd be a huge backlash, and that little restaurant in Brooklyn, funky, interesting, quirky, the one with the garden in back, would take it home.

So. Why am I here? For that we need to go back.

The term *maître d'hôtel* translates as "master of the house." It popped up around the sixteenth century and was given to the head servant or butler. We restaurant folk have continued the tradition of servitude for five centuries. It seems the role we currently think of as the maître d'hôtel—that person formally dressed, standing guard at the door, keeping the riffraff out, prowling the dining floor, terrorizing staff, and soaking guests for a good table—appeared in the middle of the nineteenth century. It's generally accepted that the term was cut to just *maître d'* in the 1940s. It seems two accents in one term was too much for Americans to deal with. In Europe this person was usually formally trained at a hotel school and well versed in all aspects of service—from knowing where the fork goes to carving a bird tableside. In the States the role generally went to someone who'd worked his way up, with on-the-job training, from busboy to captain and eventually the master of the dining room.

My uncles always referred to the maître d' of the famous Copacabana club as a god, someone everyone needed to know to get a table. To me, becoming a maître d' was the pinnacle of my restaurant career. The money was great, until, that is, the IRS decided that a maître d'hôtel was in actuality a manager and couldn't be included in the tip pool but had to be salaried. Given that most restaurant owners are among the cheapest people in the world, this wasn't going to fly, and overnight, maîtres d'hôtel went the way of the dodo. Though this may actually have resurrected the dodo since the owners then hired mostly dimwits for minimum wage to stand at the door and greet people. What was once the best-paid position in the dining room soon became the least paid, the duties essentially given over to a moderately paid manager and a team of hosts.

Brooklyn

Everything has a beginning. Mine was in Bensonhurst, Brooklyn, in the sixties. The neighborhood was mostly made up of Southern Italians whose parents or grandparents emigrated from either Naples or Sicily. My mother's mother was from Naples, her father from a small mountain town in Sicily. The best thing my mother got from them was how to cook. She saved the best for Sundays, when the aunts and uncles would come over. I'd wake up early Sunday morning to the smell of garlic and meat frying, the searing of ribs and meatballs in her big cast-iron skillet. She always left three meatballs on the side of the stove for me to eat when I got back from church.

My mother raised me herself. I was the classic latchkey kid and took myself to school from first grade on. I never knew my father. What I did know was that when the conversation between my mother and aunts became hushed, they were talking about him. I'd strain my ears to hear what they said, and from what I did hear, it was never good. He had apparently disappeared when my mother was pregnant and, according to her, reappeared at the hospital the day I was born with the promise of marrying her should she give me his last name. She did; he disappeared and never returned. Not until I found him years later did I learn the truth.

Before anyone came over on Sunday, there was church. I was an altar boy, and every Sunday I'd leave the smell of that kitchen knowing the meatballs my mother set aside would be there when I returned. I hated church. It was an hour or so of kneeling, standing, sitting, kneeling, standing, sitting again, and praying; on and on it went. While my mother made me go every Sunday, the only time she went was for a wedding or a funeral.

Frankie G, one of my buddies from the neighborhood, was an altar boy. He was the smallest, the only one smaller than me, and with a bigger nose. God that kid had a beak. He was born with Jimmy Durante's schnoz. When he entered the altar from the side, his body arrived about three minutes after the entrance of that glorious nose. He convinced me to be an altar boy. He came home one day after serving at a wedding with a five-dollar bill from the best man. It was customary, at the conclusion of the wedding ceremony as the bride and groom exited the church, for the best man to stay behind and pass out bills like he was trying to get a great table at the Copa. The priest got the most, usually $100 handed to him in an envelope. The altar boys got anywhere from one to five bucks. The first palm tip I ever received (a palm for those who, sadly, are not aware is when someone places money in your hand for good service and even more money for a better table) was after the first wedding I served. The best man came over and, with much-practiced skill, slid a five-dollar bill into my hand. Back then five bucks was a fortune! This was my introduction to the service industry.

The church was my theater, wonderfully lit, with the warm glow of the candles, the chandeliers hung low, softly illuminating the congregants beneath. The light shining through the stained-glass windows bathed the entire space in soft hues of green, blue, and red. The mood was enhanced by the statues lining the perimeter, set pieces creating the mood—from the beatific look of the Virgin Mary to the pained and tortured expressions of the martyrs and sinners. This was drama! We were told we were all here to serve God. We knew better. We were there for what we could get. The Italian American ethos of the time was espoused in the words of my uncle Joe: "You get what you can, because if you don't, somebody else will."

Altar boys "serve" at mass. Serving at a mass or serving tables in a restaurant, it's all the same. In restaurants, the first thing you do is go down to the locker room to change into your uniform. At church, I went into the rectory to change into my costume, a beautiful white robe. I loved putting on that robe, it made me feel special. Walking down the aisle, I'd hear the whispered comments from the old ladies: "Look how cute he is! He's adorable!

So handsome!" This was my stage, my moment to shine, to be seen and get what I could. I always tried to serve the later masses. They were the most crowded, and the more people, the more money you made. Had I known the term then, we'd have called the number of worshippers the same name we use in restaurants today, *covers*. The number of guests you begin a shift with is the cover count. Covers mean money. For you, the restaurant, your vendors, et cetera. Covers at mass meant more newspapers to sell and more money in the collection baskets.

Before the mass begins the altar needs to be set. In restaurants, all the work done prior to opening is the pre-shift, the polishing of silver and glassware, setting up linen stocks, folding napkins, setting tables and sweeping floors. Mass was the same. The altar had to be prepared, linens laid out, cruets filled, rugs vacuumed, and the gold plates polished. After the setup, we'd go through the motions of the mass. The endless, boring prayers, the constant kneeling and standing, kneeling and standing, over and over—my knees were chafed for years. We'd then supply the priest with his condiments for the drinking from the chalice of Christ's blood, cheap red wine, and Communion wafers.

There was always a lot of jockeying among the altar boys for the right job. It's like jockeying for the best station in a restaurant. Everyone wanted the cool jobs—filling the cruets, handing the priest the incense holder, and of course carrying the plate to put under the parishioners' chins to catch any dropped hosts. If you didn't get one of these plum positions, you wound up hanging back at the altar and trying your damnedest not to let out a killer yawn. If your job was holding the plate to catch the wafers, you got to see up close all the pretty girls in church that day and smile at all the old ladies from the neighborhood, who would, seeing your angelic presence in those damn white robes, get you an extra quarter every time they asked you to run errands for them. We were always looking for tips. By the time I started in restaurants I was already well versed in earning money from the guests.

At the end of the mass we'd retrieve the offering baskets, round wicker baskets with long wooden arms like broomsticks, used to reach across the pews to collect donations. You'd walk down the aisle and pass the baskets, each person dropping in offerings, from coins to dollar bills. Once finished, we'd take the baskets back behind the altar and dump the money into a big pot. One of us,

YOUR TABLE IS READY   11

usually the oldest altar boy, would skim a few bucks off the top. Then, once mass ended, we'd run outside and sell *The Tablet*, the Catholic newspaper. We'd each take a bunch of copies and stand outside the church, shouting, "*Tablet, Tablet*, ten cents a copy!"—staying till we sold out. Once back in the rectory we had to count out all the money we earned and hand it over. We always made sure we'd keep at least $1. We'd skim from both the baskets and *Tablet* money to reach the magic number.

Once finished, we'd head over to the candy store on the corner and sit at the counter. Frankie G and I would get two orders of buttered toast and two cups of coffee. The only toast you ever ate was white bread, and they always buttered it for you while it was piping hot, steam rising from the two diagonally cut slices, the warm butter oozing out the middle. This was my madeleine. We'd take the perfect piece of toast and dunk it into the creamed and sugared coffee. Years later, I'd hear chef David Burke refer to this simple deliciousness as "good eating."

As we got older, the coffee and toast became the after prize. Once mass ended, we'd do our best to beat the priest back to the rectory. We'd steal a bottle of unopened wine, a bag of unconsecrated hosts to snack on, and skim the pot for seven bucks. The extra five was to buy a nickel bag of pot, which we'd score from one of the older kids who always came to mass with pot to sell. We'd then hide behind the church, get high, drink a bit of wine, and finally head to the candy store for our toast and coffee, which was now even more delicious since we were high out of our minds.

Returning home from church, the first thing I'd see as I turned down my block were the double-parked Cadillacs. These belonged to my uncles, cousins, and family friends, all headed to my house for the Sunday meal. It was an unspoken rule on the block that if you needed to use your car that day, you'd better not park it on the side of the street where we lived. The Cadillac Eldorados and Coupe de Villes were all in a line, blocking any car that was legally parked. My uncles and their friends—always well-dressed, in tailored suits, shoes shined to a mirror finish, black or brown fedoras atop the heads of the older ones, slicked-back hair for the younger ones—were all connected in some way to the Mob. They'd unload the boxes of cakes, pastries, loaves of bread, wine, and Dewar's Scotch and leave their cars there. No one in the house worried about the illegally double-parked cars, since every few hours a cop car would cruise down the block to make sure the cars were safe. These guys were connected, and, as Uncle Joe always said, "One hand washes the other." They weren't the mobsters with the money and cachet flouted by John Gotti and the like. These guys were the type played by Al Pacino in the film *Donnie Brasco*. His character, Benjamin "Lefty" Ruggiero, was the sad-sack mobster, living in a shabby apartment with never enough money and always wanting to be what he wasn't and never could be, a *capo di capo*. These were my role models.

These Sundays are when I first began to serve and bartend. The men would settle in the living room, put on the game, light up their cigarettes, start dealing gin rummy or poker and wait to be served. They all smoked. A lot. My mother and many of the others would later die of lung cancer. Once the men sat, drinks and food had to be served and ashtrays needed to be emptied. This is when I'd get to work. I'd serve the food, pour shots of Dewar's, empty ashtrays, and listen to the stories and cursing as the gin rummy game commenced. I'd get everyone what he needed and, when the men finished, clear or "bus" the plates and glasses. I'd take the used shot glasses to a corner, combine all the little drops of Scotch left in the bottom of each glass, and make myself a little shot. I'd hold my breath and down it.

The Mob was a constant in my life during these years. My mother worked as a secretary in a real estate office. I'd spend days there during the summer months since she couldn't afford a sitter or camp. The four large brown desks in the office were each topped with a sheath of glass, and they were always littered with papers. The office smelled of old wood and cigarettes. I'd hang out in the office or outside, the summer heat excruciating, the days interminable. Except for Fridays. One desk at the front of the office looked out onto the street and was always unoccupied except on Friday, when "Uncle Joe" would enter like a celebrity, a huge smile on his face, kissing everyone on the cheek. He wasn't my real uncle Joe. My mother had me call him that, and it always insured a crisp dollar bill was handed to me. He'd come into the office and shout "Mikey!," pinch my cheek so hard I thought he was ripping it off, and thrust that dollar bill into my hand. He'd then sit at the front desk, which meant we were open for business. People would line up outside the office for the opportunity of speaking to him for a few minutes. In they'd come, one by one, for a whispered conversation with him. None stayed longer than a few minutes.

When it came time for lunch, he'd grab me and say, "Mikey, let's go eat!" Lunch was at the Nineteenth Hole, a bar around the corner. We'd enter and find a group of men, most wearing fedoras and smoking cigarettes. They'd come up to him one by one, kiss him on both cheeks, and sometimes whisper in his ear for a few seconds. This ritual would be repeated each week, and to me seemed the most reasonable thing in the world since I assumed he gave them all crisp dollar bills. There I'd sit atop the bar, the room dark for noontime, in the midst of all these men in their hats and suits, cigarettes dangling from their mouths, the smell of Scotch on their breath, and we'd have lunch. He'd order, shouting to the barman, "And don't forget the usual for Mikey!" My usual was the most delicious pot roast sandwich I have ever had and till this day have not had an equal. A white oval plate would come with a half loaf of crusty Italian bread stuffed with slices of pot roast and piping-hot gravy, the aroma of cooked meat wafting through the bar and cutting through the cigarette smoke. The meat tender, with a generous pouring of gravy, almost sweet with a tang of salt at the end. I loved it. I loved lunch with Uncle Joe, the men, the laughter, and the stories. This was my mother's living room all over again, this is what I knew as family. These moments, the camaraderie, the booze, the food, and the smoke, would become my life in the restaurant business.

Uncle Joe would create an organization called the Italian American Civil Rights League. He'd have my mother give me pamphlets and buttons from the organization to hand out in the neighborhood. Years later, as I was having breakfast at the counter of the East Village coffee shop Veselka, I picked up the paper and saw on the front page of the *Daily News* the headline COLOMBO SHOT—FIGHTS FOR LIFE. There on the front page was my uncle Joe, the apparent head of the Colombo crime family, shot at an Italian American Civil Rights League rally. I had no idea he was the head of the Colombo crime family, one of the legendary five Mafia families of New York. Now it all made sense.

As I read the article, the association brought me back to when my mother and I had briefly moved to Miami. She'd gotten a bookkeeping job at the Singapore Hotel, situated directly across from the luxurious Bal Harbour on Collins Avenue in Miami Beach. Again on Fridays, an elderly gent would come down to the office, and my mother would go to the safe and pull out an envelope to give to him. He said little and on his way out would hand me a dollar bill and leave. It was the legendary mobster Meyer Lansky, who was one of the owners of the hotel. I am certain few people in the world can say they were palmed by both Meyer Lansky and Joe Colombo. Years later I would learn how deep this Mafia connection was to my life.

All the neighbors knew not to interrupt anyone at my house by asking him to move his car. The one time this happened, a friend of a neighbor came knocking to ask that a car be moved so he could get his out. Unfortunately, the offending car was owned by a gangster named Mugsy. The men, as usual, were in the living room playing poker. Mugsy was losing heavily. He'd already had quite a few Scotches when one of my aunts interrupted the game to say a neighbor was outside and needed to move his car, which was blocked by Mugsy's. She may as well have told him his mother was found murdered in the street. You could see the anger rising in his face as he cursed, slammed down the cards, and went to the door.

What then happened could have been a scene right out of the film *Good-fellas*. All the men followed Mugsy out, stood on the porch, and watched as he walked over to the guy who was standing by his car, and said, "This is the piece of shit you drive? This is what you want me to move my fucking car for?" Mugsy then goes to his trunk, pulls out a lug wrench. and proceeds to smash in all the windows of the guy's car. "Now get your piece-of-shit car off this block!" Mugsy pulled his car out of the way, tires screeching, to let the guy out, then followed him down the block to make sure he wasn't coming back. The one thing you didn't do to these guys was disrespect them.

Fran and Lou's

FRAN AND LOU'S CANDY Store was a narrow sliver of a store that served my Bensonhurst neighborhood in ways the barbershop and drugstore must have in small-town America. The candy store was actually a luncheonette. Each neighborhood had at least one, but some had a half dozen or more. Aptly named after the owners, Fran and Lou, the candy store provided the neighborhood with cigarettes, newspapers and magazines, breakfast, lunch, and the opportunity to bet on a horse or a sporting event, as well as serving ice cream, egg creams, and malteds. You also got to hear the local gossip, and the chance to either run into or hide from your neighbor.

I knew almost nothing about Fran or Lou, where they came from, how they started the business, what unfortunate circumstances led them to fall in love, and why the fuck they still lived under the same roof. By the time I met them, they hadn't spoken to each other in years and the hate had dissipated into complete indifference. Lou, mid-fifties, had thinning red hair slicked back, and the few strands of it that remained were not enough to cover his freckled scalp. He was slightly stooped, always in a clean sports shirt, with the smell of Dewar's perpetually on his breath—a slight scent in the morning that built to a malodorous stench by evening. Lou could knock off a fifth of the stuff on a good day and, on the more difficult days, put a good dent in the second. His wife, Fran, similar in age, was the prototypical Brooklyn "broad" right out of central casting—large of breast, teased blond bouffant, makeup so thick it looked troweled on, chewing gum at the ready, and a thick, guttural Brooklyn accent made thicker by years of cigarette smoke.

The store was a gold mine. All transactions were made in cash. Customers were in and out of the store all day, purchasing newspapers and magazines, candy and cigarettes, egg creams and malteds, and having their breakfast or lunch at the long counter that ran the length of the store. The man himself, Lou, took charge from morning till early evening. He stationed himself at the front of the store behind a window that remained open in warm weather and closed in winter, but always slid open to give the never-ending line of customers what they needed. As you entered the store, a rack to the right was stacked with almost any periodical you'd ever want, from *Popular Mechanics* to *Playboy*. The latter stacked discreetly at the very top of the rack with all the other nudie magazines, so as to discourage browsing kids and, one would assume, short people. The two small green vinyl booths opposite the lunch counter were now used mostly for storage and Fran herself. Actual customers hadn't sat in one of the booths for years.

As the day progressed, Lou would put more and more of a dent in the bottle of Dewar's he kept under the counter, which he'd pour into and sip from a coffee cup. He usually finished by five or six, and as he was leaving, Fran would swoop in, head kerchiefed, in big dark sunglasses, makeup box in hand, and head over to her booth. Never was a word spoken between the two as they switched shifts. She'd commandeer the front booth, unpack the huge makeup bag, and from 6:00 to 11:00 P.M. do her hair and makeup. There she sat each evening, staring at herself in her battery-lit, gold-trimmed makeup mirror, applying various powders and tinctures, raising her head when the front door opened to scan each and every person that entered. You knew she had something serious to say when she looked up from the mirror and actually eyeballed the person she was speaking to. Fran putting her face on was a process akin to Leonardo painting the *Mona Lisa*, Michelangelo imagining the *David* from a piece of stone, the building of the Verrazzano Bridge, steel girder by steel girder. She only stopped to go to the bathroom or sip her coffee through a straw. Dinner would be later when her mobster boyfriend came to pick her up in his Cadillac, always at eleven and always on time. Her evening was a continuous monologue to any and all who entered the store—cursing this one, greeting that one, gossiping with another, all while never missing a stroke of putting on the many layers that would get her to that place of beauty where she knew she looked good enough to hit the town with her guy. We never knew where they went or what they did, and no one ever asked.

At the back of the store were two telephone booths and beyond that the bathroom. From his post at the front window, Lou spent the day kibitzing with the regulars and shouting out to-go orders to the two potbellied, balding short-order cooks, Hymie and Heshie, whose employment harkened back to the store's opening. Both had aged as badly as the store. Hymie, the fatter of the two, hair once red, had the classic baldness pattern redolent of monks, his face redder than his hair once was, and sprouted a W. C. Fields nose. Heshie was the shorter and wore thick-framed black glasses. His expression was a constant resigned look of "Whaddya gonna do," no matter the subject he was expostulating on. He spoke with a New York accent so thick you could cut it like a Carnegie Deli pastrami sandwich. His hyperopia so severe, that even with the glasses, he was in a perpetual bent-over position to get as close as possible to be able to see what was right in front of him. These two seemingly knew every single person that had sat at that counter for the past forty years, constantly dispensing wisdom and arguing with the customers over the local sports teams, marriages both good and bad, kids, politicians, movie stars, mobsters, and life. These two were the local sages, their words trusted and rarely called into question.

My introduction to the candy store came from Johnny, one of my neighbors on the block. He was a true Brooklyn character, a hulk of a human given his Italian roots. His girth matched his five-foot-eight height, and if not for his unbelievable speed and athletic prowess, he'd have been called fat and teased relentlessly for it. His legend was established the day he beat the shit out of a kid that was the head of a rival gang in our neighborhood. I was always the smallest kid on the block, the runt, and Johnny was like a big brother to me, my protector. He began working at Fran and Lou's when he was fifteen and hired to put together the Sunday newspapers.

On Saturday afternoon, the newspaper trucks would pull up to the front of the store and the drivers would throw bundles of papers on the sidewalk, each wrapped with a thin piece of wire and containing the Sunday sections of the *Daily News* and *The New York Times*. These sections were printed beforehand since they never contained breaking or timely news. Once built, each paper would measure at least half a foot thick. There were early editions and late editions. The early edition would be for the bettors, the guys who wanted the horse results and the numbers. The "numbers" were played by most everyone in the neighborhood, from racketeers to grandmothers, and serviced by the local bookies.

The "number" everyone was betting on was actually three numbers. These were the last three digits of the total mutual handle at Aqueduct Racetrack, which was found at the bottom of that day's racing results and published daily in the *Daily News*. Customers would begin lining up outside the store at about eight thirty every evening. The bettors waiting for the early edition of the *Daily News*, which got dropped off around 9:00 P.M., to check the numbers and the horse-racing results. The late edition, which was printed with the day's final news, would be dropped off around midnight.

Business was booming, and this is where I came in. On Saturday evenings, the queue for the Sunday paper had become so substantial, the number of papers to build so overwhelming, that Johnny, seeing me one day on the block, said he'd be needing help at the candy store and would I be interested. I ditched my shitty paper route and jumped on the opportunity. Thirteen-year-old me, already a rogue altar boy, stealing from the poor box, swiping the wine and Communion wafers, was hired to assist a neighborhood legend with the papers. I'd show up about seven and help with the stacking. Once the last sections were dropped off, I'd rush the completed copies to the window, where Lou, who always worked a double shift on Saturday, stood. By then he'd be well into his second fifth of Dewar's and would be hammered, barely able to stand, let alone count the money. He'd be screaming at me to hurry up and bring more papers, berating his customers for taking too much time to take the cash out of their pockets, or just plain insulting anyone he could. This was my first experience dealing with an alcoholic, maniacal, and angry owner. This scene would continue till the late or final edition would be dropped off at around 11:30 P.M. The last paper was usually stuffed by 12:30 A.M. A perfect time to call it quits, since that's when the bakery truck would pull up and drop off the cakes for the Sunday sales. The driver would bring the cakes in—

French crullers, cheesecakes, and assorted pastries for the morning opening. The driver would always spend several minutes trying to collect money from the now totally wasted Lou. My job was to sneak into the back of the truck and make off with boxes of sweets while Johnny stalled the bakery driver. My restaurant career had officially begun.

The busiest times at the store were breakfast and lunch; the place filled with Brooklyn denizens and misfits. There were the regulars. An old woman with long, single hairs jutting out from her face would sit at the counter, always dressed in a thin beige wool coat no matter what the weather, her nylons rolled down to her ankles, her shoes, beaten-up red high heels, the leather peeling off the sides. She'd sit there, muttering to herself, while hunched over a cup of coffee. Lou would let her sit for hours and, as far as I knew, never charged her. There was Sam the Shylock, a Hagrid-looking man, large and beastly, who wore a ratty long brown overcoat even in summer. A banged-up brown fedora was always atop his head as he incessantly chomped on an unlit cigar. After he had a stroke, he'd still show up to take bets from the back phone booth, the juice from his chewed cigar dripping down his chin, his partially paralyzed face making it impossible for him to swallow the spittle. He'd squeeze his large frame into a phone booth, and since he was never able to fully close the door, the entire store could hear him taking bets. Everyone knew the phone was off-limits during betting hours. He'd repeat this twice a day, for daytime and nighttime bets, phone dangling from his ear, nodding and repeating back what callers bet for the day. There were the three guys who sat at the counter, talking horses and sports all day long, one on disability, one retired, one chronically unemployed, always a story, a complaint, a joke.

The more wasted Lou got on Saturday, the more apparent the double shift he did was going to kill him. I think he realized this when he tapped Johnny to cover the evening shift at the "front," as it was called. My first understanding of what *front of house*, or *FOH*, actually is. Johnny was so good at running Saturdays that he was soon promoted to night manager, a move that was either genius or destructive, depending on how one counts one's losses. With Lou at the helm, two bottles of Dewar's in, it was a recipe for disaster. Johnny was certainly the lesser of two evils.

With Johnny fully ensconced as the night manager, my place at the store was solidified. I'd run errands, do deliveries, pick up money for Sam the Shy, sweep outside, put away stock. Whatever was needed, I was there to do it.

Then it finally happened. On a quiet Saturday afternoon I was hanging around waiting for possible deliveries when the fountain kid, Howie "the Jew," called out sick. I was all of thirteen, hair just beginning to appear under my arms, on my legs and balls, and I was about to do one of the most exciting things of my young life—man the soda station. It mattered little that I had no experience. I walked behind that counter and put on a white apron, which I needed help tying since I had no idea how to put on an apron that was big enough to wrap twice around my skinny body. I was so small you could barely see me standing behind the counter. The soda spigots so towered above my head that I had to stand on tiptoes to pull the handles back. I manned those spigots like a gunner on the USS *Iowa*. I may have looked like a baby, but I culled all my bartending experience with my uncles into this moment. It apparently went well because I was soon doing Saturdays regularly, day shift into the night, and a couple other nights as well. The fountain was mine and I took ownership of it. Those spigots gleamed, the counter in front of me spotless, and after putting a milk crate on the floor in front of the spigots to stand on, I now towered over them as I made my concoctions. I made it. I was one of the "boys."

Months later, after I was promoted to short-order cook, I was schooled by Hymie on how to break down the entire cook station. He trained me like he was preparing a recruit for the invasion of Normandy: scrub the grill (seltzer the key ingredient); wipe down the refrigerators, making sure to get out all the spilled milk, crumbs, and mouse poop (a sweet and plentiful family of mice had taken residence there); clean the pans and sinks; rid the meat slicer of the day's bits of meat; wipe the cutting board and knives; clean out the prep table, which was filled with meats and garnishes; scrub the sinks and wipe away as much grease as possible; wrap and store the leftover food; restock whatever was low or missing; and leave everything clean, neat, and orderly. My first night of breaking down the station, fearing Hymie's wrath if I did it incorrectly, I scrubbed everything as instructed. I left no detail unfinished, no surface unscrubbed or degreased, every crumb picked up and accounted for, all the garnishes wrapped and put away, so much so that the cleanup was probably longer than my actual shift. I even went above and beyond and took the two cast-iron fry pans, which looked like they had never been cleaned, and gave them a going-over. I took these horribly aged pans, their undersides caked with grease, dotted with what looked like tumors or warts, and scoured them like I was polishing the queen's silver. After at least thirty minutes of using soap, steel wool, and knives to pry off the built-up warts, I succeeded in making these two old warhorses look like my uncle's Cadillacs: shiny, glowing machines of sex and power, ready to fry eggs well into the next century.

When I came in the next day for my shift, ready to reap the praises of a labor never before seen in Fran and Lou's Candy Store, I suspected something was amiss when I spotted Lou at his post at the front. He had a sick and maniacal smirk on his face, almost gleeful. It being 3:00 P.M., I assumed it must have been a rough day, as he was well into the second bottle of Dewar's. That's when I saw it coming—that beautiful little cast-iron fry pan that I'd slaved over the previous night was heading toward me like a Whitey Ford fastball, narrowly missing my head and wiping out a row of magazines behind me. Hymie stood there glaring at me, red-faced, apoplectic with rage, chef's knife in hand, screaming something mostly unintelligible, but by the tone of it I knew he was going to kill me. He lunged at me from over the counter, and the ever-present Sam the Shylock pushed me out the door and told me to run for my life. Lou's bellowing, drunken laughter was all I could hear over Hymie's screams. My transgression? Those two little cancerous-looking egg pans were not cancerous at all, but, well-seasoned tools that after twenty or so years of service would put out the perfect eggs, over and over, with no sticking or breaking, little gems of breakfast perfection. As I was later informed, washing them destroyed the "seasoning" of the pans and made everything stick, caused the restaurant to waste dozens of eggs, deal with an irate breakfast crowd, and make Hymie's morning absolutely miserable. Little did I know that this would not be the first time a chef was going to want to kill me.

I was now working regularly at the candy store. This was my home, the place where I did it all—made money, met girls, connected with the neighborhood people, got high in the basement, became known, and had some local renown. Once Johnny had the trust of Fran and Lou, it became somewhat of a free-for-all as to who could get what. This was a cash business and the cash kept coming. Lou would keep all the cash in the till, which was a white money sack hidden behind the cigarette cartons under the window where he stood. At the end of the day he'd take the bundle with him and take it to the bank. On the two-bottle Dewar's days, he'd sometimes forget and leave the day's receipts in the register, which would then be added to the night business. Once the cash register was full, the front person would bundle the bills and put them in the till. On a busy Saturday this might happen two or three times, the till stuffed and overflowing with cash.

There was a marked change in Johnny's financial outlook once he was firmly ensconced as the night manager. This high school dropout was soon driving around in a 1965 GTO. I finally put two and two together and realized he was regularly helping himself to the till. Items sold through the front window were never rung in. This was a cash business and I assume Lou reported as little to the IRS as possible. When it came time to count the money and drop it in the till, Johnny would always wrap a few bundles of cash to keep for himself. With Lou's drinking and Fran's indifference to anything but her makeup and local gossip, a few hundred dollars here or there was never noticed nor missed. I soon got into the act and we started a little side work. We recruited Eddie, a neighborhood legend, to be our getaway and delivery driver. The bakery truck was the first of our little businesses. When the truck pulled up, we'd wait for the driver to enter the candy store, and one of us would act as a lookout, while another took a few boxes of pastries and brought them to Eddie's car. We then expanded to ice cream and soda deliveries. As we unloaded the deliveries and brought them to the basement, we'd make sure some went to Eddie's car.

Our most lucrative side job was cigarettes. The delivery truck would pull up outside the store, and we'd bring in the cases, putting them in the back, just past the phone booths, where they'd be ready to be stacked in the storage area just above. We'd get a ladder, which one of us would sit atop, while the other unpacked the cases below and passed the cartons of cigarettes to the person above, who would stack them by brand. As we stacked the cigarettes, Howie, usually atop the ladder, would have our little order sheet and would toss what we needed into the phone booth below, while I stood in front of the ladder, blocking anyone who might head back or be able to see our stash piling up in the booth. We'd load up the back phone booth with cartons of cigarettes and, once finished, get the big trash can that would always need to be put out around this time and fill it with the cartons of cigarettes, cover it with trash, and wheel it outside where Eddie would be waiting with his car. We'd dump the cigarettes into his trunk and off he'd go to fill the orders and collect the cash. Years later I learned that putting contraband in the trash bins to be taken out was a common way of getting stolen goods out of a restaurant.

There was another way of getting a few bucks—Saturday nights. Howie and I figured out that on this night there would be so much cash that we should be able to cut ourselves in on the action. By 10:30 P.M. the till was always overflowing with cash from Friday night's receipts, Saturday's lunch, and any drops Johnny had made from the early business. Once the rush from the early business had ended, like clockwork Johnny would head to the toilet. Fran would be reaching the final lap of her makeup application and was not to be bothered to cover the front, lest she be interrupted from completing her masterpiece. Johnny would call me over to cover the now-unsupervised front, exit from behind the cash register, grab the *Daily News* and the *Post*, and head to the toilet. This would give us about a fifteen-to-twenty-minute window to get our work done. Even better was when I'd see him sneak a porno mag in between the papers. This would guarantee a longer stay, since he'd jerk off as well as take a shit. As I stood at the window behind the register, Howie would get on all fours, crawl behind me, pull out the till, and count it to see how much we thought we could get without anyone knowing. We had to factor in how much Lou had drunk that day, how much Johnny would steal, and what made the most sense. This took about ten minutes, and on a good night we might get thirty to fifty bucks each.

This one evening, the signs were all aligned for a good haul. Fran was deep into her makeup, Johnny was in the toilet, hopefully with his dick in his hand, and we were set. Howie is down on all fours behind me counting away, when suddenly Johnny comes out of the bathroom. To warn Howie, I lifted my leg to kick him, but in my fear I kicked too hard and smashed the bottom of my foot into his nose. He let out a muffled yelp as the blood started gushing out. As Johnny turned the corner, Howie was able to back away just in time and head to the toilet to clean himself up. It was worth the bloodshed. We netted a hundred bucks.

My last year at the candy store we were able to expand our business, thanks to the beneficence of New York's finest. Lorenzo the Fag's brother was a cop and would regularly bring home drugs he'd appropriated from busts. Depending on that day's perpetrator, there'd be pot, acid, quaaludes, Seconal, and Tuinals. These party drugs were in great demand. Pot, acid, and quaaludes were the big sellers in high school, and everything was in play in the gay community. Lorenzo handled the gays, and I took care of the high school kids. Suddenly every high school kid in the neighborhood was lining up for egg creams. They'd come into the store, sit at the counter, and get served an egg cream, and under a napkin would be their drug of choice. Business was brisk. I had two ten-speed bikes, a 3.5 hp minibike, clothes, and enough drugs to get me through my adolescence.

Then things turned progressively bad—the city was in shambles, crime out of control, the police were corrupt, rapes and burglaries had tripled in just a few years, murders jumped from 681 to 1,690 in a year, and the subways were deadly—no one we knew took them at night. There were race riots in the high schools, mine included, and by noon we'd all leave the school building to get high and sell drugs with absolutely no repercussions. The school wasn't safe and we were better off outside. Two of my friends had overdosed, and Lorenzo, high on pills and driving a stolen car, ran down two elderly people and was arrested. The streets were violent—you were always one step ahead of someone looking to either steal from you or beat the shit out of you.

Then one night I had an awakening. A few of us had dropped acid, and for some reason I was separated from the others. The sun was just coming up and I was on my hands and knees in my elementary school schoolyard. I was crawling around on the pavement, convinced the pebbles in the cement were a message from God. No matter how hard I tried, I couldn't read them, couldn't figure out what they said, but I was sure God was trying to tell me something profound and life changing. The next day I understood what it was. I was seventeen and going nowhere. If I stayed where I was, I'd probably be arrested or overdose like the others. I needed to get out. I had a cousin who was like a sister to me and had moved to Hollywood Beach, Florida. She always said I had an open invitation to come live with her. In a week I was there.

PART II

Back to the City

I finished high school in Miami. One day a friend shoved a *Playboy* magazine in my face, pointed to where the University of Florida had just been voted the number one party school in the country, and said that's where we were going. Since I had no plans, it seemed like a good idea to me. We both applied and were accepted. The university lived up to its billing. After a first year of continual partying and pretty poor grades, I turned it around and got serious about school, achieving decent grades, and discovered theater. The local Hippodrome Theatre was seeking actors for a show, and after spending hours preparing a monologue for my first-ever audition, I got a part. Turns out my first role had little to do with my excellence in the performing arts, unless you count streaking naked across the stage with twelve other young actors performing. What better way to draw an audience than having a bunch of eighteen-to-twenty-year-olds parade naked across your stage. This led to a four-year stay at the theater, including doing some actual acting and, perhaps more important, meeting the person who would get me my start in the restaurant business.

A few months into the start of the theater season, we were told that the theater was going to be audited for a potential National Endowment for the Arts grant. This was a huge deal for us. Getting a grant would put this upstart little theater on the map and provide some much-needed cash. The audit was performed by Robert Moss, then the producing director of Playwrights Horizons in New York City. He inspected the theater, took in a show, and was wined and dined by the theater's directors. He apparently liked what he saw, and the Hippodrome was put on the map, soon to be recognized as the State Theatre of Florida. While I never got to meet him during his stay, I made sure to remember his name and that of Playwrights Horizons. Soon, both would change my life.

Acceptance to the master's program in the English Department at NYU was my ticket back home. Once my student loan money came through, I set about searching for an apartment. Vacancy rates in Manhattan at the time were 1 percent, which meant snagging an affordable apartment in this storied borough was nearly impossible, even though the city was broke and crime at an all-time high. But there was no way I was going back to Brooklyn. Despite the odds, I was intent on getting an apartment in Manhattan.

The Village Voice newspaper was where you looked for the cheaper apartments. I'd scan the offerings, circle the ones that seemed both affordable and in a decent neighborhood, then head over to check them out. But by the time I showed up, they were either already rented or the line waiting to see the apartment was at least twenty people long. After a week or so of this, I realized this method was futile and I needed to come up with a better way.

I tried everything I could think of. I sniffed out the locals, attempting to charm anyone with an apartment to help me get a place in his or her building. I checked the obituaries, cross-checking the names of the deceased with their addresses in the phone book and if they had lived in a somewhat affordable area. Then I'd head to the building, suss out the super, and offer to pay him off if the apartment was still available. I'd wait at the newsstand at the crack of dawn for the papers to arrive, scan the ads, and head over to the most likely apartment, which in my case meant the one that cost the least. My best idea was calling *The Village Voice* to see where the first drop of the Wednesday paper was. It turned out to be the Astor Place newsstand, which is still around today. For a couple of weeks I was the first person there. But others soon caught on (although I still think I was the first to come up with this), and by the third or fourth week about twenty people were ahead of me waiting for the drop.

After three months of looking I saw an ad—in the venerable *New York Times* no less—an East Village one-bedroom for $250 a month. Everyone told me to avoid the East Village because it had deteriorated. Many of the buildings were burned-out, crime and drug use were excessive, and the old tenement buildings that had been a refuge for turn-of-the-century immigrants were in massive disrepair and infested with vermin. All true, but I was desperate. I had seen so many apartments, most unlivable, with broken walls, appliances that didn't work, and basically closets that were called studios. One so-called apartment was over by NYU, in the basement of a building, and was a former storage room converted into what they called a studio. There was a dorm-size refrigerator and hot plate and the place could be yours for the discounted price of $200 a month if you also agreed to mop the hallways and take out the building's garbage. I passed. Another apartment was in a building on Second Street where my cousin Eddie had, at age twenty-one, overdosed and died in the hallway from the heroin he had just purchased from a dealer who lived in the building.

I spent the entire day calling the East Village landlord until someone finally picked up and we made an appointment for the following day. The apartment was on East Sixth Street in the East Village. As I walked over to see the apartment, I realized this was the block where my cousin Richie was murdered. A former junkie, he ran into some guys he owed money to, and they beat him to death on the street, about two doors down from where I stood. Despite the history, I took a look at the apartment. It was a typical East Village tenement, small, tub in the kitchen, windows that rattled with the slightest breeze, and crooked floors. It was perfect. I was home again.

Playwrights Horizons

ROBERT MOSS WAS A successful Broadway stage manager who parlayed a vivacious and engaging personality, laborious attention to detail, and massive ambition into creating Playwrights Horizons on Theatre Row. He, among very few others, saw the value of converting the boarded-up whorehouses on Forty-second Street between Ninth and Tenth Avenues into what became and is still today Theatre Row. With André Bishop, who is now the artistic director of Lincoln Center Theater, they turned Playwrights Horizons into one of the most important and renowned off-Broadway theaters. I telephoned Playwrights Horizons, was put through to Bob, gave him my name, and said we had met (not true). I let him know I was now at NYU, had five years' experience at the Hippodrome, and was looking to work in the theater. He invited me for an interview. It went well and I was immediately hired as his assistant. Well, sort of. I got a job, something of a title—assistant to the producing director—and zero salary.

Playwrights was rocking at the time. A year or so earlier, Richard Gere had left mid-rehearsal to become a star in the film *Looking for Mr. Goodbar*. Writers James Lapine, Ted Tally, Bill Finn, Christopher Durang, and Albert Innaurato had their works in development or performed there. While I was thrilled to be in the midst of this, there was one nagging problem. I was broke. But Bob didn't want to lose me, and one day he walked in the office and asked if I'd ever waited tables. I told him of my soda-jerk/short-order-cook experience at the

YOUR TABLE IS READY   31

candy store, which he seemed to think was enough. He told me he was getting me a job.

La Rousse restaurant was directly adjacent to the theater in another former whorehouse. The last remnant of those former days was a beautiful mural on the wall of a nude with red hair, lying on her back. The place was previously the French Palace, where for the ripe sum of $10 "complete satisfaction" was guaranteed. Its new name was an homage to one of its owners, Aline, a somewhat fleshy, fiery redhead who assumed the role of "madam" of the restaurant. The other partner, Timothy, a former actor, was high-strung, generally irate, and perpetually exhausted. Whatever forces threw these two together, the result was incompetence, argumentativeness, hostility, and, on the part of Aline, drunkenness. It felt like Fran and Lou's redux.

One day Bob sat me down with Timothy, told him I needed a job that would actually make me some money, and I was hired on the spot. I knew the restaurant. Bob would lunch there regularly with the elite of the theater world and me, his assistant, in tow. Across the street was the Manhattan Plaza apartment complex, two towers originally designed for upper- and middle-class residents that were converted during the 1970s financial crisis into low-cost housing for those in the performing arts. The buildings were filled with thespians, both young and old, and, sadly, decrepit and alcoholic playwrights. A decayed Tennessee Williams had an apartment there. Williams would regularly come talk to Bob in his office at Playwrights, breath reeking of alcohol, about a new work he wanted to present, though I don't ever remember seeing any of the script. The meetings would always end up with lunch at La Rousse, with me taking notes and usually eating the least expensive item on the menu. This was my first introduction to French food, and this type of cuisine would pretty much come to define my restaurant career.

Lunch with Tennessee was always fascinating and sad. He'd drink his wine and talk about the new work, albeit vaguely, and the more wine he drank, the less sense he made and the more pathetic he became. Other lunch guests would include such theater legends as John Houseman, who was in the middle of his celebrated run on the TV series *Paper Chase* and had a theater on the block named after him; the director Harold Clurman, whose book *On Directing* is

still a must-read for both actors and directors; Nancy Marchand and her husband, the character actor Paul Sparer; a young Christopher Reeve, who was
being coached for his role in *Fifth of July*; the playwrights Lanford Wilson and
Ted Tally; the director Gerald Gutierrez. The list goes on and is a roll call of
some of the greats working at that time.

Who wouldn't want to be part of the scene here, a room always filled with
exciting guests and the chance to make a few bucks? I was down with working
at La Rousse, and Timothy and I set a date for me to train.

Restaurant 101

NOTHING COMPARES TO THE energy of a busy restaurant, especially one filled with celebrities from all walks of life. The laughter, the toasts, the intensity of the alcohol-fueled conversations, the celebrations, birthdays and anniversaries, and the joy, happiness, and fun that comes from partaking with strangers—people in for a night and whom you don't really know no matter how much they act like they have known you their whole life. But for the moment, these strangers love you like family. It's perfect, partially because it lacks any of the painful connections or remembrances from your past.

When it works, it's the best of family life. For a few hours these surrogate families become what we always wanted them to be. It's the McDonald's Christmas commercials repeated over and over. But when it doesn't work and you're a server or bartender or manager thrown into the mix, it's as much fun as being waterboarded. It can be an addictive cycle and draws in addictive personalities of all sorts—alcoholics and drug addicts, sex addicts, survivors of abuse, ragers, narcissists—all thrown into an unbelievably high-pressure mix. Many of those I've worked with, including myself, exhibited at least some of these dysfunctions. Combine that with the need to serve, to be good, to please mommy and daddy, to be rewarded, all under the auspices of hospitality, and you have a recipe for the enabling of dysfunctional human beings.

Years later when I was trying to get sober, I was forced to confront my own dysfunction. My mother, who had congenital hip problems, eventually had to have surgery and was in the hospital for almost a year. None of my

Mafia uncles or their wives stepped up to watch over me, and I was placed with friends of friends in a "foster" situation. The family I stayed with had two children, a son thirteen and a daughter eleven. Much of my time there is a fog, a haze that I spent years trying to forget with alcohol and drugs. I was introduced to the household and its rules clearly on the second day. Both of the kids were caught stealing. Their mother took them in the kitchen, heated the burner on the stove, and in a rage took their fingers and placed them on the hot burners. The screams were terrifying and a portent of my year in that house. I was abused both sexually and mentally for most of my time there. It was brutal with the son, though with the daughter somewhat comforting since after she was done "playing," we'd fall asleep with her holding me close for the rest of the night. The abuse carried on outdoors as well. Being an outsider and unknown to the neighborhood kids, I was regularly beat up whenever they caught me on my way back from school. I saw no one from my family the entire time I was there. I then learned why the restaurant business fit me like a glove.

Servers tend to be attractive people thrown together to engage in this particular form of battle. Serving is a blend of toxicity and extremes, a feeling of living on the edge re-created almost every single day. We seek that which we need or think we need. Throughout my thirty-five-year career in the restaurant business, I have seen the story repeated countless times. The faces change but the stories never do. Into this little pot of egos, addictions, alcohol, drugs, and booze came I.

On my first day of training I was attached to a senior server and "trailed" her, which means following a server throughout the shift, mostly watching, seeing how things are done, and learning the particular style of the restaurant. My trainer was an actress from Utah, a reformed Mormon (I've met a lot of these over the years, fleeing their uptight homes to find some freedom in the city, with many learning some hard lessons), blond, thin of lips, attractive, and very, very efficient. She wasn't a smiler, but, man, was she good. Very good. While you might not want to take her to a party, you certainly wanted her serving you when you had a curtain to make. She was our Nurse Ratched. Her efficiency would have made her a Nazi poster child—with her blond hair, pale skin, and militaristic attitude, she certainly resembled one. She did her job by the book and took shit from no one.

The shift began with everyone doing an assigned task. One or two servers set tables, another polished glasses and silver, another folded napkins. This being a small restaurant, there were no bussers to clean tables or runners to serve the food; the servers did everything, which was a great way to learn all parts of service. In larger houses, the bussers, besides setting and clearing all the tables, do much of the setup and grunt work, which is both dirty and heavy: helping stock the bar, sweep the floors, empty and clean the trash bins, and straighten the tables. This is in addition to clearing all the plates from a table once the guests have finished. Runners usually set up the kitchen for service and deliver all the food to a table. But at La Rousse, we did it all, which was an incredibly valuable experience when I moved on to other restaurants.

The ex-Mormon, besides hating to train newbies, hated most of humanity. While she was incredibly efficient and capable, no one was more ill-suited to work daily with the public. A shift for her was tantamount to serving time, something to be gotten through as quickly as possible, unless you were in the "industry" and could do something for her. She would then turn into a mix of Grace Kelly and Katharine Hepburn, cool, sexy, suave, and snarky. I don't believe this ever resulted in her getting an acting gig (even though she did end up on her back quite a few times attempting to) as she eventually forsook the stage to settle with a rich producer and have babies. But while on the job, she would use her mediocre acting talents to the best of her ability to get through that evening's service. Her clinical efficiency separated her from the rest of the servers. She'd go to a table, flash her fake smile, take a drink order, head to the bar to order the drinks (restaurant computer systems had yet to be invented), go to the next table, and repeat.

La Rousse was a theater restaurant, so the doors opened at 5:00 P.M. for dinner service, early enough to get in the pre-theater crowd and fill the place for the first seating. There'd be a trickle of guests from 5:00 to 5:30, half the tables would be seated by 6:00, and then the restaurant would get slammed from 6:00 to 7:45, followed by a mass exodus as guests set off for their shows. Until about 6:00 P.M., she wasn't a bad teacher: follow her to get the drink orders, place the order, move on to the next table, repeat. Drop the drinks, return to the first table, get the food order, put the order in, on to the next table, repeat. This works fine when guests are seated in an orderly and methodical fashion, but sadly that is not how the restaurant business works. Guests don't get seated evenly in all the stations at fifteen-minute intervals for the pleasure of the servers. They come in when they want, order when they want, and leave when they want. The server's job is to anticipate and get everything done in a timely, kindly, efficient manner. Your livelihood and your job depend on it.

But on my second night of training we got hit hard. Every table was filled at once, and my teacher let me know, in a not-friendly way, that I needed to get the fuck out of her way. I was the piece-of-shit newbie that would not only interfere with her mechanized death process of serving tables, but would severely diminish her income, which she was not about to allow. Fearing for my life and new job, I stepped aside and watched her work. Great servers multitask and anticipate. She knew which table to make wait an extra five minutes, which would ask the most questions while she was taking an order, and which had the guy who needed all the attention and would keep her there while telling bad jokes and expostulating on how vital he was to the outside world. Meanwhile, while she pretended to listen, her mind was going—take the drink orders, place the orders, take the next food or drink order, place the orders, serve the drinks, pick up the food, serve the food, bus the table, drop dessert menus, take dessert orders, serve dessert, drop the check. Her routine was a ballet without music.

As the rush commenced, her lips pressed tighter, her smile became more forced, and her responses to guests' comments got shorter and shorter. I don't think she took more than five breaths during the ninety-minute rush. She kept it all inside, churning away, and as I soon learned, her only release was when she stepped outside to chain-smoke. She was infamous among the staff for ripping into other servers for one infraction or another—not replenishing the silver, not emptying a bus pan, not replacing a glass she unrightfully thought belonged to her. Lear's line "Come not between the dragon and his wrath" were words to heed.

Into this mix was I thrown, somewhat terrified, but it reminded me quite a bit of the candy store back in Brooklyn, and I loved every minute of it. I was home. For the third training I was given three tables to run myself. This was fun. It felt natural and I was at ease among the guests. Throughout the evening she watched me the way a predator eyes a field mouse, ready to pounce. She instantly corrected every feeble effort on my part. "Get those drinks before the martini is water! Restock the silver! Bar needs glasses, get that table bussed, you hear that ringing in the kitchen? It's your fucking order! Pick it up! You're fucking with my money! It's my money you're fucking with." Trainees don't get a share of tips. All they earn is abuse.

Despite my initial ineptness at figuring out timing, what exactly was in the food we were serving, and how to get the right dishes to the right person, I didn't do such a horrible job, and at the end of the evening, the ex-Mormon gave what for her I considered to be an accolade: "Well, you didn't fuck it up too badly."

The takeaways from my trail: stay the fuck out of the way of the other servers unless you want to get pushed, glared at, and cursed sotto voce so the wonderful guests don't realize the purveyor of such sentiment is actually a miserable, unhappy, failed actor who probably fucked up another audition that afternoon; chefs hate you; bartenders hate you unless they are trying to fuck you or need something right away to enhance the tip from Johnny Swags, who is eating at the bar and just ordered an expensive Bordeaux; get the customers their booze as fast as possible, because once the liquor kicks in your odds of success at that table increase exponentially; and the nicest and kindest folks in a restaurant are the immigrant labor—the lowest paid, those receiving the fewest perks with the shittiest jobs.

My fellow servers consisted of the same cast of characters found in most New York City restaurants. There was the Thespian Bartender—mid-to-late thirties, an arrogant prick who said little to any coworker unless, as previously stated, he was trying to fuck you. A few months back he had scored a small role in an off-Broadway play with a TV star, which he never stopped talking about. He was apparently fired from his last bartending job, either for stealing or because he left to do said off-Broadway show. Next there was the Hippie—a university student, so ditzy, yet, oh so delicious, hair under her arms, the scent of sweat and sex just oozing from her, and whom *everyone* wanted to fuck.

The Server, thirties, gay, was from somewhere in the Midwest, blond hair thinning, and the beginning plugs of a hair transplant viewable through the few strands of hair he had. He was perpetually taking acting classes to hone his craft but had yet to land an acting job. The Server's Boyfriend was in his early forties, blond, unconventionally handsome, his nose a bit too big for his face, a receded hairline with a bushy crop of blond hair atop his head, sardonic wit, hilariously funny, and whose claim to fame had been his affair with his mentor, the legendary actress Kim Stanley. He rarely spoke about it but the boyfriend always did when he was out of earshot.

The Chef was in his mid-to-late twenties, tall and skinny, shoulder-length hair, mustache, a typically French weak chin, pointy nose, Gallic accent, short-tempered, and with as much talent as a fry cook at Nathan's. The Comedienne, midtwenties, rotund, an aspiring stand-up comic/actress, hysterically funny, actually hated no one, and was damn good at her job. Aline's mother, in her late seventies/early eighties, her long, once-blond, grayed hair always in a French braid and loved by everyone. Rumor was that she modeled for Matisse in her youth.

And the owners. Aline, scatterbrained, perpetually confused, alcoholic, who was totally incompetent at running a restaurant. A consummate fag hag who was the face of the business, with a huge following, yet inherently sad and a bit broken. Finally, Timothy, the other owner, with the personality of a Chihuahua. Skittish yet loud, and when not being stroked, could be very, very vicious. He knew the business and ran it moderately well when he was not being blindsided by Aline.

My first real shift began smoothly. Aline seated a lovely couple that had been to the restaurant before, knew what they wanted, and weren't much in need of their server. They required no validation of their order, especially from me, who had almost zero knowledge and wouldn't be able to validate much of anything. My second table was a party of six. Tables of six obviously require more time than those with fewer guests. These were six women from Long Island in search of an inexpensive pre-theater meal and giddy with their bravery for having ventured into the land of crime, sex, drugs, and theater. They needed a *lot* of attention.

The drink order wasn't so difficult: glasses of wine and a couple of cocktails that I actually knew what to do with—a cherry goes in a manhattan, an olive in a martini, and lime for the gin and tonic. As I garnished the drinks, Thespian Bartender stood staring at me, arms crossed, smirking, watching like a beast of prey waiting to pounce and rip out my jugular if I mistakenly put an olive where a cherry should go. My confidence hadn't reached the point it would later on in the business when, if I had to deal with someone of this sort, I'd look him in the face and tell him to fuck off. Instead, I slowly and carefully placed each piece of fruit in the correct cocktail.

Because of Thespian, I'd taken way too much time getting the drinks, and returning to my station, I saw that three more tables had been seated, two deuces and a four top. As I delivered the drinks to my Long Islanders, I passed ex-Mormon, who, sensing disaster, snarled, "Move it," as I walked past the new tables, my tray laden with beverages, smiling weakly at the waiting guests in a pathetic demonstration of aplomb.

As I placed the drinks in front of the wrong guests, my Long Islanders, still giddy with goodwill and humor, and feeling safely ensconced in our little bistro while rape, murder, and pillaging were going on only feet from our door, began what I can only describe as a press conference. They barraged me with questions regarding the menu and all those damned French words. Not having the temerity, nor the battle experience, to ask these lovely folk to wait a minute while I took the drink orders from my now-four tables, all in search of their missing server, I began a recitation of the dishes, fading under the pressure and getting some beefy items crossed with fishy ones. My boat was taking on water fast, the ship was sinking, my heart palpitating, and I broke into a sweat as all around me I could hear desperate guests crying out for their waiter, pleading to order drinks.

While I envisioned unemployment and the imminent shame of having to explain to Bob why I was fired my first night on the job for extreme incompetence, a miracle occurred. From the corner of my eye I spot Comedienne enter my station and shout out, "Here I am, folks, just needed a piss," which made the whole station crack up as she then proceeded, with the speed of Jim Brown and the grace of Ginger Rogers, to take drink orders, serve them, and get all but one food order from my now-full station. I was finally able to get the order from the six top, fully serve another four top, and, with the help of funny girl, get my station fed, watered, paid, and out the door before their curtain.

As the six top were leaving, they called out to the already-inebriated Aline, and as I awaited what I was certain would be my imminent execution, they instead told her what a remarkable server I had been, one of their best ever, and they'd soon be back. Aline, who never missed a chance to kiss a younger man, came over, gave me an all-too-intimate hug and kiss, said, "Well done, Michel!," and marched directly back to her glass of chardonnay. She had no idea how clueless I had been, and I had no idea how clueless she was to have slammed the new guy's station, something that would have gotten her fired had she worked anywhere but in her own establishment.

So This Is What It's Like

ONCE THE EARLY GUESTS left for their shows, the restaurant emptied out completely. Those who showed between eight and ten were rare. A quiet restaurant, with servers having a couple hours with little or nothing to do, combined with an absentee or incompetent management team, is a dangerous thing. La Rousse didn't have an actual manager. The place was run by the owners. While Timothy was quite adept at this, poor Aline was clueless. She was able to open and close the restaurant, greet and drink with her friends, and, depending on her level of intoxication, was sometimes able to count money at the end of the shift. Sometimes.

Luckily, despite our prolific alcohol consumption, we were a pretty honest group. Except Thespian, the fuck, who was eventually fired for stealing. Timothy had apparently suspected Thespian of chicanery and brought in a spotter (someone hired to sit at the bar and watch every move the bartender makes, ensuring all the receipts are put in the register). One evening the spotter nailed Thespian with his hand in the till. Good riddance, scumbag.

Aline was impervious to our boozing since she herself was always somewhat half in the bag on her way to sweet oblivion. She always reminded me of Brick's lines in *Cat on a Hot Tin Roof*: "It just hasn't happened yet, Maggie. . . . The click I get in my head when I've had enough of this stuff to make me peaceful."

Her click always seemed one drink away. And things only got worse for her. As the business began to fail, she slowly descended into the alcoholism that would eventually kill her. She was desperate for money. The rumors that her mother had been a model for Matisse turned out to be true. Her mother had a sketchbook with drawings of her done by the artist. For years she had been selling the drawings off piece by piece to make ends meet.

Once the restaurant emptied out from the first seating, Aline would head upstairs to the office, supposedly to do some paperwork. The toilets were on the second floor and the office just beyond them. It was common knowledge that Aline kept a bottle of vodka on the ledge outside the bathroom window. Having already had a few glasses of wine during the first seating, she'd head upstairs, hit the bottle of vodka, and head to the office, where she'd stay till almost ten, when the after-theater rush would come. This gave us a free pass for the next hour and a half to do pretty much as we wanted.

The booze flowed. We all drank, some nights so much that someone would end up in the upstairs bathroom puking his or her guts out. Or if not to puke, for a quickie. Hippie had one or two up there with her boyfriend, who would show up between seatings for free booze and a chance to fuck his girl at work. Comedienne would get smashed and, more than once, get so drunk that, in a fit of hysterics from something she herself had said, she'd collapse to the bar floor, unable to pick herself up.

I had a thing with a beautiful pianist who lived across the street at Manhattan Plaza. She always came for dinner with her boyfriend, a musician, who worked the Broadway shows. We had a pretty intense flirtation, and one evening she came to the restaurant alone during the lull to see me. We had a few drinks and she invited me to her apartment. There was still forty-five minutes till the second rush. Comedienne was bartending, saw what was going down, pulled me to the side, and said, "If you don't leave right now and fuck her, I will." Comedienne covered for me.

This quickly became a thing. The Pianist would come to the restaurant just as the first seating was leaving, have a quick martini, and then leave. Once she was out the door, I let the crew know I'd be back and headed over to her apartment. Her musician boyfriend would have already left for his show, and we'd fuck like crazy. I'd then head back to the restaurant before the second seating while she'd shower and be ready for his return. Some nights after I'd been there, she'd bring him over to the restaurant for dinner after the show. I never asked her if he knew.

The booze didn't help when it came to avoiding mistakes, which we servers made more than our share of, increasing the ridiculously high stress of the business. One night we forgot to put in an order for a table that needed to leave to see a show—they left without dinner. When we gave a lady a steak instead of her fish, she was livid and insisted she was a vegetarian and the sight of the meat made her want to puke, even though she did order fish. We spilled a glass of red wine on the shirt of a producer, who jumped up, called the server a stupid fucking asshole, and stormed out with his party without paying the check. The servers had to come up with the cash to make it right. The litany of errors that can happen always makes you feel like a complete piece of shit and creates a cascade of more errors and the resulting irate guests.

Despite the partying, this was still the restaurant business, replete with asshole guests. There was the obnoxious, affected German homosexual, who would come with his lovely boyfriend to hobnob with Aline and use her for all he could get. He was a boor, gross, rude, and egotistical. A noted designer, he had made a splash with a cheesy leather line. The more he and Aline drank, the sadder she became, the angrier he became. He'd shout at the servers to get him drinks or to order food. *Please* and *thank you* somehow didn't make it into his heavily accented English vocabulary.

One of Aline's biggest failings was comping actors and her "friends." She and Timothy would get into brutal, screaming fights over this. At the conclusion of their public battles Aline would burst into tears and run up to the bathroom, hit the vodka, then come back down with her tear-smudged makeup repaired, smiling from the anesthetic effects of the rotgut house vodka she hid outside the bathroom window. The female waiters would seize this moment to suck up to her, be her friend and a shoulder to cry on, thus ensuring themselves a favorable schedule and the leeway to come in late from an audition or to finagle some food from the kitchen. By then I was one of Aline's favorites, having risen through the ranks to become one of the better servers, as well as a male shoulder for her to cry on. I, too, needed the right schedule and a morsel at times to balance out the booze in my gullet.

One packed post-theater night I was deep in the weeds, fueled by shots of vodka our new bartender—who would become my close friend and partner in debauchery—had given me. The German was sitting at the bar, and when I heard that grating, drunken accent, shouting to me about getting him food as I was passing him with two plates, I hit my breaking point. I stopped, turned, threw the plates to the ground, and cracked him square in the face.

The bar cleared, and sitting directly next to the German was Paul Simon, who'd seen and heard everything the German had said. Simon stood up and, as the German reared back to hit me, shoved him back, over the barstool and onto the floor. Some regulars then tossed the German out, and he never returned to the restaurant. Aline apparently harbored the same feeling for him that we all had and let him know it was best that he didn't return.

Getting bailed out of a bar fight by friendly guests was but one scene during my run at La Rousse. It was theater every night there. While the parameters of a night's service are pretty much the same, each evening has its own dynamic, and you have no idea how things will end up. The military has an expression that explains this: no battle plan survives first contact with the enemy. The restaurant is your stage, and the set is arranged by the cast, made up of the waiters and bussers. It starts the same every night. Floors swept, bathrooms stocked, silver and glasses polished, tables set, napkins folded, side stations stocked, candles prepared for lighting, paintings and photos dusted and straightened, chairs wiped down and arranged, refrigerators cleaned and stocked, bar stocked, wine stocked, everything precise, everything prepared. I love this part. I have always found a sense of comfort and safety in this, the monotony of it. You come to work knowing what needs to be done—the expectation, the repetition, the routine, never changing, unless something happens. Which it did one disgustingly hot, humid August afternoon.

The temperature outside was in the nineties, Forty-second Street backed up with traffic, the street and air filled with the soot and grime of 1980s New York City. I was playing my role, setting up the room in this former bordello, when the door opens and in comes a woman, overdressed, heavy makeup, and big hair. She staggers a few steps and collapses. I immediately run over to help, and she murmurs a few words about needing water, which I get. I prop her up and give her a sip, when in rush an army of people. She is obviously well attended to, and as I watch, someone rips off her wig. Suddenly I realize it's not a woman. It's Dustin Hoffman. He was on the block shooting the film *Tootsie*, was overcome by the heat, and stumbled into the restaurant desperate for AC and water.

It seemed the entire film crew, including the director, Sydney Pollack, came in to assist. Hoffman pulls it together and, before leaving, comes over to thank me and asks my name. A week later, he returns with his wife, walks in the door, asks for me, and they sit and have dinner. We chatted a bit throughout their meal, which he was happy to do, and as they left, he handed me a hundred-dollar bill. Besides that being almost half my rent, more important, it began to solidify my reputation at the restaurant. I was becoming known by the guests, tips were getting better and better, and I was now fully accepted by the staff. Life was getting a bit easier in the Big Apple.

A Kick in the Dick

VIOLENCE WASN'T LIMITED TO the front of house. One example was our chef of little talent, who, between cigarettes and regular shots from a cognac bottle while pretending to cook, was quick to temper. He was a rare one as chefs go, talentless and misanthropic, equally bestowing his wrath and anger on both front and back of house, on men and women alike. There's one thing that many chefs hate and despise, and that triggers their rage, even more than a guest complaining that his perfectly cooked medium-rare steak is undercooked. More than a perfect piece of prime returned as being overcooked. More than having a runner refuse to pick up a scalding-hot plate even though it's been heated to the point that touching it will leave pieces of burnt flesh on the edge of the plate. More than a server trying to correct him on anything foodwise, and more than their hatred for anything front of house, as awful as these other transgressions may be.

No, the one thing that makes a chef want to draw and quarter a server is holding dupes. A dupe (duplicate) is the piece of paper you write an order on and then bring to the kitchen and give to the chef. A dupe pad was a pad that had carbon paper so each order would have three copies, one for the kitchen, one for the bar, and the third the server kept. This was before computers, though the piece of paper that gets spit out from the printer in the kitchen with the food order printed on it is still called a dupe. A smooth service works when tables are booked at appropriate intervals in an attempt to seat the dining room as smoothly and evenly as possible. Generally, this means every fifteen minutes with a maximum number of covers or guests allowed within those quarter-hour periods. The formula for this is usually decided by both the chefs, sous-chefs, managers, and maîtres d'hôtel. This brain trust figures out the magic number of guests per time slot that can be seated for the restaurant to run optimally. The aim is to not compromise service by seating too many covers at once, so that each station in the kitchen has time to prep, cook, finish, and garnish each dish in a timely and delicious manner.

To ensure that each guest is served at the same time at a table and the kitchen runs as efficiently as possible, chefs want the orders to come in smoothly and evenly. It's the same in every kitchen. When this doesn't happen, when the orders keep coming in immediately, one after the other instead of spread out, chaos ensues. It matters not that this is a theater restaurant and getting everyone in and out at the same time is paramount to the business model and ultimate success of the venture. Chefs hate an onslaught of dupes.

But despite the years of experience possessed by all those making these decisions, restaurants are invariably inconsistent. This is the tragic nature of the business. The only guarantee is that every night is going to be different and, despite the best planning by the best minds, something will go wrong. Doom is always hovering above the well-set table. Guests are either late or early, the room is overbooked, a VIP will telephone for a table at the last minute, or a regular walks in without a reservation and must be accommodated. Or perhaps the stars will want to dine—Raquel Welch needs her dinner immediately, Lauren Bacall must have a seat at ten thirty because she is coming directly from her Tony-winning Best Performance in *Woman of the Year* and Kander and Ebb are joining her, or Christopher Reeve is bringing Swoosie Kurtz, fresh from her Tony in *Fifth of July*, and wants to sit at the exact table he spent so many lunches at being coached by director Marshall Mason. Or perhaps a guest insists on being moved to another table, no matter that the server in that station was just quadruple seated, or table one is waiting ten minutes for drinks, table six needs their food immediately, table twelve needs to be bussed, and the owner, sensing havoc, starts screaming at anyone in earshot that we're all ruining his restaurant. When this happens, chaos reigns. Orders start pouring into the kitchen one after another.

One result of such chaos is that servers, especially the inexperienced ones, wind up "holding" their dupes. Example: A station gets triple and quadruple seated, all the tables want to order at once, and just as the server finishes taking the order at one table, he turns to see the guests at the next two tables are glaring and waving at him and ready to gnaw off his arm if they don't order immediately. The orders are then taken one after the other, and the dupes get stuffed into a pocket till the server can safely make it to the kitchen to put them all in. This can then be further compounded when a server walks by the bar, pockets stuffed full of dupes, and sees his drink order that needed to be delivered five minutes ago sitting on the bar, ice melting, and the bartender about to smash the server's face in if the bartender is forced to make the drinks again. The server then has to stop and serve the drinks before putting all the orders in.

As the orders are entered into the computer and dupes keep getting spit out by the kitchen printer, the chef's rage builds. This rage reaches a crescendo when the chef realizes that the multiple tickets that are coming in one after another are from the same server. In the old days there were no computers, so servers would have to actually walk into the kitchen to put in the order, face-to-face with a now-livid chef.

One night the perfect storm was raging in the dining room and we all saw it coming. We were about to get fucked—overbooked, guests were late, all were pre-theater and had to be out at the same time, all the tables were seated at once, servers were triple and quadruple seated and were bringing dupes into the kitchen, one after the other. When this happens, no matter how big or small the restaurant, the chef sees it as a complete failure of the front of house: the host or maître d'hôtel for seating the tables, the servers for putting in multiple orders at the same time, the managers for letting these disasters happen, and the customers for actually ordering all at once. No one is immune from the blame and hatred. It matters not that the reservation book was perfectly built, or that the host or maître d'hôtel attempted to seat the room smoothly and evenly, or that the servers tried in vain to take one order at a time, or that the managers were on the floor doing their best to calm things down. No matter how hard everyone tried, the front of the house gets blamed.

On this particular night, we were all buried and going under, the entire staff scampering about the dining room, trying to pick up drinks, take orders, and serve food, running in and out of the kitchen, calling out orders one after another. The heat was rising, chef was getting angrier and angrier, screaming, "*What ze fuck! What ze fuck!*" in his French accent, slamming his fist on the pickup bell, over and over, *ding, ding, ding,* screaming, "*Peek up!, Peek up!,*" a Gauloises dangling from his mouth, cognac shot at the ready, shouting out orders for the cooks: "*On ordear, tree steaks, one medium, two medium rare, tree Dovair sole, two rack of lamb, both medium, tree aliboot, four sides of ze mashed. Peek up table fourteen!*"

As the orders kept coming, the stations overwhelmed and the anger and tension in the kitchen rising, in saunters Graham. Good old Graham. Fucking idiot Graham. Graham was hired, despite having zero restaurant experience, because he fit both Aline's and Timothy's disparate views of the perfect server. Aline's view of perfection was a gorgeous young man who was willing to sit and listen endlessly to her litany of sad stories, while they simultaneously charmed her friends. It didn't matter that his station was crashing and burning around him. For Timothy, perfection was young, handsome, gay, and flirtatious, with the possibility of a romantic encounter. Graham was all of this. He was also an aspiring actor. What he didn't have was the ability to wait tables.

Chef hated everything about Graham. His incompetence, his sexuality, his good looks, his perfect hair (chef's was prematurely thinning). Chef rode the guy hard, constantly insulting him, asking suggestive and rude questions about his sexual preferences, such as whether he was the man or the woman in the relationship, did his rectum bleed after sex, how deep could he take it down his throat—he was relentless. You had to take it back then. There was no HR, no one to go to or complain to, no social media to let the world know your chef was a maniac and your existence was threatened almost daily. Graham took it, shrugged it off, and would saunter back to the dining room, shooting shots of chilled vodka, flirting with anyone that looked rich or could give him a role in a play, anything to keep his mood happy, calm, and steady. I was standing at the pass, the narrow counter where all food is passed from cooks to servers, trying to help the chef plate and arrange the dupes while running back and forth to the disaster in the dining room, when here comes Graham. He slowly pulls three crumpled orders from his pocket and nonchalantly places them in front of the chef. I let out an "Oh fuck."

The chef looks down, picks up the dupes, hurls them in Graham's face, takes a step back, and, with the practiced aim of a soccer striker, lifts his greasy, grimy black-booted foot and kicks Graham right in the balls. It was with the precision, speed, and power of a Ronaldo. The hit itself, the screams— one from the chef as he let his foot go, one from Graham as the boot made contact—were so loud, hideous, and terrifying that everything in the kitchen stopped dead.

The force of the kick caused Graham to topple into me, plates flying into the air, charred steaks and fillets of sole soaring into the sky, flipping in tandem as though waiting to hit a hot pan but instead falling directly onto the floor. Down went Graham, screaming and writhing in pain. The chef, spent and satisfied, looked as though he just had the best orgasm of his life.

There was now absolute and complete havoc in the dining room. One server was down, a table's worth of food was on the floor, and guests were screaming at the staff. Many walked out, and the few who remained had their meals comped. Graham ended up in the hospital. When I went to visit him, his testicles had swollen to the size of grapefruits, and he was unable to leave his bed until the swelling subsided nearly two months later.

What happened to the chef? The exact same thing as when he'd pulled a knife on me a few months before and threatened me with it. Nothing.

Althea

THE MUDD CLUB OPENED as the antithesis to Studio 54. As Studio was to glitter, fashion, and class, the Mudd Club was to the punk ethos. Located on a barren street in TriBeCa, the club was void of any pretense of design. The VIP room was up a dark, narrow staircase, sealed off by a chain-link fence, and guarded by some large bouncers who separated the masses from the superstars.

I have no recollection of whom I went to the Mudd Club with that Sunday night, but I know for sure I didn't leave with them. The bathrooms in the club were the first I had ever encountered that had no demarcation for men or women. Each used the same, unaware of which was which. When I went to the bathroom, and as I was washing my hands at the sink, I felt a tap on my shoulder. I turned to face an attractive, punkish-looking woman, who asked me if I wanted to do some blow. I of course nod yes and was handed a baggie full of cocaine. She undid the coke spoon that hung around her neck, handed it to me, and I did a couple of hits. Whoa. This wasn't some shit she'd bought off a kid in the park.

She then introduced me to the two men she was with, a dapper gay couple, who looked somewhat out of place in a punk club. Whenever she spoke, I had a hard time figuring out what she was saying. I'm not sure if it was because we were both pretty fucked-up, but I asked what her name was a few times and could never quite make it out. One of the men then pulls out a small metal pipe and asks me if I want to take a hit. As I drew from the pipe, I had a coughing fit that lasted a good two minutes. When I asked what it was I was smoking, they said, "Quaaludes." Fuck. This was going to be a night.

We continued chatting for a bit, when she asked if I wanted to freebase. I had absolutely no idea what she was talking about but one of the guys explained that it was cooking cocaine so you could smoke it instead of snorting it. Now I'm thinking, This is pretty good stuff as it is, but if they want to smoke it, I'm down. She then asked if I had any ether and said it so matter-of-fact that I asked her to repeat it. "Ether?" Did they think I was a doctor? Where the fuck would I get ether from? Still in the toilet, I'm thinking I've met a trio of maniacs.

They all then try to explain that ether is the best way to get the cocaine to a form where you can smoke it. None of this is making sense. "Sorry, I'm all out of ether." One of the guys then asks, "Do you have a stove?" It seems a gas stove is a good option should one have mistakenly left their supply of ether at home prior to heading out to the club. "Of course I have a stove." I replied. "But not with me."

The next thing I know we are outside the Mudd Club and I'm whistling for a taxi to take us all back to my East Village tenement, which indeed has not only a stove, but also my sleeping girlfriend, who would soon be waking to go teach her kindergarten class. Waving off the taxi, one of the gents guides me into the back of a black stretch limo, replete with a full bar and another bag of coke. We drive off, and as I start to tell the driver my address, the attractive woman who started all this and whose name I still don't quite know, stops me and tells the driver to go back to their hotel instead. Apparently the baggie full of coke is not enough to get us through our soon-to-be freebase escapade.

We head to the Loew's Summit on Fifty-first Street, and as we drive, whatever her name is keeps sneaking glances out the back window of the limo. Eventually she asks the guys if we are still being followed. Seeing the anxious look on my face, they explain that she's going through a bad divorce and her husband has her followed everywhere. This leads me to ask the question who her husband is. The answer is Larry Flynt, legendary pornographer and founder of *Hustler* magazine. Fortunately the coke, quaaludes, and booze now coursing through my body ease me into accepting this turn of events; my fears, if I had any, are now somewhat placated.

When we get to the hotel; she leaves the limo and quickly returns with two more bags of the white powder, and we head down to my apartment. It's almost 4:00 A.M. as we enter my apartment and wake up my girlfriend the kindergarten teacher, whom I hastily introduce to my new friends and explain to her we have come home to freebase.

Now, this wasn't entirely out of the ordinary. *Time* magazine had recently run a cover story titled "High on Cocaine," accompanied by a photo of a martini glass filled with coke, and New Yorkers of a certain age were regularly taking "disco naps" so they could go out and party all night, then show up for work in the morning. My girlfriend didn't put up much of a fuss.

The boys got right to it, and the five of us were soon inhaling the sweet smoke that was about to destroy a whole generation. The crack epidemic that was about to hit Bond Street, only a few blocks away, and similar streets in neighborhoods all over America would soon be littered with so many crack vials that the sound of their crunching underfoot was like a Philip Glass symphony. This all made total sense to me after inhaling the first few tokes. It was fucking amazing. I felt like I was floating above the earth, completely weightless with an intense feeling of euphoria. I was completely fucked-up. My girl had a few tokes and was soon headed off to work, while the four of us, besotted, and as only true coke fiends know, needing to go out and continue the party.

I knew of an after-hours club on First Avenue and Thirteenth Street that our limo driver, in his absolute professionalism—and undoubtedly a stellar paycheck signed by Mr. Flynt—was only too happy to ferry us to. I couldn't say the same for the private detectives that followed us there, but I assumed they were being well cared for back at the *Hustler* mansion. The club was on the corner, the front, mostly boarded up and graffitied, the entrance, a small, nondescript doorway. It was now 7:00 Monday morning and as we entered the place was packed. We danced a bit, then headed to the basement, where the VIP room was located. The room was strewn with seedy, torn couches and beanbags. I am not sure where the boys went, but she and I headed to a couch.

As soon as we sat, she attacked me, pulling my pants down, taking my cock in her mouth, and begins furiously sucking me. This wasn't happening. No way, no how. I was so wasted, so out of my mind, that I couldn't find my cock to piss, let alone fuck.

I have absolutely no idea what happened after that and didn't return home until, I think, Wednesday. My multi-day disappearance didn't do much for my relationship with the kindergarten teacher, which soon came to an inglorious end. Nor did I think much about this mysterious lady, and my one and only experience with crack, till almost ten years later. While watching the film *The People vs. Larry Flynt*, the memory of that evening came hurtling back when Courtney Love appeared on-screen and introduced herself as Althea Flynt. Althea! That was the name she was trying to tell me, Althea! I then realized who I was with those two or three days, ten years ago.

Althea apparently died from AIDS a year or two after our encounter. Thanks to my constantly inebriated state during our time together, we never had actual sex. I am one of the few people that can say crack probably saved my life.

All Good Things Must Pass

La Rousse lasted another year till its death by mismanagement. We all had no idea. The restaurant was relatively busy, we made money, and our guests, for the most part, were happy. Our new bartender—let's call him Rick—was a jazz musician, singer, and songwriter and became one of my closest friends. He was tall, handsome, wore small, round wire-rimmed spectacles, and had a movie-star jaw. He was also a great bartender, trusted, and became a favorite of the whole staff. He was so well liked by Timothy that when a rent-controlled tenement apartment above the bar became available, Timothy helped him rent it for the sweet sum of $65 a month. This may not have been the best of ideas. Nobody in his right mind, other than a struggling jazz musician, would want to live there. It was a typical tenement: bathtub in the kitchen, toilet in the hallway—the kind with the water tank above it and a pull chain to flush, exactly like the toilet from which Pacino extracts the gun hidden behind the water tank in *The Godfather*. There were plenty of roaches, not much heat, and even less hot water.

But despite these limitations, the rent was a steal, and the apartment served its purpose as both a recording studio and flophouse. The antics we had in there rivaled its days as a whorehouse. Rick brought in musicians to play some nights, and with them came the debauchery. The apartment became the place to rehearse, get high, fuck, or pass out. Among the many lessons I learned about the business at La Rousse, understanding that restaurants aren't just about food and drink was a major one. Sex is a big part of the business—lots of young, attractive people in one small space, easy access to drugs and booze, the constant flow of guests, many looking to have a good time. The temptations are just too great.

When the musicians arrived, so did the drugs. The first drug to make an appearance was opium. A sax player would bring in balls of the dark, tarry substance wrapped in plastic, which, we were told, needed to be frozen prior to use. Apparently, without the appropriate pipe, the best way to ingest the drug is to stick a frozen ball up one's ass for the full opioid effect. The ice sink behind the bar was the perfect repository to store the frozen balls. At any time, the bin had a half dozen awaiting their final destination up the asses of select guests and staff.

One evening as I was waiting for drinks at the service bar, I watched as Rick scooped up a bunch of ice and dropped the cubes, including one of our opium balls, into a cocktail he was preparing for one of our guests. "Rick!" I screamed across the bar, pointing at the glass. It was useless, the music was too loud, the lights too dim, and Rick too drunk to see the black ball floating atop the gin and tonic. Rick serves the drink, the guest lifts the glass, and as he takes a swig, he gags and spits out the ball of opium. Rick, totally unfazed, sees the ball roll toward him, picks it up, looks at it, looks the guest straight in the eye, and says, "So that's where that went," then tosses the ball back in the ice and makes the gent a fresh gin and tonic.

The little apartment above the bar became our den of iniquity for the remaining days of the life of La Rousse. Where was your bartender? Where did your server go? Who was pouring drinks? No one was ever sure. The apartment upstairs was a revolving door of vice—servers, chefs, musicians, and guests all taking part. Were all restaurants like this? I had no idea, but for a guy in his early twenties, this was fucking amazing.

Then, just like that, it ended. I came to work one day to see the restaurant door padlocked shut. A sign from the tax assessor was pasted to the door. The taxman had caught up to our little bistro. The place I grew up in and learned the business in was done. The last thing I got from it was the night Rick, wasted on opium, looked me in the eye and said, "You're an artist, you're an actor, go do it." And at about the same time as the closing of La Rousse, Robert Moss stepped down as producing director of Playwrights Horizons. My days on Forty-second Street had come to an end.

PART III

Life on the Water

UNEMPLOYMENT SUITED ME NOT. Nor did I suit the eateries I applied to. The unemployment rate in Manhattan was about 10 percent. This was a buyer's market and this market wasn't buying me. I pounded the pavement dropping off my sad, one-paragraph résumé at every place I thought somewhat suited my meager experience.

One afternoon, after handing out what felt like my one thousandth résumé, I was about to give up when I decided to try one more place and stumbled into what looked like a new restaurant in the Union Square area. I knew immediately I was wildly out of place. This was a fancy establishment catering to fancy people, eating fancy food, who, to my eye, were certainly not the artists and denizens of Forty-Deuce that I was accustomed to. Even worse, I was dressed in black pants, a white shirt, and a skinny black tie, looking more as though I could perform alongside Elvis Costello than serve the guests here their expensive food.

Guarding the door was a stunning, lithesome woman, who smiled as though she'd known me for years. I meekly inched my way toward her and, with all the confidence I could muster, gently handed her my scant résumé, typed and carbon-copied on an Olivetti manual that had served me well while I was an undergraduate English major. I expected to be turned around and shown the door. As I scanned the dining room, I could see that those who had already gained employment here seemed well-fed and somewhat prosperous. They were all Caucasian, scrubbed clean, with cherubic, Midwest faces and gleaming-white smiles that attested to their parents' dental munificence. They were all Polo shirted, their khakis pressed to a crease so sharp it seemed as if it could slice through one of the tender steaks I assumed they were serving. The gleaming, polished shoes they all wore must have allowed them the chance to admire their gorgeous smiles every time they deigned to glance down at the floor to pick up a stray piece of food or paper. They looked like refugees from a Ralph Lauren ad. I had no fucking chance of a job here.

I was about to bolt when, through either absolute indifference, inexperience, or the results of imbibing the hospitality Kool-Aid concocted by the proprietor, the host actually told me to wait and someone would be with me shortly. I perused the upscale, two-tiered dining room as guests with pockets full of cash spooned beautifully prepared food into their well-groomed, manicured, and attired selves. That's when Danny arrived. Had this been 1989, I would have thought that Jerry Seinfeld got his start in the restaurant business, since they look so alike. Dripping with both kindness and hospitality, Danny sat down, looked at my résumé (kudos to him for not bursting forth with a belly laugh), and began asking questions. I remember three things from this meeting:

1. I had a better chance of playing shortstop for the New York Yankees than getting hired here.

2. Hellmann's or Miracle Whip?

3. What is more important, food or service?

I of course did not get the job. But thirty years later, I would once again get to meet the legend and thank him for asking me the most important question anyone has ever asked me about the restaurant business.

Danny had just reopened Union Square Cafe and was dining at Le Coucou—his reservation that evening had the staff very excited. The thrill of providing hospitality to such an icon of the restaurant industry was palpable. Some of our staff had worked for him previously and were looking forward to seeing him again. Others had read his book and were thrilled to see the man in the flesh. He arrived as Danny Meyer should—unassuming and warm, absolutely benevolent and greeted by many of our guests who either knew him or his celebrity. I let his party get settled in before heading over and introducing myself. I reminded him of that first meeting, of which he had absolutely zero recollection, and I thanked him for asking me *that* question, the one I have since referred to over and over. No, not the mayonnaise. (Of course it's Hellmann's.) To be truthful, I'd forgotten about the Miracle Whip and Hellmann's till his wife chimed in with the mayo reference. I apparently was not the first quizzed with that one.

No, it was the other question. Food or service? Food or service? Food or service? I've worked with many great chefs, have been present in the service of hundreds of thousands of meals, some wonderful, some good, some average, and some inedible. Yet the one thing that keeps customers coming back over and over is the service. Even if eating the same dish every time—the steak au poivre at Raoul's, the Black Label burger at Minetta Tavern, the rigatoni at Carbone, the *ris de veau* at Le Coucou, the Dover sole at La Grenouille, or some new concoction whipped up by the darling chef of the moment—it's still the service. *Always the service.*

Even if it's the first-time dining at that restaurant, or whether the dish was perfectly cooked or ill prepared, it's the service. Chefs who are able to leave their large egos at the front entrance have always agreed with me on this. We all want to connect, to be recognized, treated well; some of us need to be adored, "recognized" either as the movie star we are, or the billionaire titan of Wall Street, or that politician, cop, restaurant-industry professional, tailor, construction worker, teacher—all of us want to be made to feel special, to be known and acknowledged. It makes you feel good. This is where the power of the great maîtres d'hôtel comes from. They recognize this, understand the psychology of it, how guests should be greeted, how to make them smile upon entering, how to then escort them to a table; these maîtres d' know what it takes to be great. As the master maître d'hôtel Guy Sussini of the Water Club always said to me, "Give zem zee beeg blow job."

Restaurants aren't just about sustenance. We go to them to celebrate the occasions, the special events of our lives, from births to deaths and everything in between. It's pretty easy to forgive an overcooked steak when your server, barman, or maître d'hôtel knows you, remembers your name, how you liked your martini prepared, that you ordered the halibut last time, remembers your kid just graduated from high school, or that it's your anniversary, or calls you to tell you your ex just booked a table on Thursday and you might want to go somewhere else that night, or greets your fourth different date that month as if he or she were the only person you'd ever brought to the restaurant and she might just be the one.

On and on it goes, the ability to make a guest feel special, unique, and not just another of the hundreds that pass through our doors each night. We can recook the steak, reshake the martini, or heat up the bread. That's easy. Juxtapose this with the host who's texting when you walk in the door and ignores you, or the lack of anyone to say hello when you enter or goodbye as you leave, getting seated at a deuce in the coldest corner of the room when the restaurant is empty because the host is either ignorant or a lazy piece of shit for not offering you the empty four top on the banquette when everyone knows it's not going to be seated tonight. Or the server has no idea if there's butter in the fucking *beurre blanc* or forgets your wife's order on her thirty-fifth birthday, or the entrées come two minutes after your appetizers were served, or they never even brought the appetizers. Or you can't get a damn drink after standing at the bar for ten minutes because the bartender is trying to get a blow job from the woman at the end of the bar, or he doesn't even acknowledge you in the packed bar but asks others who arrived after you what they'd like to drink because they are taller or prettier or handsomer or richer, or the white wine you asked for appears as a glass of red and the server insists you asked for red even though you haven't had a glass of red wine in ten years, or once you've paid the check and your tip has been recorded you've been forgotten.

These are just some of the multitude of offenses perpetrated in shoddy restaurants, where ownership is absent, or management doesn't care or is inept or has no idea of these simple points of service. It doesn't matter that the chef has gone to Le Cordon Bleu or the Culinary Institute of America, has four stars from *The New York Times*, three Michelins, and a Beard Award. If we in the front of house can't get you the sometimes-asshole-in-the-kitchen's masterpieces in a timely manner, with a smile, a kind word, and a thank-you, you ain't coming back. There are twenty-five thousand restaurants in New York City, many of them with good to decent food.

Look, it can't be done without good food, I know this, we all know this.

When the food is good or great, it makes everyone's job easier, and chefs are some of the hardest-working people in the world. Read the legendary Bourdain's *Kitchen Confidential*; a chef's and a cook's jobs are brutal, the hours suck, and the pay can be abominable. We work as a team and need to work as a team, but it's the service that keeps you coming back to pray at the altar of these culinary masters. Thank you, Mr. Meyer.

I walked out the door after that interview knowing I'd never hear from Danny. I went back to beating the pavement and dropping off résumés to be filed in the nearest wastebasket. My well-honed apartment-searching skills were put to good use as I scoured the help wanted ads. I knew where to get the early papers, knew to show up at the crack of dawn to get to an open call early, yet despite this, I somehow missed an ad for a new restaurant that was seeking servers.

They were seeing people for three days and today was the last day. I had gone out the night before to the Pyramid Club to see the young Lady Bunny and other drag queens perform in the new club on Avenue A. I'd met the bartender, a twentysomething lady from Texas, on previous visits there. She was a somewhat punkish cowgirl from Texas, had hair bleached white, Buster Brown bangs, a nose so thin it looked sharpened and was adorned with a silver ring through the right nostril, black horn-rimmed glasses, a plain cotton dress always, hem falling just below her crotch, thin white legs, black socks, and black boots. I loved her.

I had sat that night at her bar being plied with Gibsons, as the bejeweled drag queens, wigs so tall they barely missed scraping the leaky water pipes hung just below the tin ceiling, strutted their glamorous selves to the DJ of the moment. Lying in bed the next morning, my head pounding from the excess of the evening before, still nauseous from cocktail onions and gin, the paper open on my lap, I spotted the ad and initially thought it best to not present myself in such condition, figuring that by the third day they would have filled their needs. Though something in my still-gin-addled brain clicked. Perhaps it was that I was broke and had spent my last twenty at the bar last night and needed a fucking job.

I decided to get dressed and drag my sorry ass to the call. The restaurant was the Water Club on the East River. On this hot, humid July day I walked the thirty-plus blocks there to save cab fare. As I approached the restaurant, I spotted the long line of at least five hundred of my fellow unemployed. Yes, five hundred needy souls. The men dressed in the requisite black pants and white shirts, the women the same, or in dresses and heels, each waiting for a chance to be once again rejected and set off into the crime-riddled streets. The line moved slowly in the sweltering heat. My white shirt was soaked through with sweat as we finally reached a side deck and were ushered, like cattle waiting for the bolt gun to the head, to a set of metal stairs that led to the upper deck.

This was restaurateur Michael "Buzzy" O'Keeffe's soon-to-be-mecca to WASP cuisine and the yacht-club lifestyle, the Water Club. Two white barges, formerly used to transport trash up and down the river to the aptly named Fresh Kills dump on Staten Island, sat adjacent to each other and were connected to land by a grand windowed entrance in the center that allowed access to either barge. Sitting in the East River, this was going to be a much-larger version of O'Keeffe's majestic River Café, which sat on the other side of the river about a mile south and under the Brooklyn Bridge.

As I entered, my first thought was that this construction site might never be a restaurant, and if it did become one, the opening would be well past my imminent bankruptcy. Nauseous from the gin, the sun pounding on my hungover head, the stink of the putrid East River filling my nostrils, with the ridiculous amount of sweaty, desperate people looking for work and the slim chance of my actually getting hired here, I decided to make a run for it before I puked all over the new deck. Just as I'd made up my mind to leave, I was ushered to a round banquette table and handed an application. At the end of the deck was a rectangular table, behind which sat a man and a woman with a stack of résumés in front of them. Directly behind them was the unseen East River and a panorama of midtown Manhattan, the UN, and the newly built Citicorp building. The table where they sat was right at the edge of the deck, the polluted river right below. I thought how easy it would be to take those who were about to be rejected and just push them overboard. With this heat, and given that I was about to vomit, it wouldn't be a bad alternative.

As I sat there, it felt like high school as we each filled out an application, surreptitiously trying to check out the others' qualifications. I was soon led to the deck edge and introduced to the general manager, a tall, Waspish woman in her late twenties, sleekly attired in a well-fitted suit with a string of pearls around her neck. Next to her was this little guy with a cherubic face and a thick, guttural New York accent. He sounded like one of the Bowery Boys, from the films popular in the forties and fifties about a group of Depression-era kids on the Lower East Side. As I later learned, he was aptly nicknamed Ratso, was already a legend in the world of NYC dining, and was to be the restaurant's head steward. He was the first of the many characters I would meet that inhabited the world of Buzzy O'Keeffe.

Ratso peppered me with questions about service, some of which I actually knew the answers to; the others may as well have been about quantum mechanics. The height of my ignorance came when I was asked what Port Salut is. I had zero idea of what he was talking about. Figuring I was about to head overboard and had nothing to lose, with a sickly smile I asked, "Is that when a ship docks and all the soldiers stand at attention and salute the commander?" The belly laugh that burst forth from Ratso meant that either I was about to be ridiculed for my complete ignorance of not knowing it was cheese, and heaved over the edge, or perhaps I might have gotten myself a job. The latter was the case.

About a year later, I got hired to serve at a party for *Rolling Stone* at magazine owner Jann Wenner's apartment. The organizers needed a bartender as well, and I got my bartender crush at the Pyramid Club the gig. The bar was set up in the kitchen, and when I went in to get a few cocktails, I saw her, hips pressed against the corner of the kitchen island, rubbing herself quite vigorously against it. "What are you doing?" I asked.

"Masturbating. I always do this when I'm bored."

Another World

ON MY FIRST DAY, I was led through a construction site that would soon be the main dining room of the Water Club. Saws were whirring, nails were being hammered, painters were painting—an army of workmen were doing what workmen do. The floor was covered in sawdust, with not a table or chair in sight. In the midst of this, standing in a circle, were my soon-to-be fellow servers and bussers. This group—all Caucasian except for the one Chinese captain, whose perfect English attested to his Hong Kong boarding school— was an assemblage of very, very attractive people. If O'Keeffe tried to assemble such a group of Caucasian lovelies today, there'd soon be a line of attorneys at the door with lawsuits in hand.

In the midst of this young, curated group stood Ratso, laying out the laws of the O'Keeffe kingdom as though he were planning a bank heist. I would soon begin to learn some of the details of his legend. He worked at the original P. J. Clarke's and had the distinction of being the recipient of prefolded $100 bills from Frank Sinatra which were bestowed to most of the floor staff each time he ate there. During Ratso's stint at the storied Maxwell's Plum, he'd also been made to fire future restaurateur legend Keith McNally. Apparently the young McNally, then a server, was caught with his finger in the ice cream by the chef. Ratso was forced to fire McNally on the spot. When Ratso protested that McNally was a good server and should be given another chance, the chef, in a logic that could be formulated only by someone who'd spent a lifetime working in kitchens and detested every single individual not dressed in kitchen whites, replied that everyone knew that a waiter's finger would soon be up someone's asshole and had probably already been up one. When Ratso let the illustrious and grandiose proprietor, Warner LeRoy, know of the impending dismissal, he retorted, "Well, at least it wasn't up my asshole." Aside from the news of the stringent dress requirements—Brooks Brothers shirts and slacks, J. Press ties, and black leather shoes that were to be polished to a military shine (all paid for by us)—my biggest takeaway from Ratso's monologue was the warning for us to stand clear of Mr. O'Keeffe. Ratso described him as difficult, ill-tempered, sometimes mean, and to be avoided at all costs. Ratso put the fear of God into us nonbelievers.

Having never opened a restaurant, I had no idea what to expect. Restaurant openings are a life unto themselves. After my experience at the Water Club, I swore I'd never do it again and indeed did not, until we opened Le Coucou in 2016. Each day is trying, the construction timeline a fantasy, everyone is in a rush to open and the delays in receiving parts and equipment, or the wait for workers to finish something before they can move on to the next step, cause constant frustration and a toxic environment.

The stress was evident when the inevitable screaming would start, from worker to worker, contractor to owner, owner to GM, GM to the managers, and from the managers to we lowly servers. The chef waits for his stoves, and once he gets them, he has to wait for Con Edison to turn on the gas, which could take as long as a month. And since there is no gas, there is no cooking, and the entire kitchen staff, who were hired to begin on the date the stoves were to be installed and the gas turned on, is now on payroll, trying to make themselves busy while the kitchen is completed. The floor guy needs to wait for the bar to be installed. The bars can't be installed because the plumbing fixtures are imported from Europe and stuck on a boat somewhere in the mid-Atlantic. The carpenter can't do the window trim because the windows are too large for the space and either the wall needs to be enlarged or the windows remade. And on it goes.

The FOH staff were being paid minimum wage, which at the time was $3.35 an hour. For the first few weeks we did little serving. Instead, we unloaded trucks with boxes of dishes of every shape and size, silverware, glasses, knives, forks, spoons, and everything else needed to get a dining room open for business. We swept, mopped, and cleaned up after the workers to set the dining room for training. Some did windows, some polished silver, some did the heavy grunt work. This was basically free labor to get the restaurant open and, in today's world, entirely illegal. We didn't see a guest for weeks.

Back then, restaurants were run like the military. No bullshit. You do as you're told or you got your ass handed to you. The hierarchy went like this: owner at the top; if the chef is renowned, he comes second; if not, the general manager is next in line; then the maître d'hôtel, followed by captains, waiters, and bussers. Bartenders are and will always be in a world of their own. Especially bartenders in the Buzzy O'Keeffe world. They tended to be older, experienced, and Irish. He knew many from his days of owning a group of saloons and took them with him whenever he could.

It was becoming apparent that the restaurant world I knew—the theater, the struggling actors, and the stars that inhabited my little world at the fifty-seat La Rousse—was about to become a distant memory. I was now thrust into a world I had no idea existed. This is where I made my bones in the industry.

My biggest lesson in those early weeks? It's all in the details and the details are paramount, especially in an O'Keeffe restaurant. He misses nothing. That first week, once we had unloaded the deliveries and cleaned up after the workmen, we would set the dining room, polish all the glasses and silver, fold napkins, lay out the linen, and arrange everything as though we were about to greet a roomful of customers. The silver needed to be polished to a bright gleam, glasses had to be spotless and reflect their surroundings as brilliantly as the decor. Tablecloths had to be perfectly pressed; if the crease wasn't perfectly down the center, if the length wasn't cut to where it hung just so, or if there was one spot on them, it had to be tossed. If the maître d'hôtel or manager came around to inspect and the tables weren't perfect, they'd push everything aside and you had to do it all over again. Chairs had to be dusted, tables leveled, floors swept. The goal was perfection and nothing less.

Once the grunt work was completed, we engaged in "mock" services. This is where half the team acts as guests while the other half are customers. This was repeated over and over, ad nauseam, because it's the only possible way of figuring out what you may or may not be doing in an actual service.

As we got to know one another, alliances formed, and we were allowed to pick our own teams. Some of this was driven by who we thought were the stronger servers, but a lot of it was driven by lust. Servers are just that—servants. You find few rich kids waiting tables and cooking in restaurants. Our staff (like that of most restaurants) was composed of the working class—misfits and artists, drunks and druggies, beauties and predators, gay, bi, and straight. Many had fled their hometowns to pursue their dreams in New York City. Here was a place to get lost in, experiment in, to play in, to work in, to cry in, and sometimes to die in. This was a city where anything anyone could want or desire was seemingly at one's doorstep twenty-four hours a day. At the Water Club we had entrée to the big city, to discover things we had no idea existed, to fall in love, experiment, and embrace a new style of living. This was at times to fatal effect, but if it's about the journey, for many of us it began here.

Partners in Servitude

We quickly got bored of the routine. We'd yet to have a customer, and the little money we were making had our patience wearing thin. This ample time allowed personalities to emerge. There was the Al Pacino look-alike, whose motto was "God hasn't made a woman I wouldn't fuck." He was fond of taking out his massive penis whenever he could and letting it hang down to his kneecap. There was Claire, beautiful, short dark hair, translucent skin, green eyes, and a damn good server. I found her one of the most beautiful women I had ever seen and instantly fell in love with her. Rumor was that she and O'Keeffe were dating. I glued myself to her throughout training and did everything possible for us to be teammates. She was married and I was engaged. Neither of these circumstances would impede our soon-to-be-apparent lust for each other.

We weren't the only ones. Restaurants, as I have said, are not just about food. Yes, we go to them to dine, celebrate, party, and drink, but, perhaps more important to some, also to pursue intimacy. We go to restaurants on dates, to meet others, sometimes to seduce. We take our significant other there to celebrate, get a bit liquored up, then go home and hopefully fuck. The meal is not the main course. The possibility of sex is. This is as true for the staff as it is for guests. Staff get hit on regularly. Many men give their cards to that moment's object of desire, hoping the beautiful host or waitress serving them will call. The men seem to think professional hospitality extends to the bedroom. Gifts are given, liquor and drugs plied, in hope of favors. We had a host who was beautiful, lovely, incredibly charming, gregarious, and sought-after by everyone, guests and employees alike. One guest sent her a mink coat, another a diamond ring, all props to lure her. None of it worked, though she did keep the gifts.

Customers pick up servers, servers pick up customers, and bartenders pick up everyone. The major players at the Water Club were the Ice Queen, a gorgeous Brooklynite, replete with accent, of Norwegian descent, with princess-blond hair, cold, efficient, and perhaps our best captain. She paired off with the writer from California, who soon came to be known affectionately as Uncle Rob. He had had success with a screenplay in LA, a remake of *Where the Boys Are*, but his deal had gone sour, and he'd migrated East. He was handsome, incredibly smart, and, as we were soon to find out, a massive alcoholic. There was the Dancer, tall, with iceberg-blue eyes, a pixie haircut, who was here for the money, easily distracted, and sidled alongside the cabaret singer Rick McKay, who spent most of his time singing throughout the dining room and talking constantly to anyone who would listen. Rick was an awful server, but his personality got him through the shift and everyone loved him. He would go on to make the heralded documentary *Broadway: The Golden Age, by the Legends Who Were There*.

Next there was the Jock, Brian Straub, corn-fed, farm fresh from the Midwest, handsome, kind, and charming. Women threw themselves at him. In fact, most everyone threw themselves at him. He was one of the genuinely nicest human beings on the planet. He came East to be an actor, and like most actors, was waiting tables. His former stint was as a barback at Studio 54. Joining him were the Three Sisters, our male bussers, all incredibly intelligent and all über-gay. They were mediocre at their jobs and spent most of their time dishing on everyone. Their main goal was to get through a shift by having as much fun as possible. They earned the nickname the Three Sisters when they descended the stairs one day with stacks of linen, their heads draped with napkins to make them look like nuns, singing "Dominique" in chorus, as they unpacked and unfolded stacks of napkins.

Also on the roster was Aunt Chip from Florida. He came to NYC to be openly gay and was the kindest, sweetest, and most loving individual I've ever met. Everyone, and I mean absolutely everyone, loved and adored him. At his funeral a few years later, after succumbing to a long battle with AIDS, the crowd was so large and varied that people spilled out the doors of the chapel and onto the street. Next was Boyd Black, a boyhood friend of Uncle Rob's who came East with his wife, the soon-to-be major movie star Kelly McGillis, who promptly dumped him and his heroin habit when she went off to star in *Reuben, Reuben*, and then to superstardom with *Witness* and *Top Gun*. And there was Guy, the maître d'hôtel, tall, French, with the perfect Gallic accent, dashingly handsome, mustachioed, with slicked-back black hair. He always arrived to work with a cigarette dangling from his mouth (the cigarettes would kill him a few years later), his bow tie undone, hanging rakishly down from his collar.

Behind the bar was Dr. Dewar's, a grizzled ex-cop who couldn't say no to the few extra bucks or drugs he could get his hands on at every stop or bust he ever made. He was subsequently tossed off the force, only to be rescued by O'Keeffe. The ex-cop's nickname was earned for his ability to easily polish off a bottle of Dewar's a night. With bushy red hair and a mustache, he was a bartender's bartender, old-school and could talk the paint off the wall. He lived out of his station wagon with his German shepherd, who would often sleep behind the bar, unbeknownst to the guests, while Dr. Dewar's worked his shift.

As training wound to a close, alliances with our fellow workers set, our motley crew was as ready as we'd ever be to open the restaurant. Despite the woodwork and trim sitting unfinished, various lighting not hung and sawdust everywhere, Buzzy needed the revenue and we needed it more. The gas was finally turned on, and for the last few trainings we worked with actual food. We learned how to fillet a Dover sole, shell a lobster, and debone a baby chicken, all tableside.

Throughout training, O'Keeffe always sat at the first booth next to the entrance to the dining room, a place that we soon learned would serve as his de facto office. The table was atop a platform about three feet high, which created a perch from which he watched over his domain like an eagle, hovering and waiting to pounce on his prey, whether they be contractors, the managers, or the waitstaff.

O'Keeffe is a tall man, always impeccably dressed in his Savile Row best, his thin hair parted to the side, with a beak-like nose just below his beady eyes. During the first few weeks of our employ, his screaming was focused on management and contractors. He did his best to make them all feel incompetent, as if the greatest mistake of his life was to have hired them, and everything they did was with the purpose of destroying his as-yet-unfinished restaurant. We, the floor staff, were left alone. I later realized this was because we had yet to become real people to him. We were the coolies who did the grunt work, and had yet to don a uniform. Once we did have our uniforms and would actually be responsible for taking his orders and serving his food, our status went from trash to prey, putting us on equal footing with the others.

The first time he addressed us was to chime in on the deboning of the baby chicken. This, we were soon to learn, was near and dear to his heart. We were taught in precise detail how to pull the leg and thigh away and cut through the connective joint, separate the thigh from the leg, remove the breasts from the breastbone, and, most important, flip that little sucker over and make sure we removed the "oysters," the two small rounds of dark meat on the back, which, Buzzy imparted to us, were the most flavorful and tender parts of the bird. He ordered the chicken many times just to test how well the server could carve it. If it wasn't perfect, you got reamed.

Whatever all the years of Catholic schooling had taught Buzzy, it seemed his greatest lesson was on how to rip someone a new asshole. The vicious and sadistic nuns of yore had nothing on O'Keeffe. Not only would he dress you down verbally like you were a smarmy little piece of shit, but he'd also make sure a manager would call everyone off the floor to witness the execution. The first server to commit the infraction of omitting the carving of those two little balls beneath the chicken was not only humiliated, but also got a two-week suspension to think about it while at home eating TV dinners, since his income was now less than nil.

Each day brought new infractions. If the butter was served at an inappropriate temperature, if there weren't enough scallions or pepper in the potatoes colcannon, that we'd mix tableside, if the aforementioned chicken was improperly dismembered, if our shoes weren't shined to a military polish . . . if your shirt wasn't the required J. Press or Brooks Brothers white button-down . . . if a lampshade was crooked or a piece of paper lay on the floor for more than two seconds, or if the drink straws were not black (he hated colored straws because they did not match the food), Buzzy would grab a manager, have them gather the *entire* staff in the kitchen or pull us to one side of the dining room, and basically tell us what pieces of shit we were. In no uncertain terms he'd let us know how we were destroying his restaurant and how he could get monkeys to do the same work.

He was also fond of telling us that since we made our money on tips, in a space he provided, with a kitchen that he staffed and paid for, we should pay him for the right to work in his restaurant. In his pique of anger, he would repeatedly tell the story of some mythic bathroom attendant at the Plaza Hotel. Apparently, this gent actually paid the hotel to allow him the honor of overseeing the toilets because of how much money he earned in tips while handing over fresh, starched white towels for the swells to dry their soft white hands with.

Despite all this, I desperately needed this job and was going to do my best to remain here. We were hearing the stories of the guests at the River Café, across the river—the actors, models, and stars, the Wall Street tycoons, the absolute beauty of the restaurant, how well it was run, and most of all the money that everyone was making. The River Café was the high temple, and if we succeeded, we'd at least be on equal footing with them or maybe just a notch below. If I was to succeed here, I knew I had to get the boss on my side.

One quiet afternoon, I spotted O'Keeffe sitting alone at his table and went for it. I walked up to him, introduced myself, and told him we had all been warned to stay away from him if we didn't want to be eaten alive. I let him know (and lied) that I couldn't imagine anyone being so awful and that it was an honor to work for him, adding that he couldn't be any worse than those in Bensonhurst where I grew up. A little chutzpah didn't hurt, and it worked. The other servers stared at me in disbelief as Buzzy started to tell me a few stories of his growing up in the Bronx. Buzzy talks at you and does little listening, but it didn't matter. I had cemented my position and survival at the restaurant and wound up working for Buzzy for eight years. Of course it also didn't hurt that I was pretty damn good at my job.

How Soft Is an Opening?

THE FIRST CONTACT THAT most new restaurants have with the public is what's called a "soft opening." It typically lasts three days and is also sometimes referred to as "Friends and Family" because the specially invited guests are actual friends and family of the owners, chefs, managers, and so on. Prior to the official opening, they are invited to dine, sample the food and service, and many times are asked to fill out comment cards on the experience. This is when we get to put into practice what we have spent weeks training for. The kitchen gets to put out food, the front gets to serve it, and we all give the guests a preview of what the restaurant will be like. The servers are still learning the systems and mistakes are plentiful. Hopefully the guests will be somewhat kind throughout the disaster that is about to befall them. It doesn't hurt that the meal is free.

Everyone is nervous and the objective is to screw up as little as possible. On the first day of Friends and Family we arrived early to set up. It was a disaster. The floors were still covered with sawdust, the tables were in disarray, and the silver and glassware was still racked and unpolished in the kitchen. Linen had to be retrieved from the deck two floors above, and all the tables and stations set and prepared for the onslaught. The pressure was enormous and, to make it all worse, Buzzy was at his table, phone in hand, intermittently screaming at someone on the other end of the line and, in turn, spewing his venom at either the contractors or managers, whoever was closest. He'd then whisper to the minions around him, some covert piece of information that was to be kept as secret as the nuclear codes, all while being continuously interrupted with last-minute details requiring his yea or nay.

With two hours to opening, the team assembled for this night had to come together and work like mavericks. Al partnered with Boyd, both attacking the "clean" silverware, which came out of the kitchen in flat plastic racks, covered in grease and bits of food. When they went back to tell the chef this needed to be rewashed, he promptly sent them back to the dining room, saying his dishwashers were too busy and this is what servers were for. I would soon realize this was the status quo for large restaurants: racks of supposedly washed, cleaned, and sanitized silver, still laden with grease and bits of food, are sent out for the floor staff to wipe them free of the previous evening's detritus.

To achieve a state of cleanliness and shine, servers have to fill deep metal hotel pans with scalding-hot water, dip a rag in, and wipe the grease and food off each piece. It's disgusting. The bond Al and Boyd created while picking away at bits of greasy potato, steak, eggs, and so forth was to last for their duration at the Water Club. To be honest, I am not sure if this was the moment that they both discovered their penises were magnificent specimens akin to those of stallions, but double exposure soon became the norm for them. They carried trays laden with food, their pants covered with starched white aprons and their penises hanging out underneath, flopping up and down under their aprons as they tread the aisles to drop off trays of food.

Glasses were in a similar state, spotted, sometimes greasy, but all needing a hot-water bath and a good polishing. Linen was brought down from above by, of course, the Three Sisters, the trio bitching every step of the way as sawdust was swept, tables laid out, napkins folded, and finally the tables draped and set. As the sun began to set, we realized not all the lights had been installed and the bulk of the restaurant would be dark. When O'Keeffe overheard in pre-shift that there would not be enough light to fillet the Dover sole and ensure all bones were removed, he shouted out from his table, "Get another waiter to hold a damn candle over it!"—and with this rallying cry leading us into battle, the first night began.

The fact that most friends and family stay friends and family after a restaurant opening is shocking. It's a disaster. The wait can be intolerable, the service helter-skelter, and the menu limited; the guests are basically guinea pigs. The owners, investors, and managers wind up squeezing into the dining room everyone they are indebted to—friends, family, other investors, the cognoscenti, and those whose blessing will be absolutely necessary for the success of the restaurant. This means the initial thirty or so covers that both the front and the back of house feel could be accommodated reasonably well quickly blossoms to seventy or more.

Then there are the foodies, that group of people who live and die by their restaurant experiences. They are rich and make it their life's goal to have eaten at every three-star Michelin restaurant around the world. These individuals feel they *must* be among the first to dine at the restaurant of the moment and will spend the equivalent of the GDP of a small country to have the pleasure being the first to wine and dine at these establishments. Thanks to their largesse, they'll also always get the pièce de résistance—the mandatory visit by the chef at the end of the meal, when he walks through the dining room and stops at certain tables to see if everything he and his team have created that evening was satisfactory.

Of course all feign shock that his eminence has actually left his domain, that being his kitchen, where an army of cooks in their spotless whites, their jackets laden with tweezers, spoons, testers, and knives have painstakingly spent the last three hours fawning over every piece of meat, fish, vegetable, and garnish and plated as though Picasso, Matisse, and Pollock had all collaborated on the dish. The fact that the chef would actually pry himself away from his crew and creations, greet them with the humility of St. Francis, and make sure everything was to their satisfaction is what they all crave.

This group's masochism demands that they be invited to a Friends and Family so they can tell everyone that, "Yes, of course we were invited, dahling, and of course it was awful. It needs so much work. We won't be returning anytime soon." Of course they will return instantly once the word is out that the restaurant is indeed great or recognized as that moment's place to be and a reservation is now all but impossible. Since they suffered through Friends and Family, they will demand a reservation and expect to be treated like royalty.

Then, since anyone who is anyone must dine at seven thirty and only seven thirty, since they'd never make it from work any earlier and must jet off by nine thirty to attend *this* party or *that* social, the reservations increase exponentially at exactly the worst time. The thinking by the big-money guys who have invested a small fortune in the place, and who have no fucking idea how to run a restaurant, since their only experience is making reservations and knowing which side of the plate the fork goes on, will tell you, "It's a two-hundred-seat restaurant, what's a few more covers?" These "few more covers" equal absolute and total disaster. The kitchen runs out of food, the waits for food and drink are intolerable, and servers spend most of the night explaining why everything is taking so long. The servers are still learning the systems and mistakes are plentiful.

On this first night, the collapse began when Ice Queen incorrectly ordered twenty-two steaks for a table of two. It didn't matter that this table only seated two and that everyone knew the largest table in the restaurant was an eight top. Not one person questioned the order—not the chef, the expediter, the cook, the runners who served it, no one. Three runners came out of the kitchen, arms aloft, trays laden with a cow's worth of steaks and plopped them down in front of two shocked diners. Two steaks were served, and the rest were taken back to the kitchen. Seconds later the whole dining room heard the expletives emanating from the kitchen and the crashing of plates, as the chef tossed all the plated steaks across the kitchen and at anyone within throwing distance. This was only worsened when, once the guests cut into their prime pieces of beef, they saw that each was cooked to the incorrect temperature. The captain, sensing imminent expulsion, begged the guests to keep the steaks, brought them another bottle of wine, and didn't go into the kitchen for at least another week.

The downward trajectory of the evening was thus set, and no one would be able to right the sinking ship. The limited menu notwithstanding, both food and drink orders were taken incorrectly. Waits for food were up to an hour and guests accepted the wrong food just to be able to eat something. Guests were furious, and the most we could do was to keep plying them with alcohol to soften the misery.

The entire staff was in a tizzy. The Singer couldn't find his captain mid-service, and she was finally located in the banquet barge practicing her ballet to alleviate her stress. So in an attempt to mollify the guests, who were now acting as though they'd only recently survived the Biafran famine, the Singer broke into a Richard Rodgers ditty as though he were performing at the Café Carlyle. Dr. Dewar's was well into his second bottle, which brought the making of drinks to a standstill since he spent most of his time trying to keep himself upright. As we were soon to learn, the drunker he became, the less pouring he did, instead reminiscing about the old days on the force, oblivious of the catastrophes around him. Al, who attempted to fulfill his motto every possible moment despite what might be happening in the dining room, needed to be constantly corralled from out at the main bar, where he'd emigrate to try to pick up the front-door hosts, all Ford model wannabes, or the cocktail waitresses who were serving in the main bar. The chef was unapproachable, sending out food in any manner possible, no matter the quality, the correctness of the order, or where the table was in courses. Desserts were served as appetizers, appetizers as main courses, and entrées were being plucked by guests from trays as soon as they were set down.

In the midst of this disaster sat Buzzy, oblivious of the typhoon around him as he wined and dined some of the investors, his table being the only one served appropriately since every available manager was there to oversee it, the rest of the dining room be damned. This is where I learned another valuable lesson that would serve me well throughout my restaurant career: no matter what anyone tells you, the guests are not the most important people in the room and the customer is not always right; the most important person in the room is the owner and if he is taken care of perfectly, he rarely notices anything else in the room. And that's how, despite the calamity of our first night, we all got to serve another day.

Success

IN NOVEMBER OF 1982 the recession ended, and this coincided with the opening of the Water Club. O'Keeffe had nailed it. Despite the dirty silver and glassware, sawdust and lack of lights, poor computer skills and eccentric servers, the Water Club opened and succeeded beyond anyone's expectations. Wall Street came roaring back, and like in the twenties, booze, drugs, and sex came with it. The crowds arrived, swells from all facets of New York, the elite of politicians, publishers, magazine editors, movie stars, musicians, bankers, lawyers, fashionistas, you name it. And with them came the money. On a typical night we'd each walk out with $200 to $300 cash in pocket. This was a month's rent made in one evening. Those who had coupled off would have double that to play with. Claire and I would leave with about $500 or $600 in our pocket and hit the town with many of the staff in tow.

To say sex, drugs, alcohol, and cash fueled the restaurant world in the eighties is an understatement. Prices were high and we soon found ourselves making more money than we ever had before. Besides getting a 20 percent or more tip on your check (15 percent being the standard at the time), the big shots, especially the Wall Street guys, would come in, greet you with a hug and a kiss as though they'd known you their whole lives, and slip a folded hundred-dollar bill into your hand, usually wrapped around a gram of coke. Cristal and Dom Pérignon would follow, and we'd be beckoned to join in a toast to life and all its splendors.

What put restaurants at the fore of the celebrity world was the closing of Studio 54 in 1980. This left a void; the beautiful people needed places to go, to be recognized, and the restaurant world was only too happy to oblige. Restaurants became the new Broadway, places to be seen, to gawk, and, for many, to try to establish oneself in the social pecking order. Keith and Brian McNally understood this, and their first venture, the Odeon, began a run of restaurants that has continued to this day. They staffed their eateries with beautiful people at the door and on the floor, and all the beautiful people followed. Everyone wanted in. It was a party, and if you could afford the entry fee, all were welcome. Well, almost all. If you were not a some-body or didn't know someone in the "industry," the only reservations you could get were at either 5:00 or 11:00 p.m. The best tables and the most sought-after times were kept for the stars, the wealthy, and the connected. Stardom and money were the passes through the door. Those not blessed with celebrity or wealth were happy to be relegated to the outskirts, feeling lucky to be in a room with such vibrancy, or took being put in "Siberia" as a personal affront.

This is when the maître d'hôtel becomes either the most loved or most hated person in the room. It's somewhat of an art form to not only curate a dining room but be able to keep from being murdered by the guests who arrive at the dreaded five thirty, have waited a month for this particular booking but all they could get was a five thirty reservation, and are then told that all the choice banquettes in the middle of the room with the best views are unavailable in a completely empty restaurant.

Here's how it works. Most successful and hot restaurants release reservations at only the dreaded hours of five, five thirty, six, ten, and later. All the other openings are held and disbursed to the owner, chef, VIPs, celebrities, great regulars, and the best tippers. Restaurants need celebrities as much as celebrities need the restaurants. Celebrities want and need to be seen, be talked about, and know that they have the swag to get a table at any time, any hour, no matter how full the restaurant may be. Who gets these tables? DiCaprio, De Niro, Woody Allen (yes, still), Beyoncé and Jay-Z, Clooney, Oprah, Pitt, all the sports stars, the great chefs, bigwig politicians, models, "old" Wall Street, great regulars (those that dine more than twice a month, spend lots, and tip generously), and neighbors. You always want the neighbors to feel welcome since they're the backbone of the business and will keep coming once DiCaprio and crew have moved on to the next hot thing.

The Wall Street guys were always the most welcome, some receiving legendary status. The best of them were kind, unassuming, always asked if a table was possible and never demanded it. They would order the most expensive wines, know when to give the table up, and, as was the case with the best of them, could make your rent in one visit. These guys had their names marked with *Always gets a table* no matter how full and overbooked the restaurant was.

While working the door, I've been threatened, cursed at, punched, and called every name imaginable, from "shorty" to "arrogant prick," by those unable to get the choice booth or window table. For some, to not get a piece of prime real estate is tantamount to emasculation, and the rage it engenders is something to behold.

So, how does one get a prime piece of real estate without being from one of the protected classes? Honestly, starting with being nice always helps. I've risked having a VIP wait a few extra minutes because a lovely couple came in to celebrate their anniversary and asked for that particular table. Unless every table is being held for superstars, which is rarely the case, any maître d'hôtel worth his or her salt will give that nice couple or four top a great table. And if not, if the maître d' shakes you down for a tip, leave! No restaurant is worth that. Money will almost *always* get you a great table. Just as money (and celebrity) gets the box seats at Yankee Stadium, courtside at the Knicks, on the fifty-yard line at a Giants game, the same is true at restaurants. If a guest comes in, gives their name, and hands you a hundred-dollar bill, are you not going to give them a great table? I like to think this largesse has come to me, for the most part, because I generally love people and treat them all fairly. I care about them, their families, partners, businesses, and so on. I go out of my way to make the guest experience as wonderful as possible. The great doormen and restaurateurs understand this. It is for me what makes this business so special and addicting—the hundreds of thousands of people I have met over the years. It changes every night, and while some nights can be downright awful, the majority are not.

Our chef, Neil, a great horse handicapper, would take bets on the horses from anyone interested in laying down a few bucks as well as covering the spreads on football and basketball games. One busy Saturday evening (a night when we could easily hit four hundred covers), he came to me and said he had just gotten a tip on a horse in the last race at the Meadowlands Racetrack in New Jersey. He needed the carfare to get to and from there so he could put all he had on the horse. He made us a deal that if the floor staff would cover the carfare, he'd place bets for us on the pony, which, according to his guy, was a guaranteed winner. At first I told him he was full of shit and I wouldn't give him a dime, but he was persistent as only degenerate gamblers can be, saying this was a lock, he was risking his job by leaving in the middle of a Saturday night, and that we were crazy not to follow his lead.

I took the bait and Uncle Rob and I stirred up a gambling fever among the staff, made the rounds on the floor, and raised $1,500 from just about everyone who had cash—the servers, captains, bussers, waiters, cocktail servers, valets, cooks, everyone. We covered the carfare and packed the chef off, already coked up and somewhat inebriated, with a few thousand in cash in his pocket, and little time to make it there for the last race. One of the sous-chefs took over running the kitchen. Chef returned around midnight with a shopping bag stuffed with cash. The horse killed it—came in first by a mile.

And They Came . . .

YES, THEY CAME. FROM all walks of celebrity, business, the arts, and fashion. The gossip columnist Liz Smith, closeted at the time, would regularly dine with her partner, Iris Love, their two dogs encamped under the table, holding court and mingling with other Water Club guests. Liz was instrumental in the success of the Water Club, regularly writing about the celebrities that she saw dining there. Calvin Klein came with Roy Cohn and Malcolm Forbes, replete with their boys du jour—blond, milk-fed studs, imported from some magical farm in Iowa, blond gods who were of course "friends" since they were all closeted at the time. Roy Cohn would sit and leer, his pallor yellow, eyes dead, half paying attention to the boy with him, constantly scanning the room for those he knew, worked for, or had fucked over.

The rock stars came. Springsteen, Mick Jagger, Dire Straits, and Rod Stewart. The evening Stewart came, he was so noticeably nervous as he awaited his first date with the model Rachel Hunter that he asked the captain if she thought Rachel would like him. John Fairchild, the legendary publisher of *WWD*, dined regularly with us, and once the copious amounts of wine he consumed became too much for his bladder and a trip to the upstairs toilets too daunting, he would slide open the glass doors that led onto a small balcony and piss over the rail and into the river in full view of the guests. Other regulars included the gracious Walter Cronkite; Ed McMahon, who doled out hundred-dollar bills to any staff member that passed his table; Brooke Shields, celebrating her eighteenth birthday and getting most of the staff on the dance floor with her and her friends; Eileen Ford, who brought in the supermodels of the day and was also Buzzy's pipeline to the endless supply of gorgeous hosts that were stationed at the front of the restaurant. If you weren't beautiful, you had no chance of getting a host position.

On any given night the dining room was a who's who of New York. Geraldine Ferraro lunched with one of Buzzy's partners after she accepted the vice-presidential nomination. Billy Joel, a chronic 10 percent tipper, courted Christie Brinkley here. Joey Heatherton, decked out in diamonds, would show up with manager-boyfriend Jerry Fisher (who she also wound up stabbing), and get so coked up and drunk she'd regularly fall off her barstool. Mel Tormé, Diane Keaton and Warren Beatty, Faye Dunaway, Mary Tyler Moore, Bob Dylan, all came to dine. Mob bosses and crooked politicians had their last meals here before heading off to prison—Howard Golden, Donald Manes, Meade Esposito—it was a complete snapshot of the eighties, at its best and worst.

It's five thirty on a Saturday evening. I'm late to the floor from changing into my tuxedo. As I enter the dining room, Guy grabs me, gives me the you're-fucking-late look, and tells me to get my ass over to table one, where he had already seated a special guest. As I approach the table, I see a couple staring out at the view of Manhattan. I walk around to face the guests and find myself staring at the legend himself, Jackie Gleason. Gleason, rotund as ever, red carnation jutting from his lapel, face gleaming from a fresh shave, with a hint of expensive cologne, sat beside his wife, the picture of elegance. I welcomed them and was about to ask if I could get them a drink (these were the days before every conceivable type of water was offered prior to getting a damn cocktail), but before I could utter a word, Gleason, in his New York Ralph Kramden accent, piped up, "I'll have a J and B on the rocks. The lady will have a glass of Chablis."

With that I was off. It was the Great One himself, the king of Bensonhurst. Returning with the drinks, I placed the wine in front of his wife, and after I put the J&B in front of him, he lifted his glass to sip, reached out with his other hand, grabbed my arm, and held me there as he promptly downed the Scotch. After the famous Gleason "Aaaahhh!" he looked me in the eye and said, "I'll have another!" I returned with the Scotch, and this time, after I placed it in front of him, I waited. He shook me off as I stood there: "Nah. Doctor says only two." He tapped his heart with his free hand. When I returned to the table to talk about the menu and give specials, once again before I could say a word, he blurts out, asking, "Do you have hash browns?" I replied no. Hash browns were not something we'd ever serve. "Do me a favor, ask the chef. Tell him it's for me."

With a huge smile I let him know I would and went straight to the kitchen. Chef Neil, our horse handicapper, was in the kitchen. "Chef, I have a guest that wants to know if you'll make him hash browns." Neil, a Brooklyn boy himself, looked at me and without batting an eye said, "Azzolina, get the fuck out of my kitchen!" I said, "Chef, it's a PPX, it's Jackie Gleason!" Neil again told me to get the fuck out of his kitchen and added that I was just looking to get a hundred-dollar bill from one of my Wall Street guys. "Chef, it's for Jackie fucking Gleason." He again screams at me to get the fuck out of his kitchen. Exasperated, and not wanting to disappoint Gleason, I told Neil to go and see for himself. He dropped what he was doing, gave me the if-you're-fucking-with-me-I'm-going-to-stab-you-in-the-heart stare, marches into the dining room, and sees the Gleasons sitting at the table.

Neil returns to the kitchen and this time gives me a good old, simple "Fuck you" and shouts out to a cook to bring him potatoes. I returned to the table and let Gleason know the chef would be delighted to make him hash browns. Gleason looked at me, smiled, and replied, "I thought so." He and his wife could not have been more pleasant and gracious—both obviously in love—and they had a wonderful dinner. They were the first table of the night, and as their dinner was coming to an end, the restaurant was now packed. The Water Club is a long rectangle, with the maître d'hôtel stand at one end and table one at the other, far end. As the Gleasons were leaving (a stellar tip was of course left on the table), they walked arm in arm down the long aisle toward the exit. As they passed, the diners began realizing who it was, and you could hear the gasps and "Oh my God!" and "Holy shit!" As if choreographed by Busby Berkeley, the guests at the tables rose as though doing the wave at a sporting event and gave him a standing ovation. He reached the maître d'hôtel stand, turned, took an elegant bow to the guests, and, with that big Gleason smile, was gone.

Mimi

EVEN THOUGH THE RESTAURANT was succeeding beyond anyone's expectations, one fear hung over the head of Buzzy O'Keeffe. No, it wasn't the line of tradesmen and purveyors that would come knocking every day to get paid. O'Keeffe is notorious for not paying his bills and one disgruntled chap actually brought in a team to begin dismantling the stairways, promising to take the whole place down if he wasn't paid. A check appeared before he left the building. The fear wasn't of the idiot waiter who couldn't remember to carve out the oysters on his baby chicken, or of the bartender who got caught dealing coke to the rest of the staff, or of the rotating litany of chefs, or of the constant threat of theft of food from the walk-ins and storage. No, the one fear that gnawed at him, that he kept bringing up, was a five-foot-tall Jewish woman from Brooklyn named Mimi.

Mimi Sheraton was the first female food critic for *The New York Times* and had an eight-year run at the paper. Now in her nineties, she still dines out and writes about food for *The Daily Beast*. Her reviews at the time were uncompromising, and her passionate analyses of food, service, and value dead-on. No matter how long a restaurant had been open or how popular it was with the cognoscenti (her review of Regine's was a punch in the face to that establishment), or how many stars it had in the past (Le Cirque was demoted to one star), she focused on the experience, sometimes going back to a restaurant seven or eight times to get it right. Her reviews were well written, honest, and to the point.

O'Keeffe would beg to differ. So much so that he put a $100 bounty on her head. The first person to spot her would get a fresh, crisp C-note and ostensibly be in his favor forever. Of the many diatribes he'd launch on any particular day, the one constant was his disparagement of Mimi Sheraton. He said he had proof she was paid off by other restaurateurs to secure good reviews and was convinced she'd come in before we were "ready" for a review, potentially damaging his reputation and that of the newly built, much-thriving Water Club. Perhaps it was her one-star review of the River Café that had put fear into his restaurateur's heart and pocketbook. She wrote:

> Earsplitting noise and inadequate lighting mar the beauty of the setting. . . . Time lapses between courses can be agonizing, and the management sometimes offers wine as an apology. Once the food arrives, the staff hovers around, snatching plates away and pressuring slow eaters to hurry. . . . But too many dishes arrive tepid or downright cold, and there are a number of misguided combinations in every course.

O'Keeffe had it in for her and wasn't about to let her write a review that could potentially destroy the empire he was building. He approached Claire and me one day and asked us if we'd be willing to surreptitiously wait outside her apartment in the West Village and try to get a photo of her. He wanted to pass it around to the staff to make sure she was spotted the moment she walked in the door. Desperate to solidify my reputation with O'Keeffe and actually honored he entrusted me with this task, Claire and I sat for hours across the street from her apartment one crisp fall morning, camera in hand, awaiting either her entrance or exit, neither of which occurred. We finally gave up, defeated by the cold and the boredom of waiting, and went for breakfast.

It turned out the photograph wasn't necessary. One of our servers had worked at Regine's restaurant, where Mimi was spotted while doing recon for a review. That review is one of the most quoted of Sheraton's lengthy career and definitely worth a read. Spotting her was this server's high point at the Water Club. I hoped he saved that hundred-dollar bill he received from

Buzzy for identifying her, since he was fired shortly afterward when he was caught stealing from the tip pool.

It was a Thursday evening. We were as busy as usual when word spread that she was spotted sitting in the dining room. This was it. The entire staff was made immediately aware. The energy in the room, already heightened by an effervescent Thursday crowd, was made even more so as we awaited the decision—would he actually throw her out or let her get through the meal? Prior to her being recognized, her party had already been seated and served a bottle of wine. After an executive huddle led by Buzzy, the captain was told to return to the table and inform them he would not be giving them menus. As Mimi later wrote, when the captain returned to the table, he said, "We have reason to believe a restaurant critic is at this table and we are not yet ready to serve critics."

A number of flags are perched atop the Water Club; one has a green background with two gold balls on it. After asking a number of times what the flag represented, I was finally told that this was made to represent Buzzy's testicles. There they were, for all to see, detractors and fans, his Irish nuts hanging high above the Water Club. They were certainly on display that night, both above and in the dining room. Well, somewhat on display. True to form, he ran out of the restaurant as soon as he passed his dictum to not serve her. This was something I learned he would do time and time again when things got dicey in one of his restaurants—leave the dirty work to everyone else. Mimi left gracefully, never to return. Buzzy had one of his henchmen immediately call Page Six of the *New York Post*, which reported the episode in the next day's paper. The story went viral. The publicity the Water Club received from this was unbelievable. We were now internationally known. Business was never better.

Extracurricular Activities

LIFE AT THE RESTAURANT was raucous. We settled into a routine of serving for an eight-to-ten-hour shift and then reconnoitering at the bar of the moment to have a postmortem on that evening's service. Wherever we wound up, the alcohol flowed and sooner or later one of us would head out and find the nearest dealer for grams of coke. The nights regularly extended to four, five, and sometimes eight or nine in the morning, as we usually headed home as the sun was coming up and all the nine-to-fivers were heading to work.

We had our favorite haunts. Marylou's on West Ninth Street was one. This basement restaurant was lorded over by Marylou herself, a rather large, vibrant woman who would host that evening's celebrities and then lock the door at 4:00 A.M. so the party could continue into the early morning. The legendary jazz club Bradley's was a few blocks away on University Place, and the musicians—some of the great jazz artists of the time—after a set, would head to Marylou's, where they drank for free and the blow was handed out like candy. The place was filled with mobsters and stars. Jack Nicholson, Jay McInerney, Robert De Niro, Oliver Stone, and Eric Roberts—all were regulars. After the servers and bartenders at other restaurants quit their shifts, they would head over, grab drinks, and then fight for space in the toilets to break out bags of coke.

J.S. VanDam was another legendary spot, located across the street from the renowned Heartbreak club and just a few blocks up from the Odeon, both of which are memorialized in McInerney's *Bright Lights, Big City*. This was the booze and drug alley of TriBeCa. Whatever you needed was there to be had. The bar at VanDam was run by two legends, Jed and Danny, who were master bartenders; their mastery extended from being supreme mixologists to their remarkable ability to down considerable amounts of alcohol and coke while working a bar that was three deep with drinkers. This was another spot where the toilets below were as popular as the bar and restaurant above. The lines were so long that most of the men just went outside to pee, while the women would go to the restaurant next door, since the VanDam's stalls were filled with groups of people either snorting coke, having sex, or both.

Up above, when the stress became too much, the boys behind the bar would pull out their bags of coke, lay out lines on the sink, and do what were termed gaggers. This is when they'd inhale so much coke at once, that the rush would be so intense, their system so apparently overwhelmed, that they'd puke in the sink behind the bar, down a shot of chilled vodka, shake it off like a dog in a park, and get back to work. Then, at 4:00 A.M. they'd lock the doors, and the poker games would begin, usually lasting till noon.

All our bad habits were not limited to after work. The debauchery was rampant at work as well. Al was on fire every night. I've never met another human being who managed to screw as many women as possible at his place of work, yet also be so open about letting those he was screwing know that he was screwing everyone else, and no one seemed to care. Al would regularly take out his penis and show it to whoever wanted to see it—and even some who didn't. You'd turn a corner and there he'd be, penis out, dangling almost to his knee, as he polished a glass or some silverware.

One of his gimmicks was to tear a hole in his pants pocket and place his penis in the pocket. During one setup, as he polished a glass, the sommelier came walking into the dining room, asking if anyone had a corkscrew. Al, glass and rag in hand as he kept polishing, told the sommelier to reach into his pocket to get his. As the sommelier did, he let out a scream of surprise as all he got in hand was a large penis. His smile made us all know he would love to go back for more.

Another night, Al told me to wait ten minutes and then go to the front bar and stand across from the service bar so I could get a clear view of it. At the appointed time I headed there, abandoning my busy station, because if Al said to do something, it was probably worth any penalty incurred. As I stood with a clear view of the service station, there was Al, with one of the cocktail wait-resses whom he was having a fling with, standing next to him, her hand in his pocket, giving him a hand job. Both stood smiling at me as she jerked him off.

Boyd was a sometime accessory to the exhibitionism. His penis matched that of Al's in size, though at almost a foot taller than Al, the initial impression was not as awe-inspiring. Both of them were runners. One of their tasks was to wheel out a hurdy-gurdy, one of O'Keeffe's little enhancements to dining room service. The hurdy-gurdy is a music box on wheels, in the shape of a wheelbarrow. On one side was a hand crank that, when turned, emitted the "Happy Birthday" melody from the box. The runner's job would be to wheel this contraption out from the kitchen for every birthday celebrated at the restaurant, along with a piece of cake and candle. Boyd and Al would jump at every chance they could to bring out the cake and music box. Boyd wheeling, and Al, with cake in hand, would reach the table, and one of them would begin cranking the box while the other presented the cake. What all the servers knew, but the guests were unaware of, was that, under their long kitchen aprons, they would have their penises out and as one spun the crank and the other sang a vigorous rendition of "Happy Birthday," the motions from spinning the crank and from singing would have both their penises flapping up and down under their aprons in time with the music.

I understand that, as times have changed, all this behavior may seem nothing short of horrible. Perhaps we really fucked up, but as far as I knew, the antics were freely partaken by everyone involved. No jobs were threatened, no one was pressured into doing anything. We were all in on it, and if there was any discomfort, it was never mentioned. I now understand that there are some, who, for fear of retribution, might not have spoken up. The industry has, thankfully, gotten better at this. These wild and raucous times were fueled by alcohol and drugs. It's not an excuse. This is how it was.

We had a new manager join us soon after the restaurant opened. He was a buttoned-up, red-faced, by-the-book Irishman from New Jersey. Up till now, management was weak, and we servers pretty much ran the room. I was elected headwaiter by the staff, and this allowed me to do the scheduling, which meant the original crew got pretty much what we wanted. We were all incredibly popular with the guests, and with business doing so well, we afforded ourselves many liberties. Perhaps too many. Red Face was brought in to take charge and rein in our little team. He immediately took over the scheduling and tried to crack down on the drinking, though with the likes of Dr. Dewar's behind the bar, this was a losing battle.

One evening after service, the Jock convinced me, Uncle Rob, Claire, and a couple of other servers to go with him to the notorious sex club Hellfire, located in the old Meatpacking District. Back then, slabs of meat hung from the trucks and racks outside the butcher shops, and the streets were filled with prostitutes of all sorts—straight, gay, trans—you name it. The abandoned docks just a few blocks away were notorious gay sex playgrounds. Just a few doors down from Hellfire was the now-legendary gay BDSM sex club the Mineshaft. While the Mineshaft was men only, both straight and gay, both sexes were welcome at Hellfire.

The club was in a mostly unfinished basement and as you entered the club, the bar was right at the front. Both bartenders, a man and a woman, were dressed in leather harnesses, and each had enough piercings to set off metal detectors from ten feet away—nipples, navels, ears, face, genitals—it was a piercing extravaganza. We ordered drinks and settled in. The Jock had been here before. He told us a model he was dating was a regular—her thing was being collared and leashed and led across the floor on all fours by a midget.

Red Face had told Jock that he would join us after he got off work. We had all laughed and thought this would never happen, but sure enough, he showed up a little later, still in suit and tie. Eventually Uncle Rob and I stepped away to go to the toilet. The stalls were up three small steps in the back and on the bottom step lay a man in a white Izod cable-knit sweater and white pants. To get up to the bathrooms you had to first step on him and the now-soiled white Izod sweater. Once in the bathroom, there were no urinals, only a bathtub with a guy lying in there naked. It was the only place to pee.

When we returned to the bar, Claire and I decided to check out the back. It was a typical, unfinished NYC basement—dirt floors, exposed pipes, and small rooms that were made of brick or cinder block, which in the past had housed the building's meters, storage, et cetera, but were now crumbling and being used for various types of trysts. It was quite dark, and you had to squint to make out the figures, all in various forms of copulation or S&M acts.

As I turned a corner, I could make out three figures, and as we got closer, I recognized one of them. There was our red-faced, by-the-book, shit-ass manager on all fours, in the dirt, one cock in his mouth and another up his ass. I was fucking floored. I immediately ran back to the bar, asked the bartender for pen and paper and just got back just as Red Face was peeling himself off the floor. I handed him the paper. "Here's our schedules for the next month." We never had a problem with him again.

The habits and predilections of the staff were becoming more apparent every day. Little side businesses sprang up to feed off the cash that was plentiful in everyone's pocket. The coke would come from guests as tips, or from either of the two cooks in the kitchen or the head bartender. The bartender was eventually caught and fired, though after a long enough cooling-off period, someone would eventually step in and fill the void. Some servers would go shopping at the end of their shift, which meant they'd stop off in dry storage and fill their bags with tea, jams, salt, pepper, whatever they might need at home. In the handicapped bathroom and the upstairs linen room, one could steal away to do lines or a quick fuck. The linen room was a favorite because of the stacks of soft white linen you could lie on. When no drugs were available at the restaurant, the nearby Lower East Side (LES) provided a fast alternative, especially for the ones who needed a quick heroin fix.

Boyd had a heroin habit, as did one of the line cooks. When the need got bad, he'd suddenly disappear from the floor and get one of the other runners to cover for him. Still in uniform, he'd sneak out into the street, take a taxi down to the LES, score his drugs, and head back to the restaurant. He could do the trip and be back on the floor in thirty minutes. He'd shoot up in the handicapped toilet, the drugs would kick in, and he'd go into the silver room, which was adjacent to the kitchen, and puke his guts up into a silver wine bucket.

He'd also score for a couple of servers as well as the cook, who was a large, sweet, gentle giant of a man. I have no idea where or how he'd shoot up, but we all knew when the drugs kicked in. He was in charge of the lobsters and the Dover sole, the most expensive items on the menu, and the higher he got, the more orders he'd drop on the floor. Since we loved both of these guys, everyone covered for them and, to cover up his cooking errors, would just keep cooking the sole and lobsters so that when one hit the floor, he'd have another waiting. At the end of the shift there would be so many leftover lobsters he had cooked to replace the dropped ones that we'd all get to feast on lobster after the shift. Chef Neil was always kind enough to try to help him out. Knowing the cook had drugs stashed in his locker, he went to the locker room, broke into the locker, and sure enough, it was not only filled with coke, but also a gun. He tossed the gun into the East River. I have no idea what happened to the coke.

Of course the Three Sisters were also involved. David (dubbed Screecheeta due to his high-pitched voice) loved to cruise the bathrooms at Penn Station and would regularly miss his shift because he'd get arrested for either giving or getting head in the toilets. Another of the Three Sisters was best friends with Keith Haring and hung with the Basquiat crowd. He was another who'd hop a cab between shifts to score heroin and then return to work. Then there was the Bi-Boys Club, a group of supposedly "straight" men who sometimes slept with other men. None of them admitted to being either bi or gay, though the Singer was a member and apparently thrown out for never having slept with a woman. Some were in the club because they were in the closet, like the Jock, others because they were actually bi, and others because they'd get so fucked-up on whatever substance was being used that night that they'd fuck anyone.

Sadly, this would turn fatal for many of them. In 1981 the first cases of what would soon be known as AIDS occurred. One of the first was a friend of mine at the University of Florida, someone we all thought was straight, had a girlfriend whom I'd slept with, and died in 1981. By 1982 the fear had started to spread but did little to alleviate the promiscuity. During summers, a group of us would rent a house on Fire Island. By the late eighties four of our roommates would be dead. The Jock was dating a lovely female server while active in the Bi-Boys Club. They would both eventually die of AIDS as well.

Today it seems difficult to imagine the fear that many had about catching the disease. Little was known about how it spread, and rumors abounded. Was it possible to catch it from a sneeze, a kiss, touching the hand of someone that was infected, mosquitoes, blood? No one knew. One night, Claire and another captain were shelling the two-to-four-pound lobsters tableside, which was essential to sell these expensive monsters, when one cut herself on a shell. The guests freaked out and said they wouldn't accept the lobsters since the captains weren't wearing gloves and accused them of trying to give them AIDS.

Screecheeta was one of the first to show symptoms. Already thin, he began to lose weight while Kaposi's sarcoma lesions were beginning to appear on his body. He had soon lost so much weight that one of our captains, who was also in the fashion business, took a few busser coats and sewed in shoulder pads so Screecheeta wouldn't appear so emaciated. One evening when the phone rang in the dining room, Screecheeta, seeing no one at the maître d'hôtel stand, picked it up. Ratso saw this and screamed across the room, "Don't pick it up! You're going to give everyone AIDS!"

We saw the signs in our fellow workers as they began to succumb to the disease. First a cough that wouldn't go away. Then the Kaposi's sarcoma lesions would appear. Then the hospital stay when they'd be quarantined, and when you visited, you had to be robed and masked. Then the funerals. Scores of them. Screecheeta and his boyfriend, the Jock and his girlfriend, all died. In my building there are eight apartments. Six of them were inhabited by gay men. In two years all had died.

The All-Star

When one of our bartenders was fired for selling coke at the restaurant, Buzzy soon hired a renowned bartender to replace him. I am not sure if Buzzy was aware that not only was he renowned for his dazzling skills behind the bar, but for his insatiable appetite for women, booze, and drugs. Let's call him Ciaran.

Ciaran was a legend at the SoHo eatery La Gamelle prior to becoming the maître d'hôtel at Keith McNally's infamous Odeon. The fact that he was looking for work after his two prior, stellar jobs should have raised a red flag. But Buzzy liked the fact he was getting a star, and one from McNally at that, so he didn't look too closely at his prize. At La Gamelle, he oversaw a bar that was packed every night, customers five deep, waiting for their booze. He worked it alone, gripping bottles by the neck, two in each hand and making two, three, or four cocktails at a clip.

With his striking, half-Italian, half-Irish looks, tall, built, and like me, spawned from a Mob family, his incredible blue eyes had seen more by the time he was ten then most will in a lifetime. Perhaps this is what made us friends. When you went to La Gamelle you knew you'd watch a master at work, never pay for a drink if you were "family," and once past 10:00 P.M., when the bottle of Jameson he kept on the side for himself was half emptied, the lines of coke weren't far behind.

I doubt Buzzy knew all the details of his career, but he was already a legend and hiring him seemed inevitable, especially given his Irish ancestry. He began at the service bar, the front, main bar, already stocked with Buzzy's men. This in itself should have been a warning sign; great bartenders have many opportunities and wouldn't settle for a service bar job unless this was the only one he was able to get.

He wasted little time in making his mark at the restaurant. While his proficient skills were made little use of at the service bar, his storytelling and his alcohol and drug habits were soon apparent. The women loved him. Some nights, when things began to slow down, he'd disappear for a bit, usually to do some lines in the linen room with either a hostess, reservationist, or cocktail server in tow. It was easy to figure out who he was having sex with. You just needed to see who was missing from the floor when he was and for how long. The reservations office on the second floor directly above the main bar was a favorite spot of his, as was the reservationist. You knew he was there when: 1) the service bar was unattended; 2) the phone at the maître d'hôtel stand was ringing off the hook; and 3) you could hear a repetitive, bam, bam, bam, on the ceiling above the main bar. This meant that he and the reservationist had snorted their lines of coke on the massive desk (that doubled as Buzzy's) and were now copulating on top of it. Each thrust so vigorous, the desk's bouncing on the floor above the main bar could be heard by all. Management would have by now either gone home or, being the recipient of his largesse, turned a blind eye to his antics and this, together with his reputation, made him almost untouchable. Though this wasn't surprising since the GM was himself a frequent cocaine user, as were his inner circle. He wasn't about to rock the boat, though he was eventually caught and convicted of embezzlement.

One Sunday evening, it was approaching 10:00 P.M., the main bar was dead, and there were only a few tables in the dining room, all lingering and past desserts. We'd soon be closing. The bartender at the main bar would usually leave at this point, and the service bartender would close his bar and take over in the front. The dining room staff would then get what they needed from the main bar. The entire evening had been slow, allowing him to start drinking earlier than usual and he'd already put a large dent in the bottle of Jameson he usually consumed during a shift. I watched him finish off the bottle as he headed to the front.

The room of the main bar is a long rectangle. At one end and through a doorway, is the entrance to the restaurant where a security guard kept watch after ten. At the other end of the room is a fireplace with a few tables around it. The only guest sitting at the bar was an employee who worked in the finance department, was gay, and who never ceased showing an obvious affection and desire for Ciaran. I went to pick up drinks when I noticed Ciaran had cracked open a second bottle of Jameson. As I stood there garnishing the drinks, I see John X, a friend of Buzzy's, arrive and take a stool at the bar. This was an oh-fuck moment. X was universally disliked by the staff, especially Ciaran. X was rude, a drunk, never shut up, and the more he drank the louder, ruder, and more belligerent he became. His behavior was tolerated by the staff only owing to his relationship with the owner.

This wasn't the night to sit at Ciaran's bar. His frequent absences from it attested to the amount of coke he had done and at this point he was pretty fucked up. X sits, Ciaran eyes him, and instead of going over to ask what he'd like to drink, he turns, walks over to where I am standing, rests one arm on the bar, and with the other hand lifts the bottle of Jameson and takes a long swig. He puts down the bottle, returns to X, and leans in very closely to his face. They say a few words to each other, Ciaran then walks back to where I am, reaches down and picks up a five-gallon bucket that usually holds the iced house wines. The bucket was now empty, except for the icy cold water that had yet to be disposed of. He lifts the bucket over his head, stares at X, and dumps the entire bucket over himself. "Oh my god." I say to myself. Dripping ice water, he walks back to X, reaches for a martini glass from the back of the bar, chews it, and spits the glass in X's face. He then rips open his shirt, beats on his chest as though imitating Tarzan, lets out a bloodcurdling scream, jumps over the bar, grabs X, and begins dragging him toward the fireplace. X is screaming, Ciaran is screaming, I start screaming, when our gent from accounting leaps from his stool, screams "Ciaran!!!!!" and throws himself on his bare back either to try to stop him, feel his bare skin, or both. Then another scream in a thick Haitian accent, "Ciaran!!!!!" It's our beloved security guard, a six-foot-six behemoth, running toward them, screaming "Ciaran, no!!!!!" and with the speed, finesse, and aggression of Lawrence Taylor, traverses the distance in seconds and pulls the trio to the ground just before X was shoved into the fire.

The River Café

ONE AFTERNOON I WAS called into Buzzy's office (the front table by the door). He told me that the River Café needed a captain and asked if I would be interested. I was stunned. For me this was the opportunity of a lifetime. Stifling my desire to scream, I said of course I'd be interested and he left it at that.

The River Café is one of the most beautiful and romantic restaurants in the world. It sits on a barge in the East River and under the majestic Brooklyn Bridge. Located on the Brooklyn side of the river, it provides unparalleled views of lower Manhattan. This is restaurateur Buzzy O'Keeffe's ode to New York City. You can almost hear the strains of Gershwin as you look out the windows at capitalism's tribute to itself, a view of Manhattan Island as glorious, romantic, and iconic as the opening of Woody Allen's *Manhattan*. This is New York. The roaring eighties, Reagan's America. Wall Street is flush. Trickle-down economics is trickling down like the leaky faucet in my East Village tenement, slowly, a bit rusty, probably full of lead, and gradually making its way to those fortunate enough to rub elbows with the beneficiaries of this decade's boom.

The River Café began as a red-sauce joint, replete with red-checked tablecloths. Buzzy aspired to more and hired Larry Forgione (from master chef Michel Guérard's restaurant Regine's, in New York City) to run the kitchen at the Café. This would be the first of the many incredible successes O'Keeffe had with chefs here. Forgione turned it into a serious food restaurant. When

Forgione moved on, the kitchen was taken over by Charlie Palmer, under whose stewardship the restaurant received three out of four stars from *The New York Times*.

This was another dimension of the restaurant world. This was serious shit. Buzzy's maniacal running of the Water Club was nothing compared to how he was here at the Café. He sought absolute perfection, both inside and out. From the beautifully landscaped entrance at the front of the restaurant to every aspect of the dining room and the kitchen, he was in control and expected all his employees to share his strive for perfection. The valets up front, bow tied and white jacketed, wore the same uniform throughout the year. It didn't matter how cold or hot it was outside; the look was paramount. Once guests disembarked from their vehicle, the polished brass handles on the entrance door of the restaurant were pulled open and they were escorted through a small room, where two lovely hostesses (as at the Water Club, if you weren't beautiful, you didn't get a job greeting guests) would check them in and send them down a gangway to the dining room and bar.

If the Water Club was hot, a seat here was even hotter and more difficult to acquire. Reservations opened two weeks prior, and by 11:00 A.M. of the morning the books opened, the restaurant was totally filled. That is, the seats that were available to the general public. Like most restaurants I've worked, the best tables were held for regulars, the cognoscenti, and the well-heeled.

The room was helmed by two maîtres d'hôtel, Nicky and Rodney, both Italian Americans, and both defying Buzzy's dictum that the maître d'hôtel be the tallest person in the dining room. Each stood below five feet, eight inches. Rodney, whom I'd befriended from the times I had dined here and he at the Water Club, had spoken to Buzzy about me once he knew one of the captains was leaving to open his own restaurant.

If La Rousse was off-off-Broadway, this was now Broadway. The lure for me was both egoistic and monetary. The Café was famous for both food and service, the guest list surpassed that of the Water Club, and since the River was smaller, much more beautiful, and had its third star, guests had a much tougher time getting a table. The harder it is to get into a restaurant, the more the swells want to be there, and they will pay handsomely for that privilege. The restaurant was slowly climbing to legendary status because of its food, service, and stunning views, and its soon-to-be all-star lineup of cooks and chefs would solidify that standing for years to come.

This was also validation that I was very, very good at my job—a job I loved. The other lure was the money. We earned excellent money at the Water Club, but with the higher prices and smaller staff at the Café, and with the captains getting a bigger cut of the tip pool, this was the gold standard of captain jobs. Apparently, the captain that was leaving was about to open his own restaurant, Provence, in SoHo, which itself became ridiculously famous and one of the best French bistros in the city. While he had given plenty of notice, his time to leave was getting near. Each time I saw Buzzy at the Water Club, I watched for any inkling regarding the move. He gave away nothing.

Complicating this was the service director of the River Café. Rodney forewarned me that this particular gentleman was, on a good day, not only disagreeable, but hated interviews and rarely hired someone he didn't know from a previous restaurant or someone that was recommended by an authority in the restaurant business. He was also a misanthrope. In addition, he was aware of the anniversary lunch some of us from the Water Club had had there and its aftermath.

On the Water Club's first anniversary, ten of the original group that opened the restaurant went to mark the occasion at the River Café. Since we all worked evenings, it would be impossible for each of us to take off on the same night, so lunch was our only option. At this celebratory affair, the cost of the liquor we drank far surpassed the cost of the food. While I do remember us being somewhat well-behaved, we were all trashed by the end of the meal. That was the first offense. The second was that Buzzy picked up the entire check. This didn't help our already dicey reputation, since he'd apparently never done anything similar for the staff at the Café.

Once finished, we all piled into taxis for the trip back to Manhattan and work. When we arrived at the Water Club, I realized I was so smashed that there was no way I'd be able to captain a station. Uncle Rob decided it was best for me to run food that night. He figured that I'd be able to make it through the shift by carrying a few plates to a table with the assistance of him and the other runners. Things began pretty smoothly. Dr. Dewar's was behind the bar, and once he saw my state of inebriation, he insisted I follow doctor's orders and kept plying me with shots to keep me on an even keel. A couple of lines of coke provided by one of the runners didn't hurt, and by midshift I felt like King Kong—whisking plates through the dining room with an inflated confidence and a compromised dexterity brought on by the coke and booze.

Just as I was about to pound on my chest in the kitchen and let out a roar, an order came up for a ten top my station. This wasn't unusual, and our practiced runners did it regularly. Plates were carried on trays and stacked with lids on top of each plate, which made stacking a tray relatively easy. All the plates were round and fit nicely on top of one another. I made three stacks of three plates each, but the tenth plate was going to be a problem. It was chef Neil's evening's special, a whole coho salmon *à la nage*, which translates to "in the swim." The entire fish was swimming in a lobster sauce. It was plated on an oval and not a round plate. The oval plates had no covers and couldn't be stacked. The only way to get the whole order out on one tray was to set the oval on top of the rounds and make sure that I kept the tray balanced as I walked the length of the restaurant.

Our expediter and the other runners saw this and didn't want me to carry the tray. They pleaded with me to let one of the bigger guys do it or at least to break it down to two trays. But the King Kong in me was having none of it. Belligerent and feeling no pain, I stacked the tray, balanced the uncovered fish on the top, and lifted the entire thing as though doing a power lift and headed out of the kitchen to the horror of those watching.

Needless to say, the table I was carrying the food to was at the complete other end of the restaurant. I set off on my journey. The dining room is packed, guests spilling out into the aisles, and as I got about a third of the way down, I realize that this tray is fucking heavy. My arm starts to tremble from the weight of it, and I can hear the plate on top rattling as I keep walking. I'm now two-thirds of the way down and I break into a sweat. An entire day of booze and coke is seeping out of my pores, my arm is shaking, and the plate with the swimming fish is now rattling so much that it's all I can hear. As I make my way to the end of the aisle, I see the look of terror on the faces of the other servers—all of them are staring at the plate that is quivering atop my tray. I finally reach the table, set down the tray stand, raise my arm to lower the tray, and as I do, the oval plate—which had slid to the end during my walk—tips over. The fish goes flying into the air and the sauce it was sitting in now following. I turn and see the host of the party, sitting with the fish atop his head and lobster sauce dripping onto his suit. Mortified, I was ready to be fired when suddenly, one of his guests lets out a belly laugh that is so guttural and so infectious, that everyone around begins to laugh as well, including the host, who now has the salmon sitting in his lap.

The Call

My DISASTROUS NIGHT AS a runner certainly didn't bode well for me moving to the River Café, and I became less hopeful. But at the proverbial eleventh hour, the call finally came. My interview was set for the following week. I told no one at the Water Club for fear of some sort of alienation if I got the job, since so many there would die for the opportunity, but also the humiliation if I failed.

On the day of the interview I shaved, donned my best Armani, and sprung for a taxi across the East River. I didn't want to take the subway and arrive in a sweat on this hot August afternoon. As the taxi approached the gardens at the front of the restaurant, I saw the gold nameplate embossed with THE RIVER CAFÉ gleaming in the sun, no doubt polished three times a day by one of the Haitian porters Buzzy employed at all his restaurants at minimum wage. I may as well have taken the subway and saved the fare as I broke into a nervous sweat as the taxi crossed the entrance and stopped at the front door. A valet in a starched white jacket opened the door of the taxi and then held open the restaurant door for me.

Entering, I introduced myself to the bombshell hostess gracing the entryway and was escorted to a corner table to await the service director. Knowing Buzzy's parameters for hiring his floor staff—generally men, tall, handsome, and fit—I was somewhat shocked to see the tuxedoed figure that approached me from a distance. He looked like a cross between *Young Frankenstein*'s Igor and Dracula's assistant, Renfield. Shuffling toward me, slightly stooped, thinning hair atop an egg-shaped head, as unattractive a human as was ever born, he reached out to shake my hand. As he did, I couldn't take my eyes off the pronounced, saggy black bags under his eyes. It looked as though he slept restlessly on a banquette in the restaurant at night, having nightmares of the errant fools on his staff making horrible mistakes—putting a twist in a martini when an olive was requested, placing the plate holding the fillet of sole at a slightly wrong angle in front of a guest, or a server's not being on the floor at the exact moment he was needed. The possibilities of infractions, real and perceived, were limitless.

As I placed my hand in his, I was jolted by the cold yet clammy palm attached to a limp wrist. It was as though I were holding the hand of a dead man. When he separated his dry, cracked lips to smile, I caught a glimpse of his gray and crooked teeth. With a look of utter disgust, which I soon learned was his usual look, he said, "So you are employed at the Water Club." The name of the restaurant, dragged out so slowly that it took about thirty seconds for him to get the words out, was uttered with such repugnancy, one would think that this particular eatery was the perpetrator of the worst possible ills that could ever befall a diner.

He was obviously aware of our reputation. His entire restaurant existence was based in fine dining, and to him, the Water Club might as well be a McDonald's, with those employed in such a shameful locale unfit to serve anything but fare prepared for cattle. In addition, here I was the first to break Buzzy's dictum that there would be no crossover between the restaurants. I believe the service director resented me for this more than anything else. Whatever drew such an uncongenial individual to hospitality escaped me entirely.

I wanted to run, but as I looked at that view over his shoulders, at the city that has lured so many to it with its promises of riches, sex, and fame—while also crushing an equal amount—I knew I wanted to be here. I instead sat there obediently, as though I were back at church, in my starched altar-boy robes, awaiting the priest to drunkenly slur his words through another mass. I nodded and smiled through all the affronts he attributed to the Water Club, and how such would never be tolerated here in his precious gem of a dining room.

But I knew I needed to get him off the subject of the Water Club, so I pivoted and went right for his ego. I agreed with every calumny and slander he hurled at my current place of employment, concurring with his assessments, telling him how difficult it was to work in an environment with such a perfid-ious and amateur staff. I told him how I aspired to better, a restaurant filled with professionals such as himself, a place where I could not only learn, but thrive under his renowned tutelage. Having eaten here twice, I told him how remarkable and flawless the service was under his dominion, and that it was what I aspired to most in my career. To be mentored by a true professional.

The deception seemed to be working. The flattery penetrated his dead heart. He asked quite a few questions about service, which I aced. I knew he was aware of the rampant drug and alcohol use at the Water Club when he asked the dreaded question: "So, do you ever drink or use drugs while at work?" I stared straight at those gray teeth emanating from a now-gleeful smile as I lied and said that I knew it went on, but I never partook of such since it was not only unprofessional, but I was also taking acting classes and didn't want anything to interfere with that.

The interview felt like it lasted a month. I was once again soaked through with nervous perspiration when he at last stood to dismiss me. As I bid my goodbye and was exiting the dining room, I noticed it had filled up with the evening's staff starting their shift. All had their knowing eyes on me, each having survived Renfield's inquisition, and now employed and raking in the cash in this, his precious dining room. One gent polishing silver struck me in particular. A small, curly-haired fellow with an extremely high forehead, who gave me a knowing grin and smirk as I exited.

It Begins

I HEARD NOTHING FOR two weeks. I reached out to Rodney, but he had zero news other than to say Renfield had confirmed my interview. I spent the next couple of weeks just going through the motions at work. In my mind I was already out of there. Then, finally, I received a call from Renfield. He said he'd spoken to Buzzy, and my training would begin the following week. This was my shot and I wanted it badly.

This time I took the subway to Brooklyn. I figured I'd save a few bucks and knew I'd be able to change prior to the shift. Brooklyn wasn't yet the Brooklyn of today, famous, replete with hipsters, artisans, distillers, craftsmen and craftswomen, and renegade restaurateurs who had fled the high rents of Manhattan. The neighborhood the River Café was in, now named Dumbo, was barren, unsafe, most of it burned-out, and little remained of its days as a mercantile area. Manhattan still housed the artists, punks, anarchists, and those that made up the counterculture, but they would soon either flee or die off, and Manhattan would become the borough of the elite.

With a new Bill Blass tuxedo in tow, I entered the restaurant, introduced myself to the lovely host guarding the door, and let her know I was here for training. She listlessly raised her arm and pointed me to the dining room.

As I entered the sun-drenched room, that glorious view, Manhattan in the distance, the Brooklyn Bridge towering above us, blew me away. The staff was setting up the dining room, some in partial uniform with shirts unbuttoned at the neck, others with ties undone, hanging rakishly down. I saw the captains' tuxedo jackets draped over chairbacks as they busied themselves with side work, polishing glasses and silver, folding napkins, straightening and leveling tables, and setting up the server stations. This scene is played out daily in restaurants throughout the world. What was atypical was the remarkable view of lower Manhattan—the Woolworth Building, once the tallest in the world, the World Trade Center towers dominating over the Financial District, the stock exchange, the Federal Reserve, the seats of power and money—and the glorious span of the Brooklyn Bridge, which held aloft the thousands of cars going each day to and from the storied borough of Manhattan. You could almost smell the cash as it headed over the bridge to this barge in Brooklyn, where the swells fought for the privilege of spending their hard-earned capital right-fucking-here. The entire scene made me want to shit my pants. If things went well, I'd be witness to this daily.

Whether it was utter panic or the aftermath of the lines of coke and three martinis I had at J.S. VanDam the night before to quell my nerves, it didn't matter. I pivoted from this glorious scene and headed straight to the toilet, where I puked my guts up. Thank God I had a toothbrush in my bag. I pulled myself together as best I could, once again passing Ms. Lovely at the front desk, who barely acknowledged me with a dismissive half smirk as I reentered the dining room, neither of us aware at that moment we'd be fucking in three months, falling madly in love, and that our tempestuous relationship would last five years.

Through the corner of my eye I spied Renfield. He saw me entering and headed toward me. His stooped shuffle and unrushed gait made traversing the distance a drawn-out affair, taking twice as long as it would take anyone else. This caused me to hold my smile, a frozen grimace that made my jaw ache, a residual effect from the incessant grinding as I vainly tried to fall asleep the night before. A result of the coke. My head was pounding, and by the time Renfield reached me, I was ready to puke again.

He looked more Quasimodo than ever, and as he spoke, the stench of what smelled like goat cheese and wine on his breath nauseated me, precipitating a tiny drip of bile to escape my stomach and settle in my mouth. My only choice was to re-swallow the acidic liquid as he motioned for me to sit.

In his dolorous monotone, he explained what the training was going to be like. I did my best to stay as far away from his reeking breath as possible, as he let me know that prior to taking a station as a captain, I was going to have to train as both a front and a back waiter. Since I was to lead a team and run a station, I'd better damn well know how to perform everyone's job equal to or better than them. I knew from my previous experience that you train with the best person in each position, and if you don't perform, management will hear about it *tout de suite*. Nothing was guaranteed.

I also knew that Renfield preferred that I, of the inferior Water Club, not work in his sacred dining room. It was apparent I wasn't his first choice, and he was being forced to train me. I also knew he was going to quiz each person I trailed, looking for ways to not get me hired. Pros will know on the first night if you have it or not. Depending on the restaurant, you may spend days or even weeks doing a position trail prior to becoming a captain.

Finishing his recitation, he pointed me to the other end of the dining room, telling me to join the staff, who were just about to have family meal. As I stood to thank him and get as far away from him as quickly as possible, my suit bag caught on the edge of the table, and as I started off, it yanked the tablecloth from the table, bringing the glasses, plates, and silverware with it, all hitting the ground with such a piercing crash that everyone in the dining room stopped what they were doing and stared at me and the scene at my feet. I heard Renfield utter, "Oh my fucking God!"—and then suddenly, "We got this!" It was the server that had smirked and smiled at me the day I was exiting from my interview. He had two bussers in tow, and they graciously began cleaning up the mess. My new savior ushered me out of the dining room to escape the wrath of Renfield.

He introduced himself as Jimmy and told me he was the boyfriend of one of my former (I hoped) coworkers at the Water Club. I then remembered her telling me he worked here, and that I should introduce myself to him once I arrived. He led me out to the back of the restaurant to where the ice machine was kept, grabbed a cup, filled it with ice, and, from a flask he pulled out of his back pocket, poured me a stiff shot of vodka. It was as though we were in a fifties melodrama, with the orchestra playing, and angels descending from above. He looked knowingly at me. "Looks like you had a rough night. Nervous?" My reputation had obviously preceded me. I laughed as I downed the vodka, thanked him profusely, and slowly began to come back to life.

The Family That Dines Together . . .

FAMILY MEAL CAN BE the most alienating of meals. Its homey name intimates that a restaurant's staff is a family that dines and shares together or, as is sometimes the case, fights, bickers, and isolates. It is usually served right before the FOH staff changes and meets for the pre-shift meeting. In most restaurants, the food at family meal may include the previous night's unfinished family meal, leftovers from the service the evening before, food that is about to turn rancid and be tossed, or food purchased specifically for this meal. It's usually composed of the cheapest protein available at the moment. Fine-dining restaurants never give you the food they purchase for the guests. It's too damn expensive, and the few dollars the house takes from your salary each shift isn't able to cover the high-quality food our guests receive. Chicken generally leads the pack, with hot dogs and pork a close second. Many times it's from a clearing out of the walk-ins of everything that is about to go bad and cooked up for the staff.

Many cooks hate preparing family meal. Chefs want to spend as little as possible on buying the food, and on nights when the kitchen is behind and the cook designated to make the meal is deep in the shits, what you get may as well be shit. If it's fish, never, ever, eat it. Staff get fish only when it's impossible to sell to a guest because it's outlived its shelf life, and it's usually fried to disguise the rank smell as much as possible. Vegetables or salads are unheard of. This meal is as fast and basic as it gets.

Three stars notwithstanding, the family meal at the River Café was disgusting. This evening's fare was impossible to discern; bits of what looked like chicken, celery, carrots, and other indecipherable pieces of what one hoped was edible all floated like flotsam in oil. In my current state, a bite of this would bring up everything that was remaining in my gut. I grabbed a piece of bread and some water, took a seat, and tried to mentally prepare myself for the evening. On your first day, most of the staff ignore you, except the ones sitting closest to you, and due to proximity, introduce themselves, make small talk, and then turn back to their friends or newspapers. I was sitting a few chairs away from everyone and was thankfully left alone.

One afternoon, the family meal that was put up before the shift was another in a string of daily detestable offerings. It was a large pan, containing some indecipherable pieces of protein, floating in what looked like remnants of the oil spill from the Exxon *Valdez* disaster. We'd had enough. Rodney, in a very ballsy move that might have cost him his job, decided to wrap up the pan and get one of our runners to take a taxi to the Water Club, deliver it to Buzzy, and let him see the garbage we were being given to eat. Thirty minutes later a dozen pizzas arrived.

The Trail

THE FIRST NIGHTS OF a trail, everyone is checking you out and sizing you up. Are you good enough? Are you a team player? An earner? Do you drink? Drugs? Are you a rat? A plant of the owner who will tell him of all the horrible things his staff is doing to undermine his business?

I certainly knew I was good enough. I was definitely a team player, could make money with the best of them, was not a rat, wasn't a plant (though not beyond selling out an incompetent server or thief), fit in with most people, and, most important to a lot of the restaurant's staff, drank and liked my drugs. You want to find out as soon as possible who the drinkers and druggies are, which bartender you can safely procure drinks from, who the teetotalers are and who will rat you out. By the end of my first week's trail (another was forthcoming), I was fairly certain I knew the drinkers and druggies, the bartenders who aided and abetted, and the ones who would sell you out for an extra shift.

When a person from the outside is hired to take a position of authority and none of the existing staff is chosen to move up, there's going to be resentment. The two weeks you train can be like navigating a minefield of ego and jealousy. The only way to succeed is to show them you are better than they are. You work harder, treat everyone with respect, and, once hired, make as much money as possible. Surviving at the Water Club gave me all the necessary skills to succeed here.

Luck was with me on my first trail. Rodney was at the door and the captain assigned to train me that evening was Captain Gabe. My relief at not having to trail Renfield was enormous. In fact, during my two weeks of training he never trained me once, though he was always present and ever watching, waiting for me to fuck up.

Gabe was one of Buzzy's favorites. He perfectly fit the Buzzy mold: tall, handsome, curly black hair swept back, and had a seductive, charming, and dangerous, smile that rivaled Ted Bundy's, though he certainly wasn't a killer. Once at a table, he'd throw his head back and with a huge toothy smile let loose with a most charming laugh, one that made you feel you were loved, special, a part of the family—that you'd made it to the inner circle of the River Café. He was certainly not threatened by me, and with the imminent departure of Michele, the captain who was leaving to open Provence restaurant, Gabe wanted to ensure my success, mainly so he didn't have to pick up any extra shifts. Meeting him set me at ease as much as is possible on one's first day. He was as gracious and charming to me as he was with his guests. He said he'd heard quite a bit about me and was thrilled to have me as part of the team. Renfield, in the next station over, a look of disdain on his face, obviously had a different perspective.

Watching Gabe work his station was magical. He maneuvered around the tables in his black tuxedo loafers as though he were dancing the role of Basilio in *Don Quixote*. He'd greet a table with menus, get their drink order, and, if another table was seated, pirouette over, give them that seductive smile, and with a lovely "Good evening!" let them know he'd be back in a second to take their drink order. He'd then kick his leg high into the air and be off to the next table to recite the evening's specials. He'd approach the table beginning with a "Ladies and gentlemen," then recite the day's offerings as though Olivier were delivering a soliloquy. Once his recitation was complete, there were almost never any questions since he'd already enlightened the guests as to all the necessities. He'd garnish the recitation with that incredible smile and panache, and wind up taking the order immediately. He'd then return to the table for wine, usually directing the guest's finger to the bottom of the page, where the bottles were in the high-three or four-figure range, and a great majority of the time get them to purchase that bottle. He'd then finish off their superb meal by presenting the check, even if not asked for, and with such gracious aplomb, the guest would pull out his credit card and pay immediately.

It went like this throughout the evening: smile, drinks, order, check . . . smile, drinks, order, check. That night he was the best show in town. I followed him throughout the shift under the scowling and watchful eye of Renfield. Each time he was at the bar, Gabe always took a quick shot of wine, winking at the bartender beforehand. A couple of times, as if preordained, a shot of whiskey would already be waiting. It was as though the bartender knew the exact moment that a bit of anesthetic would be needed for Gabe to proceed with the shift. He'd give a nod to the bartender and me, then down it. That gesture made me know I was not only safe with him, but already welcomed. By the end of the shift he'd have a nice buzz on, prior to continuing the party wherever the crew had decided to go that evening.

The service style of Gabe versus Herr Service Director in the next station could not have been any different. Renfield would shuffle to a table, white napkin draped over his tuxedo sleeve, and with the obeisance of a Potter elf, head bowed, deferentially ask the guests if they would like to begin their meal by enjoying a cocktail. His recitation of the specials was done so obsequiously, with the humbleness of a Victorian butler, and was so mind-numbingly detailed, most guests took the specials just to shut him up.

This made Renfield a favorite of the chefs. Chefs want their specials sold. Specials make money. They are made of the best cuts of meat and of the freshest fish available at market, infused and garnished with big-ticket items—foie gras, caviar, truffles—and composed to show off the artistry and genius of the chef, and of course they carry a hefty price tag. The clientele here could not care less about the price of a dish. They were there to either impress or gorge themselves à la Frederick of Sweden, whose last meal was his undoing. A great special makes the chef a star and the house makes money. Renfield was a master at selling this. I think one reason is that those who couldn't stomach him at their table took the path of least resistance and ordered what was the quickest. He sold specials like Mercedes-Benzes at a dealership in Beverly Hills. What the rest of the staff hated about him, was that it took him so fucking long at a table that he never turned his station and ended up making the least amount of money, while doing the least amount of work. Since all the tips were pooled, this meant everyone made less.

At the end of the shift Renfield came over, sat me down, and asked me how it went. I replied, "It went really well! Gabe is an amazing captain; the support staff was on point and the food looks incredible."

"You haven't done anything. Be here tomorrow at four for a kitchen trail." With that, Renfield stood and shuffled off.

The second night began much better than the first. This time I ate before leaving home and chatted with the other servers at family meal, while Jimmy and others gave me tips on how to act with Chef Charlie Palmer. The bulk of the advice was to stay out of everyone's way and speak only when spoken to. Copy that. I had no desire to do anything but that. Palmer had gotten the restaurant three stars in *The New York Times* a couple of years prior and was now one of the most heralded chefs in America. Was I nervous? Fuck yeah. Intimidated? Absolutely. The chef has a huge say in who gets hired to serve his masterful cuisine. I knew I needed Charlie on my side and had to impress him to make the cut.

During a kitchen trail, the trainer is in a catch-22 situation. Most chefs detest the FOH staff, excepting the runners. The runners are the chef's boys (back then it was rare to see a woman on the floor of a three- or four-star restaurant, and they were almost nonexistent in the kitchens). Runners have to lift trays laden with as many plates as it takes to feed a table of six, and the trays can be ridiculously heavy. This is not to say that a woman can't do the job; back then they weren't even considered for it. The exception was the one woman server here. She was as good as any man on the team, could carry a tray laden with food with the best of them, and shared her sexual escapades as though she were a dockworker. She'd regularly jump in to carry out a tray when needed. Once she showed how good she was, it broke the barrier, and quite a few women servers followed, some eventually becoming captains.

Runners are at the chef's beck and call and rarely out of sight of the chef except when running food to the dining room, fetching something from the walk-in, or refilling drinks for the cooks. A chef trusts his best runners as much as he trusts his best cooks. Great runners get the food down quickly, in the proper position (protein generally facing the guests), make sure the guests have all they need, and return immediately to await the next table. They also assist in the garnishing and wiping down of the plates as they are set on the pass, the counter where all finished plates are set, as well as setting up the pass at the beginning of the evening with various condiments and garnishes for that night's service. Most chefs hate someone other than a runner training in the kitchen. That person is in the way and asks too many questions, and when the shit hits the fan and the chef loses his temper, will be the one run out of the kitchen and back to the dining room.

A good trailer knows to stand back; to have a notebook to write down all the ingredients he sees on every dish, as well as whatever the chef says to him about the ingredients in that dish; to never touch anything; to make himself as invisible as possible; and, most important, to speak only when spoken to. I have seen many chefs throw a trailer out of the kitchen for standing in the way or asking a question just as a cook puts up the wrong dish, and then both get ripped new assholes.

Palmer, however, was as much a gentleman as he was a great cook. He showed patience with me, poked fun at my experience at the Water Club, asked the requisite questions—Was the food there any good? Were the rumors of alcohol, drugs, and champagne flowing among the staff true? Was Buzzy a Nazi there as well?

We chatted briefly, Palmer being a man of few words. I readied myself, and soon the kitchen was up and running. Orders started spitting out of the printer, Palmer called them out in a calm and steady cadence. The only thing you heard was the chef's voice and the "*Oui*, chef!" response from the cooks as a dish that was prepared in their station was called out. It was a ballet and Palmer was the choreographer and conductor. Unlike at the Water Club, where errors were constant and chefs and cooks yelled at one another while runners, cooks, and servers were usually high, drunk, or on their way to being so, this A team of cooks only asked the most important questions, and the runners silently went about garnishing, wiping, and loading their trays.

I stood back and watched. The cooks in Palmer's kitchen would soon be some of the best chefs in America—the legendary David Burke and Rick Laakkonen (both of whom would succeed Palmer once he left), Rick Moonen, Gerry Hayden, George Morrone, Donnie Pintabona, Steven Levine, Pat Trama, Frank Falcinelli, Dan Budd, and Diane Forley, all went through the kitchen at the Café, becoming recognized in their own right. It was a kitchen lineup equivalent to the 1927 Yankees. That these folks worked upwards of twelve hours a day, sometimes six or seven days a week, for $5 an hour is mind-boggling. Buzzy O'Keeffe, while never hesitant to spend hundreds of thousands of dollars on lamps and chairs, custom-made in France, the finest wood for the floors, and gleaming hardware for the bathrooms, hated parting with his dear money to pay an employee. That's what tips were for. We all worked for $5 an hour. You also got paid for only an eight-hour shift, even though ten to twelve hours was the standard. You worked it because you had to. You were expected to do it since you were being given the privilege of working and learning from a great chef or were raking in the bucks from tips. Like other restaurateurs, Buzzy got away with this for years because no one wanted to rock the boat and risk getting fired by complaining. Buzzy finally did get caught many years later. In 2013, he was sued by his employees and settled for $2 million for misappropriating tips and not paying for full hours worked.

The IRS eventually caught on and in the early nineties cracked down on restaurants. They picked a few top restaurants and audited them, the famed Petrossian among them. Petrossian was a ridiculously expensive caviar emporium, just below Central Park, furnished with banquettes made of mink. A captain at the River Café had left to be the general manager there, and I was well acquainted with the staff. Most of the FOH were called in by the IRS and nabbed for back taxes, which were in the range of $30,000 to $75,000. Once word got out, the days of taking your tips home in cash, never to be reported, were over. Restaurants began holding the tips, and paying them weekly by check. The days of traversing the city with pockets stuffed full of cash had ended.

My kitchen trail that night went beautifully. The food looked incredible, the team in the kitchen was extraordinary, and at 10:00 P.M. Palmer looked at me, shook my hand, and, with a "Well done," sent me on my way. As I walked back to the dining room, I passed a scowling Renfield on his way to the kitchen. I waited for his return to see what else he had in store for me. As I stood to the side, some runners passed and gave me a thumbs-up. Renfield then approached me, still scowling and confirmed the success of my trail. "Tomorrow at four. Server trail." I was done for the evening.

I was beginning to feel good about things despite Renfield and my third trail was a charm. I was assigned to Jimmy, who was an amazing server. It was easy. I knew how to wait tables, and the only issue in a new house was geography and timing. Geography means navigating the space, learning where everything is so that you can accomplish as much in one trip across the dining room as possible. The geography is easier than the timing. Jimmy had it down and following him was as beautiful as watching Captain Gabe dance through the dining room.

It went like this: Table 1 is waiting for drinks, table 3 is expecting appetizers and needs silver for that course. Table 7 needs a bread refill, so we flag down a busser to bring more. Table 6 just had appetizers cleared, let's get the drinks for 1, then drop the silver for dessert on 2 and get ready to drop silver on 3, since they finished their appetizers in record time. We go to the silver drawer, it's light on dinner forks, so Jimmy grabs a busser to refill the silver in the station. At the bar the house wine is low. Jimmy shouts out to the bartender for wine and more glasses, and while he's there, a guest asks where the bathroom is. In fine-dining establishments, you walk the guest as close to the restroom as possible, which can cause a clusterfuck in your timing because entrées are now about to drop on 6, the silver hasn't been set there, and the captain is desperately trying to flag you down with a stare that is so glaring you feel it in your nuts, and then you see two tables were just seated, and protocol dictates you have two minutes to greet each table once they are seated, but you still need to walk the guest to the fucking toilet. It's like this every evening. It's an addiction, the adrenaline rush you get trying to execute all the necessary steps to serve a meal. You run your ass off and then suddenly it's over. Done. You've got through another night. Time to count the money and walk out, hopefully, happy.

Through it all, Jimmy let me know who the cool bartenders and servers were. Which ones to suck up to, to get a drink. Which bartender to check in on and make sure he had all the things he needed, so that the vodka I so desperately needed at nine o'clock would be there. Which of the staff had the coke habit, which ones were useless and lazy and which ones to watch out for because they'd sell you out in a second.

The one thing Jimmy didn't have toward me was resentment. He was obviously captain material and that I was picked over him should have made him resent me. It certainly didn't. It didn't hurt that we were two guineas from Brooklyn, former altar boys, and both in the restaurant business. Renfield, of course, always had an eye on me so there was absolutely zero misbehavior on my part. Jimmy knew it as well and we both toed the line. Two altar boys doing their thing.

"Do Not Fuck Zees Up!"

THE TRAILS WENT SMOOTHLY till the final week. I used my two days off to study and memorize the menu and learn the wine list. As far as I can remember, there was no service manual or handbook. Everything back then was taught by trailing. Now with HR and all the harassment training, the service manuals, and handbooks that can run over fifty pages, it's like having to go back to school to get a job waiting tables.

My first day back I immediately knew something was off. At the door was someone I'd never seen during my short time at the restaurant. When I walked past the maître d'hôtel stand to enter the dining room, my "Good afternoon" was met with a look of *Who the fuck are you?* and a grunt, which was either his way of saying good afternoon or "keep moving, person I have never seen before and have no desire to know anything further of."

Jimmy soon filled me in on the details. This was Maurice, a maître d'hôtel here for many years, who'd been on leave. He'd gone back to Paris, where he would soon be returning for good. He was a favorite of Buzzy's, and to Maurice's customers it was akin to having Maurice Chevalier at the door. To the staff he was greedy, narcissistic, ill-tempered, and as odious a person as one could be. In short, a classic French maître d'hôtel. He was back for a couple of weeks, and Jimmy's advice was to finish out my trail and stay as far away from him as possible since he'd soon be leaving.

At the daily pre-shift meeting, when the staff was given the evening's specials by the chef and service pointers and criticisms of the prior shift by Renfield, the maître d'hôtel then went through that evening's book. The number of covers, a roll call of VIP guests expected, the number of large parties and time they were due, the list of birthday and anniversary celebrations, and any special requests that would need to be dealt with throughout the evening. When the maître d'hôtel went through the guest list, the staff regularly commented on each guest's reputation. It could be a "Yes!" and clapping when the name of a high roller or a wine whale (the term used for someone who spends big on wine) was mentioned, or grunts and groans when the name of an insufferable or parsimonious guest was called, or one that everyone despised. Since I was still in training this night, I spent some of the time off the floor and learning various steps of service—computer skills, closing checks, seeing where the wines were kept, watching reservationists, greeting guests, et cetera. I've had to rely on others to fill me in on some of what happened and having repeated the story of this night many times, it may have acquired a few additional details, but in essence the night went as follows.

This was a Saturday night, and we were going to be packed. Over two hundred covers were on the books, which meant an average of three turns on a table. Then Maurice broke the huge news: there would be three six tops that evening. This elicited "What's?" from the servers and captains. "Do not speek when I am!" shouted Maurice in his thick Gallic accent. With this reprimand all conversation ceased. The servers and captains were incredulous as we awaited the reasoning for this apparently stupid and impossible turn of events. What I didn't know was there was only one table that accommodated six guests. Since all the other tables were booked, there could be no putting other tables together to create an extra six top. That one table was going to be occupied by three different parties that evening, one right after the other, with zero time in between.

This is virtually impossible. Each table in a restaurant is allocated a turn time depending on size. Here, it was two hours for a deuce, two and a half for parties of four, and three hours for those of six. Service ran from 6:00 P.M. to 11:00 P.M. Since the kitchen is open for five hours, the table for six is allotted two turns and gets seated at 6:00 P.M. and 9:00 P.M. When an error of this caliber is made, heads roll, and blame is usually put on the reservationist or maître d'hôtel.

When the chef heard this, he exploded. "What the fuck is going on? There's no fucking way we can do three six tops. Who took the fucking reservation?" No one was more shocked than the captain, Rick, whose station contained the large table. Rick was a fragile human being, mid-forties, small of stature, thick-rimmed glasses, with a slightly bent-over walk that protected his easily wounded heart, gay, shy, and the least capable of all the captains. He was a holdover from before the three-star days, and apparently no one had the heart to fire him. Since his skills as a captain were minimal, Rick always worked the smallest and slowest station, the one with that one table of six, which during a normal service would be turned a sensible and leisurely two times. Sprinkle this in with a few four tops and some deuces, and it's a pretty easy night.

To the tuxedoed hotshots such as Gabe, this station would be a piece of cake, a languorous evening, allowing time for a few shots at the service bar, lots of kibitzing with the guests, and generally an early out. Not so for Rick, who always began service with a discreet tipple at the bar and had a stash in his station, a bottle of white wine, placed in a bucket and kept perfectly chilled to be sipped throughout the evening. A bit of booze to kill the pain of service.

Maurice preferred his captains to be like him, a panzer *Oberführer*, barreling through the room and getting things done as quickly as possible. He wanted a guest's dinnertime to be as short as possible. Gabe was his king, Renfield and Rick his nemeses. Maurice had apparently tried to get both fired many times but failed. He thrived on nights with as many turns as possible, thus allowing him to sell tables and fatten the pockets of his tuxedo. Maurice was apparently building a restaurant in the south of France, and he wanted to make a killing his last few weeks at the River Café. Rick was certainly not an *Oberführer*. Neither tall nor handsome nor suave, slow of service and hence a liability to the restaurant.

"Reek!" he snarled, eyes filled with hatred. "Toonight you have ze seeks top at seeks P.M., e seeks top at eight P.M., and e seeks top at ten P.M.!" The room was hushed; with looks of shock and disbelief on the faces of the staff. From the back came a few sniggers from the other captains, whose income was also diminished by Rick since he was a contributor to the tip pool. They smelled blood. "At ten o'clock," continued our leader, "Monsieur Jee will arrive!"

This was the knife to the heart. The death knell. The first stop to unemployment. You could see the look on Rick's face turn from disbelief to abject terror. As Jimmy later explained to me, Maurice was referring to Mr. G, the Café's best customer, a CEO of one of the biggest financial firms in the city. He kept his own stash of Baccarat champagne flutes to sip his Cristal champagne in, and rumor had it, his handshake to our maître d'hôtel would equal a one-month payment on the five bedroom he was selling in Westchester.

"Monsieur Jee," Maurice continued, "ees dining with Andeee Warhol, Dayborah Haree, Monsieur Sprouse, and *deux* others. Zey *must* seat at exactly ten P.M. Zey ave only *deux* hours for dinner and then zey leaves for the party! *Eef you want to continue in zees restaurant, do not fuck zees up!*" With that, Maurice turned on his heel and left. I'd swear he swaggered, almost goose-stepped, back to the maître d'hôtel stand.

I was stunned. Rick was in shock and seemingly about to cry. As the meeting broke up, we all avoided Rick. From the corner of my eye I saw him heading back to the bar with the bottle of wine from his bucket. After a few words with the bartender, he shoots back another tipple and swaps out the bottle for a magnum. He was going to need all the help he could get.

Six P.M. The dining room opens. Our maître d'hôtel marches over the first table of the night and seats them as Rick stands ready, menus in hand. As Maurice walks by Rick, I hear Maurice whisper, "Six, eight, and ten!" As Rick rapidly hands each guest a menu, the host tells him they have theater tickets and must leave by seven thirty P.M. This is a fucking miracle. This never happens. Because of the distance to the Theater District, no one ever did pre-theater here. We were in another borough, for Chrissake. The gods were seemingly with Rick. So far. Rick takes the order, sends it to the kitchen, returns to his station, and begins to hit the magnum.

Seven thirty P.M. As requested, the table is out the door. While the table is reset, Rick pours himself another glass of wine. Our maître d'hôtel walks over to Rick, points at the table. "Eight and ten!"

Eight P.M. Maître brings over two women who will be part of the next six top. They are alone. This is not good. Rick pours from the magnum. As two more in the party are seated he asks the women when we can expect the rest of the guests. "On their way!" he is told.

Eight fifteen. Still only four at the table. Breaking protocol, he hands them menus, which are pushed aside.

Eight thirty. The host and his wife arrive, and the guests immediately wish him a happy birthday. Shit. A birthday? There's no way Rick is going to get them out by eleven, let alone ten. Rick looks like he's about to cry. Maître d'hôtel is circling, staring at him with utter hatred and disgust. Maurice walks up to Rick and under his breath says, "Get zee order!" Magnum is now half-emptied. Rick is soaked with sweat under his rumpled tuxedo.

Eight fifty. The order goes in. Rick is desperate. I see him go into the wine room and exit with a bottle of an expensive burgundy under his arm. He goes over to the chef and lies to him, telling him it is a gift from the host of the six top and they are requesting to leave by ten. Chef looks at the clock and tells Rick to take the wine, shove it up his ass, and get out of his kitchen.

Nine thirty-five. The entrées are served. The restaurant is packed, the bar is three deep, every table is filled to capacity. Our prosperous guests are all happy and smiling, sipping expensive wine, eating this glorious three-star food, and pleased with themselves to be dining in one of the most beautiful restaurants in the world. At the other end of the spectrum is our Rick. He may as well be in a slum in Bombay. The magnum is almost finished; the effects of the wine apparent as he wobbles from one table to the next. This portends to be his last night at this majestic restaurant.

Then it happens. G arrives a few minutes early, magnificently attired, celebrities in tow, and enters the dining room like royalty. The piano player sees him and immediately switches songs. The opening notes of G's favorite tune wafts through the room as a hundred-dollar bill is placed in the brandy snifter that sits atop the baby grand. G then turns and hugs our maître d'hôtel, and I see a wad of bills pass from hand to hand. Kisses, thank-yous, and hugs. The restaurant in France can now afford glassware. The sound of champagne corks popping at the bar. The Cristal opened and poured into the Baccarat glasses, each shimmering in the candlelight. G raises his glass and toasts his guests. Life is perfect, wonderful, being lived the way it is supposed to be.

Nine fifty. Back at the 6-top, the host rises and lifts his glass to toast

himself and his guests. He's a fat cat from Wall Street. Rolls of flesh ema-
nate from his stomach, pushing and stretching the fabric of his custom-made
Anderson & Sheppard shirt, past his belt and headed toward his knees. His
cheeks are a doughy red from a lifetime of expensive single malts and rare
Bordeaux. He lifts his glass and opens his mouth to speak. Rick is in the corner, broken, nearly drunk. He gets the death stare from Maurice as he heads
over to check the table.

At that moment, as Fat Cat opens his mouth to speak, he suddenly sputters,
grabs his chest, and collapses onto the table. Our maître d'hôtel, seeing this,
his own face with a momentary look of *What the fuck is happening?*, immediately recovers and bellows out across the room, "*Docteur, docteur!* We need a
docteur!" With the speed of Jim Brown and his own, practiced years of Fred
Astaire dining-room maneuvers, Maurice rushes to the table, gets behind the
now-slumped-over titan of industry, and screams, "Air! Eee needs air!" And
with that he pushes the fallen guest, still slumped in his chair, through the
dining room and out the door, screaming back at the guests, "Follow me! Air!"

The guests quickly jump out of their seats and follow him out the door.
As if pre-choreographed, our Chinese head busboy, a multiproperty owner in
Queens (and, whispered among the staff, a tong member), has his team reset
the table with absolute perfection. G and retinue sit down at exactly 10:00 P.M.

Guilty

RENFIELD NEVER TOLD ME I was hired. He let Rodney do it. Renfield was apparently so disgusted with himself for letting this happen that he was unable to utter the words to my face. I was in. This was now the be-careful-what-you-wish-for moment that would track me for most of my restaurant career. I was just hired for a dream job that was full-time. I'd also recently completed acting and speech programs and was beginning to audition. What happens if I get cast in a play? Will the restaurant let me take time off? Do I quit? Can I get my shifts covered? I was about to make excellent money. Do I give it all up for a play that will probably be shit and that I won't get paid to do? No other actors worked the floor at the River Café. These were all professionals. The restaurant business was their life. They were making money, had health insurance, and were working at one of the top restaurants in the country—how would they feel if I left to do a play? I couldn't worry about this now. I had a new job and would play it by ear until I was actually cast in something.

Life was good. Money was rolling in. We were at the top of our game. The kitchen was humming, service was top-notch, and many of our guests had no limit on how much they'd spend for a meal. Captains did the wine service, and under the tutelage of legendary wine director Joe DeLissio, my knowledge of the juice increased exponentially. This is hugely important to a server's bottom line. Wine sales drive tips. The prix fixe dinner menu we served—appetizer, entrée, and dessert—was $45 per person, or $90 for a party of two. Our tips were usually 20 percent, so on this we'd be tipped $18. Add a couple of drinks at about $15, the tip is now $21. This is where wine makes or breaks the night. An inexpensive bottle would be in the $30 to $50 range. That's another $10 to the tip, which is now $31—nearly a 50 percent increase. Now, get in a big spender, a wine connoisseur, or someone wanting to impress his guests, someone who has enough cash that he could give two shits about the cost of a bottle, and the tip increases dramatically. If we add a modestly priced premium bottle of wine that costs, say, $175, there's another $35. Our tip just went from $18 to $66, nearly a 267 percent increase!

Restaurants want to sell wine. This is why a prime table might be empty for an hour or so as we wait for the guest who we know will routinely spend $300 and above for a bottle of his favorite juice. It's all economics. It's a free market and we know our market well. The great disappointment is when a guest we don't necessarily know dines with us. He asks for the wine list, scans it, and picks an old Bordeaux, let's say a 2000 Château Lynch-Bages, which is about $400 today. This guest, though, is from the I-don't-tip-on-wine school. While this doesn't happen often, it happens enough to be an issue. In a restaurant that prides itself on service, to not tip on the wine service, which is given by a trained professional who presents, decants, and pours each glass of that wine till it's finished, is insulting to that server. We work on tips. We make no money on the bottle of wine you just purchased if you don't tip on it. To not tip is to not acknowledge the expertise and effort of serving that bottle.

Now, if you go to a restaurant, order a bottle of $500 wine, and the server doesn't offer to decant it, but instead opens it, pours the first glass, and plops it on the table for you to deal with throughout the meal, well then, you have a case for not tipping on it. I guarantee you, though, if we give proper service and no tip is left, this is noted in the reservation system, and the next time that guest comes in to dine, if he can actually get a reservation, he will certainly not get a prime table, nor will he receive the service he did the first time.

We not only want to sell wine to make money, but to have a guest who knows what she's doing and orders a great bottle is fun, and we become part of that experience. Many guests will gladly offer you a taste, and with great wines this is an incredible privilege, since few of us can afford to have the chance of tasting one. Supplies are finite, and to have the opportunity to taste a great bottle from a vintage that may quickly be disappearing is a rare experience.

We were among the first restaurants in New York City to build a cellar around American wines. Windows on the World atop the World Trade Center, led by Kevin Zraly, was perhaps the first and most famous for doing this. DeLissio, our beverage director, spent time as a cellar rat in California and met and made friends with the biggest names there, giving him access to their cellars. Robert Mondavi and his wife, Magrit, would come to dine and bring bottles of their wines for the staff to taste. The Heitzes, Joe and Alice, also came.

During one dinner, I was the captain of their table when Joe Heitz said, "Michael, I have a special bottle of wine for us to taste." With that, he handed me a bottle of 1972 Heitz Martha's Vineyard cabernet sauvignon to decant. To that point in my career it was the greatest wine I'd ever tasted. The legendary winemaker Mike Grgich would come bearing his wares for us to sell, and it wasn't above him to flirt with every female he encountered. Our cellar was stacked with gems from these and many other winemakers, and our guests consumed them copiously, fattening our wallets.

Three months into my tenure, Bryan Miller wrote a piece in *The New York Times* titled "As Service Standards Decline, a Few Restaurants Still Excel." It was on the front page of the Food section, with a photo of the River Café staff, led by Renfield himself with a captain and four waiters. We were cited as giving some of the best service in New York City. In the article, Miller noted that captains and maîtres d'hôtel are deserving of an added gratuity if service was exemplary. While our share of palm tips was damn good here, this article increased it tenfold. We'd finish a service with our pockets stuffed with cash, a dangerous situation for a group of young men and women flying high with their reputations in the New York dining world. This article put us at the top and gave some of us license for misbehavior.

Jimmy introduced me to the partiers, and we were soon getting regular cocaine deliveries to the restaurant. Being in Brooklyn, most of our clientele lived in Manhattan and many of them would take limos across the bridge. The valets up front, always a rogue group, befriended many of the limo drivers. The drivers that took care of the valets (slipping them a few bucks to let them know when their party was finishing up or letting them park in a desirable spot) got preferential treatment when they arrived with their high-profile guests. The drivers were like us, basically blue-collar workers in suits, always looking to make extra cash. Once a diner was dropped off, the driver was there for the duration of the dinner, which could sometimes go on past three hours. When guests left the restaurant and requested a taxi from the valet, these enterprising gents would suggest a limo, and if the guest accepted, the driver would give the valet a cut. This relationship developed to where we had one or two drivers making drug runs. We tipped them well for this and they were more than happy to make a run, since they also liked a hit every now and then.

Being true professionals, we staff would wait till around 9:00 P.M. to begin drinking and hold off on the coke till near the end of the shift. By midnight, many of the staff were high on either pot, coke, booze, or a combination of the three. It was the eighties and seemingly everyone partied. One of the longer-tenured captains would sometimes have a hard time waiting till the end of the shift before hitting the blow. By the time his last tables were being seated, he'd be so fucked-up that he regularly screwed up his orders, many times weaving at the computer terminal and unable to hit the correct key for what he was trying to order. He'd then have to go to the kitchen to explain the mess he made of the order, except that he was so high and had done so much coke, bits of the coke would get stuck in the back of his throat. As he tried to speak, he'd only be able to emit snorts as he tried to clear the coke from his throat, and everything else coming out of his mouth was unintelligible. We all knew when this was happening and would surreptitiously line up outside the kitchen, laughing hysterically as David Burke would get apoplectic and throw him out. Renfield was long gone by the time the partying started, and since both the kitchen and FOH were partaking, no one complained to management, and this captain remained working there for many years.

The party continued after work. We'd go where we knew the bartenders. The Horseshoe Bar, or 7B, on Avenue B, was a favorite. By the time we got there the bartenders were already high and would slip us coke when we arrived. We would then reciprocate; the booze would be free, and the party would continue after hours. Some nights we'd still be scoring bags of coke in Tompkins Square Park as the sun was beginning to rise and either take them back to the bar well after the 4:00 A.M. closing time or head to someone's apartment.

One night as I was leaving to score some coke, Rockets Redglare, the downtown character actor and comedian, was standing outside, wasted, barely able to stand. He saw me leaving, hit me up for money, and when I told him to fuck off, he sucker punched me. I fell into a row of garbage cans, picked myself up, grabbed a can, and slammed him over the head with it. It must have knocked some sense into him. He left, weaving his way toward Avenue A.

We'd all pass out at someone's apartment and get a couple of hours of sleep before shaving, changing back into our tuxes, and making it back to work just as the shift was starting, our faces nicked from the shaking of our hands as we shaved. It's a miracle that we managed to keep it going, but we did. Business was better than ever, and in our cockiness we pushed things even further.

After the restaurant closed at night, with the manager and Renfield gone, and the last guest out the door, we'd sit to do paperwork. The captains and the maître d'hôtel were now in charge. We'd pour ourselves drinks—within reason, we left the $50 shots of cognac and port untouched. One night, led by one of our wasted captains, the staff who were still there stripped naked and jumped into the East River to cool off and sober up. I stayed on deck since I can't swim a stroke, but I did get naked. I wasn't going to be the odd man out. Sometimes we'd let a regular guest or two remain as we broke down the restaurant, serving them drinks because we knew there'd be another hundred-dollar bill left on the table.

One evening a renowned real estate broker and his guests remained at the table after closing, something not uncommon for them, since they'd regularly have three- or four-hour dinners, tip handsomely for the extra accommodation, and keep ordering bottles of wine. This continued and, depending on whom the broker was with, toward the very end of the evening when most of our guests had left, we'd let them pull out a deck of cards. They played the card game Acey Deucey, while we kept their $300 or $400 bottles of wine flowing. All on the bill. This began to happen more frequently, with some of the staff joining in and this eventually led to all-out late-night poker games.

Soon, friends from other restaurants, hearing about the games, would come to join in. This went on for a few months. We'd play, drink, do a few lines, then head out before anyone knew what was happening.

On another night, one of the female servers decided to do a striptease on the bar. While nothing sexual happened, it planted an idea in the head of one of our high rollers. During our next poker night, two women showed up in the middle of the game and were greeted warmly by him. We got them drinks and resumed playing. We're in the middle of a hand when they both stand up and start to strip. He'd apparently hired a couple of pros. High Roller took one of the women into the bathroom, while others went behind the bar and began hitting the expensive stuff, and a few started dancing on the bar. In the middle of this, the morning porter showed up. We were usually long gone by the time he arrived for his 6:00 A.M. shift. Not tonight. He spotted me, gave me a look, and I immediately knew we were fucked. Buzzy would know within hours.

The next day as I arrived for work the manager grabbed me and pulled me into his office. "What the fuck were you doing? Are you out of your mind!" This was it. I was about to be fired. Everything I'd worked for was about to end. I waited for him to say, "You're fired," but he instead said, "Buzzy is heading over. You're about to get your ass fucked so deep, you're going to bleed for a month while pondering unemployment."

I wanted to throw myself off the barge. Besides my Catholic guilt making me feel like the biggest piece of shit in the world, the feeling of humiliation I'd have once I faced Buzzy, and then to be fired by the boss himself, was too much. I was about to leave and avoid disgrace when in walks Buzzy. He immediately spots my cowering figure and motions me over to sit. "What happened? What did you do?" I said, "Buzzy, we fucked up." I explained to him the history of the guest who stayed late, that he was one of our best guests, told him of the Acey Deucey games, how he'd keep ordering expensive wine, which we charged him for, and that he would keep spending and tipping. When he'd offer us some wine, we not only felt obligated to oblige but knew he'd keep buying bottles once we joined him. He was having a blast, was spending a lot of money, and, yes, things got out of control. I told him about the poker game, denied there were call girls but said some attractive ladies did show up. I admitted to the staff's drinking but left out the coke. He then asked how much the check was. I told him it was four figures. Story over.

As I sat there, head pounding from my hangover, ashamed, and waiting for the ax to fall, he asked, "What did the girls look like? Were they sexy?"

Whoa. Did I hear him right? I lifted my head, looked him straight in the eye, and said, "They were fucking gorgeous."

Buzzy, an inveterate storyteller, loved a good one. I laid it on thick and told him everything. He asked how long this had been going on, and I lied and told him that other than for a couple of Acey Deucey games, this was the first time. He asked who on staff was there. It was a good portion of our A team, and if he fired us all, the restaurant would be without most of its *New York Times* heralded team. I could see the wheels spinning. I knew then I wasn't going to be fired. This would be a great story for him, and he wasn't about to fire his best team for an indiscretion. He stared right at me. "Don't let this ever happen again."

"Yes, sir."

"Okay. Who's coming in tonight?"

At the River Café, the room just before the entrance to the main dining room was called the Cappuccino Room—aptly named since that's where the espresso machine was, along with a few tables where guests could sit for drinks. Just off this room was an outdoor deck that would open for drinks and light fare during summer months. Once the weather started to turn warmer, it was time to get the outdoor area open. Buzzy wanted it staffed with as many gorgeous young women as possible and management was only allowed to hire such.

One afternoon as I entered the restaurant for my shift, I see the Cappuccino Room filled with beautiful young women, résumés in hand, waiting to be interviewed for a summer position. It looked like a modeling call. These women were stunning. Walking into the dining room, I saw our manager, maître d'hôtel, and chef, all sitting at a table, interviewing one of the ladies. Even in a room full of beautiful women she stood out—just jaw-droppingly beautiful. As I was setting up my station, I eavesdropped on the interview. When asked if she had a résumé, she apparently handed over her modeling résumé. When asked if she had a résumé with her restaurant experience, she replied no. When asked if she had any serving experience, she again replied no. The maître d'hôtel then asked her if she had any cocktail experience; again no. When the chef asked if she'd ever dined in a restaurant, she laughed and said, "Of course." She got the job. During my time at the Café the actresses Julianna Margulies, Geena Davis, and Mia Sara were all employed. Men were never hired.

Jumpers

ONE OF THE BIZARRE features of working at the Café were the suicides. The Brooklyn Bridge seemed to be a favorite of jumpers, and while the restaurant was not directly under the bridge, it was ever so slightly south of it. It's an iconic structure, and if I was going to jump off a bridge, I'd probably pick it as well.

The first inklings that someone was up there and portending to end his life by throwing himself in the East River were the police boats. They'd park themselves on either side of the bridge, the boats bobbing up and down, lights flashing, waiting for the inevitable splash. As cold as this might sound, once those boats appeared, we knew our seating would be fucked.

The protocol for a jumper was to stop traffic on the bridge. Cars and pedestrians were unable to cross till the police either coaxed the person off or he jumped. This can take a very long time, upwards of an hour or more. After sitting in traffic, meters running, no one was going to cut short a meal to accommodate our later guests. We would have to seat the later arrivals. Try telling guests who just sat in traffic for over an hour that they won't be able to dine, since the time allotted for their reservation had now passed. Never mind that someone was up on that bridge, his life in such turmoil that he was considering ending it. Our guests came to eat and would not be deterred.

One evening as I was delivering a drink to a table at the window, I watched as a body fell from the bridge. The first time you see this it's shocking and stomach turning. I wanted to vomit. It's awful to witness someone fall and hit the water. I watched as the police divers jumped in and attempted to rescue the person. From what I could see, it was a young woman, and this time she apparently survived. Most didn't.

Sadly, after a few times the shock is lessened. To our guests seeing this for the first time it's gut-wrenching, though most are unable to identify what just happened. The few that do let out audible gasps that can be heard throughout the dining room.

It wasn't just the jumpers that were dying. Many of my current and former coworkers were dying from AIDS with alarming regularity. At the Water Club, five servers—four men and one woman—succumbed to the disease, none over thirty. A similar number would die from it at the Café. The first to go was our beloved maître d'hôtel, Rodney. Thankfully it was a short illness, and during the latter part of it he developed toxoplasmosis, a brain infection not uncommon in those with HIV, which made him seemingly unaware of what was happening to him.

The last time I saw him in the hospital, I had to be garbed, head to toe, in protective gear since no one was sure how AIDS was being transmitted. The effects of his brain deterioration had begun, and I was never sure if he recognized me. As I sat by his bedside, a strand of mucus suddenly dripped from his nose and hung there. Here was a man who was so proud of always looking his best, the consummate storyteller and schmoozer, someone loved by all, in the prime of his life, lying there, unaware of who and where he was. I reached over, cleaned him off, and left. It was the last time I would see him.

And yet this man, the person responsible for getting me the captain position, even in death, made certain I would succeed him as maître d'hôtel. When he passed, I was given his position.

One evening a guest had a heart attack and collapsed in the aisle in front of his table. On this ridiculously busy evening, Rodney, desperate for tables, was unaware a corpse was in an aisle. Rodney spots a table by the window get reset and ready for the next guests. As he leads the new guests to the table, he sees the body lying prone on the floor, steps over it, turns to one of his guests, takes her by the elbow, escorts her over the body, and without missing a beat asks, "Have you ever dined with us before?"

The Door

RUNNING THE DOOR OF a famous restaurant is to constantly juggle the demands of a clientele that was not just local cognoscenti, but a global manifest of guests. There were the dilettantes of the food world, A-list actors, artists, musicians, rock stars, tycoons, doctors, scientists, and politicians. Many world-renowned, many whose self-importance exceeded what anyone else may have thought of them. This is not an exaggeration, but the typical pedigree of guests dining on any given evening. They all had one thing in common—they needed to sit at a coveted window table. I couldn't blame them. Who wouldn't want to sit up against the floor-to-ceiling windows that faced the river?

This entire section is a wide-angle view of the city, towering over the churning East River, bathed in gold, pink, orange, and purple pastels each night as the sunset dwindles on the skyscrapers. Framing this on one side is the massive and Gothic Brooklyn Bridge. While all of this is visible from every seat in the restaurant, with all booths oriented toward the mecca of Wall Street and the downtown skyline, it didn't matter. Everyone that showed up needed one of the tables right at window side. They wanted nothing blocking this magical view.

There were nine of these tables. Buzzy's dictum was that other than for the exceptional VIP, window tables were to be given first come, first served. If it were only that simple. While maître d'hôteling is stressful in any restaurant, here, where seats were limited, especially at the window, much of the maître d's evening was spent explaining why this person or that person couldn't get one of the prized spots in the dining room. Who did get the tables? Always the famous, and Hollywood, rock stars, television personalities, politicians, friends of Buzzy or the chef, some industry folk, and the ones who paid for the privilege.

Buzzy was constantly warning us to never sell tables. What he wouldn't or couldn't comprehend was our salaries. The captains and I were paid $5 per hour. The tip pool was structured so that the three captains on the floor would each get a full cut from the pool and then those three shares would be divided among the maître d'hôtel and the captains. Essentially, three shares were divided among four people. If the maître d'hôtel made no tips at the door, the captains and maître d'hôtel would make less than the servers. Five dollars an hour is not exactly the salary the person overseeing service in a three-star dining room should be paid.

Thankfully, the demand for tables was high and those willing to shell out a few bucks to the maître d'hôtel for the honor of sitting at one were numerous. Very numerous. Restaurants generally seat a third of their seats each half hour, which allows for an orderly service so that the kitchen and floor staff have enough time to do their jobs without being overwhelmed. Seating the window tables first come, first served, as Buzzy wanted, was impossible. Those tables had to be held for the cognoscenti, who all wanted to sit at the prime seven-to-eight-thirty time slots.

On a typical night, when a guest arrived for the early seating, most, if not all, of the window tables would be empty. I'd have to hold them for the guests assigned to them, which was almost never at 6:00 P.M., when the dining room opened. This meant that almost none of our six and six-thirty reservations could get a window table. There is no way they'd leave in time for the VIPs that began to arrive at 7:00 P.M., though I did always try to seat the first table at a window since the earlier guests tend to eat fairly quickly and I'd be able to reseat the table as the prime guests arrived.

The rest was a negotiation. Try telling people who have arrived at 6:00 P.M. and are about to drop a couple hundred dollars on dinner that they cannot sit at any of the empty tables next to the windows. Many of these guests were celebrating an anniversary or birthday and when they called for a reservation, they'd probably been kept on hold by the reservationist for ten minutes or longer and were, when finally connected, informed no tables were available at the prime hours. Only 6:00 or 11:00 P.M. would be available. Most took 6:00.

On the evening of the reservation, they'd arrive, walk in, and see a mostly empty restaurant. A typical conversation would begin like this:

> Me: "Good evening and welcome to the River Café. Have you a reservation this evening?"
>
> Guest: "Yes, we do. We're the Robinsons at six P.M. We are celebrating our anniversary and so happy to be here! My wife woke up early the morning the reservations for tonight opened, and waited almost thirty minutes to make the reservation. It was ridiculous that all we could get was six P.M., but we are so happy to be here. We'd like a window table, please."
>
> Me: "That's wonderful, and a happy anniversary to you both. Right this way then."

I walk the guests to one of the tables closest to the window, though not at the window.

> Guest: "Excuse me, I asked for a window table."
>
> Me: "I am very sorry, sir, but all the window tables have been spoken for."
>
> Guest: "What? We called the minute your phones opened! There is no one in the dining room. How could we not get a window table?"
>
> Me: "I am very sorry, sir, but all the tables have been spoken for."
>
> Guest: "By whom! There is no one here!"
>
> Me: "I am so sorry, sir, but we have quite a few regulars coming in this evening. They have specific tables. Some are also held by the owner. This here is a lovely table."

At this point I would say, "Here, have a seat, let me send you some champagne. Happy anniversary!" and then walk away. Some never said a word and accepted defeat, the bubbles a nice consolation.

Now if there was a host with me at the door, the scenario changes. Back then we didn't have one. Having one would have made my life so much easier. When I finally did have a host in other restaurants, it went like this:

Host walks the guests to the table.

Guests complain, state they requested a window and want to sit at one of the empty window seats.

Host then says in the sweetest way possible, "I am so sorry, those are already spoken for."

Guest won't take no from a host, wants to speak to the maître d'hôtel.

Host tells guest, "One moment, sir, let me speak to the maître d'hôtel."

Guests remain at the unwanted table, looking at it as though we were trying to seat them in a coal mine.

Maître d'hôtel and host confer at the podium.

Host returns, tells guest she is so sorry, but while those tables are not available, she can offer them this lovely table over here.

She then offers guests another table nearby, but not at the window. You always, when you can, want to leave an option. This way the guests feel they have a choice. It's also less humiliating for the guests to take a different table than to sit at the table they obviously despise. Even if it's not a better choice than the original. The psychology being that if the guest is made to feel that he can actually choose that table, then it becomes the better choice, and he will take it. He feels like he won.

If I thought the guest would be really difficult, and there was no way I'd be getting palmed for a better table, as the host returned to offer the guest the other option, I'd conveniently disappear for ten minutes or so. After that, the guest would already have sat, had a drink, and realized it wasn't so horrible and not worth a fight.

But there was no host here, just me. Some guests became so enraged that they would call me every invective imaginable. I've been called an asshole, a little fucking piece of shit, a horrible human being, a liar, a scumbag, a mercenary, and on and on—all over a table. If they didn't accept their fate, they might ask to speak to a manager, who always backed me up.

Then there were the guests who would walk back to the maître d'hôtel stand with me, reach into their pocket, pull out some cash, and say, "I'd be very appreciative if there was something you could do."

Would this get them the table? Sometimes. It depended on who was actually coming in that evening and if I had a table available, which I usually did, especially at that hour. It also depended on how much they gave me. A practiced maître d'hôtel can tell the difference in the denomination of a bill just by how it feels. Twenties are generally a bit worn, fifties not so much, and hundreds, the crispest. A wad of ones is always a no. You can also tell by the guests themselves how much they are going to give. Those that give a hundred or more have that special smell to them, the confidence and worldliness of knowing what they want and how to get it. They also will give you the look that says, "You're going to like what I just slipped into your palm."

Would a twenty get you a table? Sometimes. It depended on who I knew was coming, or if I wanted to gamble on a better palm from another guest. If it felt like a bunch of singles or a five or a ten, I'd respectfully hand it back and let the guests know how sorry I was, but that it was truly impossible for me to give them an already-held table. I'd then send over a round of drinks to placate the rejection.

Most of the time I knew I'd be given money for the window tables. I wouldn't have to sell them. I'd just wait it out. Depending on the night, if it was a twenty, the guest would have little chance. Fifty, maybe. A hundred? Always.

Our other maître d'hôtel was, one evening, told by a guest he would take care of him if he gave them a window table. As he seats them, the guest hands him a dollar bill. He took the bill over to the bar, asked for four quarters, walked back to the guest, handed him the quarters, and said, "Here's your change for the pay phone," and stormed off.

Most guests who want a specific table will gladly pay for it. It gives them the feeling of power, knowing how to get what they want. They get it. They know how to play the game. They know a hundred-dollar bill gives them access, the special attention, "zee beeg blow job." Those guests love getting their cock sucked by the most powerful person in the room. It makes them the king, and I was very willing to give up the keys to the kingdom for the right price.

Also, not everyone who plays the game is in it for a power trip. Most are actually happy to give an incentive for the extra attention, to be recognized the next time they come in, to have the feeling of being known. Many were actually happy to do something nice for me, for themselves. The palm would be an actual thank-you for a job well done, for seeing me there, for always remembering them, for always being kind to them. These are the easy guests, the ones we all love, become friends with, and are genuinely happy to see each time they come in. Yes, it's a game, but when it's played correctly, everyone wins.

Restaurants are certainly not democracies. It's impossible for us to treat everyone equally, especially when it comes to seating. Service-wise, we try our darndest, but, come on, who's going to get the extra attention, the free dessert or drink sent to the table? The asshole? The rude one? The 15 percent tipper? Fuck no. It's the ones who come in, treat you with respect, are easygoing, and leave you the proper tip. We work hard, put up with long hours, take a lot of shit, so the guest just being nice goes a long way. I'd say 98 percent of all guests are truly lovely people. It's the other 2 percent that we in the business hate.

> **Uncle Rob had soon** joined our staff. He and I, along with some of the valets, started betting heavily on college basketball. We bet every night, spending much of our days scouring the sports pages and gambling sheets for any information that would help us with our bets. Don't ask me how, but we never had a losing week. Payments were made weekly by a money runner who would drive to the Café and drop off shopping bags of cash with our winnings. This lasted the entire college basketball season, right up until the playoffs. Uncle Rob and I were partners, and we each cleared about $35,000 that season. Once the playoffs hit, I stopped betting. Conventional wisdom dictated that the playoffs are too risky to bet on; with so many unknowns, the odds would surely be in the bookie's favor. There's a reason conventional wisdom is conventional. I stopped but Uncle Rob didn't. He bet through the playoffs, lost, and then kept going.
>
> When baseball season arrived, he bet on those games. By that August, he'd lost his entire share of what we'd won, plus so much more that he was unable to pay the bookie back on his enormous losses. Things got so bad he left to hide out in California. Wanting to return, he eventually saved enough money to pay off his debt and moved back to the city.

Mr. Debonair

It's Saturday evening. The restaurant is packed. I'm standing at the maître d'hôtel stand. To my right on a raised platform sitting behind the baby grand is Richard Kimball, our piano player, who just moments before disembarked from his kayak after his usual commute down the Hudson River from Nyack, playing some of the sweetest Gershwin ever. Chef David Burke is in the kitchen, having replaced the recently departed three-starred Charlie Palmer. We are so popular that reservations, which became available two weeks prior, were all taken within an hour. This was all done by hand and over the telephone. Online reservation systems wouldn't arrive for another decade.

It's 8:00 P.M. The bar is three deep with guests waiting for their tables. My tuxedo is already stuffed with cash from those who understand what it takes to sit at the window. I'm working the room, excoriating the bussers to clear and reset courses as soon as possible so we can keep the tables moving, imploring the captains to hustle.

"Get me tables!" I shout to no one in particular. I then directed a server to jump in and take a dessert order, since I needed that table as fast as possible. Some guests have been waiting an hour, and I was quickly getting into the deep shits. I regularly crossed from the podium to the bar, glad-handing guests, lying as to how soon a table would be ready, telling the bartender to send drinks to some, an appetizer to the couple whose wait would be nearing an hour and a half. I'd already sent many drinks because of the long delay, and I would have little leverage once an hour or more passed.

As I returned to the maître d'hôtel stand, a debonair gent, in an expensive blue suit, the perfect complement of gray streaking his jet-black hair, walks up to me. In tow are two gorgeous twentysomethings, bejeweled and showing just enough skin that everyone they pass takes a second look. Behind the women stands another striking gentleman. They stink of money. I greet the gent, "Good evening, sir," and before I can utter another word, Debonair speaks up and asks for a table for four. "Do you have a reservation, sir?" He did not. Then, with a smile that's maintained by the greatest dentists in the world, he said, "Do I need one?"

My stress level had been building for the past hour. Two shots of vodka had done nothing to ameliorate it, and when he said this, despite the scent of money wafting in front of my nose, I had to laugh. "I am so sorry, sir. The restaurant has been booked for weeks. I have absolutely nothing available." He again flashes that smile (one that has to have seduced scores of women, as well as grabbed the attention of men, myself included) and, completely unperturbed by the rejection, replies, "I am so very sorry. I was not aware. Do you mind if we head to the bar and have a drink?" Bam! Now that was a move. "Of course not," I reply. As he passes me to head toward the bar, he reaches out, shakes my hand, and presses a couple of bills into my palm. I am about to return them because I know there is no fucking way I can possibly get this guy a table when he stops me and says, "No, no, sir. This is for you. You're a gentleman." I thank him as he walks off, and I stuff the bills into my tux.

Just then I am waved down by a guest. He calls me over and demands to know where their food is; they've apparently been waiting thirty minutes for entrées. I apologize and tell him I will find out what the problem is. I know what the problem is. I not only overbooked the room, but more guests had handed me money than I had window tables for. I had to get out of that jam first.

I knew that as soon as I entered the kitchen to see where this guy's food was, I'd be reamed by David Burke. Burke had been at the helm for almost a year now and was blowing the city away with his towering creations that were as beautiful to look at as they were to eat. As I entered the kitchen, he immediately set on me: "What the fuck are you doing!" The pass was filled with orders, and as I stood beside him, the printer was painfully spitting out more.

"You greedy motherfucker! You have no fucking idea what you are doing. We will never feed all these people." He had a point. I was being a bit greedy, but I did actually know what I was doing. "I'm sorry, chef, it's a clusterfuck. I had regulars walk in that I couldn't say no to. It also seems the new reservationist forgot to enter some reservations, and I'm getting people showing up saying that they had booked a table two weeks ago. I can tell when people are lying; these are not. I promise you; I will slow it down and let you catch up."

All lies. With that, I made a hasty exit out of the kitchen as he began screaming at his cooks. Walking to the dining room, I remembered the money handed to me by Mr. Debonair. I reach in my pocket and pull out two crisp hundred-dollar bills. That's about $500 in today's money. I race through the dining room as a four top is getting up from a window table. I knew that all those waiting at the bar hadn't taken their eyes off the dining room. They were all waiting for someone to leave so they could finally sit. I was under a microscope and had to work fast.

"Henry!" I shouted to my head busser. "I need this now!" I made a beeline straight to the bar, ignoring all those who were waiting, some for upwards of an hour, grabbed a startled Mr. Debonair, and said, "Sir, please, right this way, your table is ready." There was that smile again. Showing zero surprise, acting as if he'd known all along he'd get the table, he bowed his head ever so slightly and said, "Thank you, sir."

I could feel the eyes of those waiting locked on me, their anger penetrating my back as he and his guests followed me to the table.

"Do you have Cristal rosé?"

"Of course, sir."

"Good. Do you have Le Montrachet?"

"Why, yes, sir."

"Excellent. I love Le Montrachet. It's like Evian. I will take both. The champagne first, please."

These were two of the most expensive bottles on our list. I immediately grabbed Gabe, who luckily was going to be this gent's captain, let him know the deal, and headed off to do damage control with the guests still waiting at the bar. Though I first detoured to the service bar, held up two fingers (my signal for a cold shot of vodka), downed it, and prepared to enter the abyss.

Luckily things were finally moving, and I was able to seat the guests who'd waited the longest. When I returned to the podium, Mr. Debonair, on his way to the bathroom, walked up to me and said, "I want to thank you again for your graciousness, sir." With that, he placed two more hundred-dollar bills into my palm.

He and his guests spent the rest of the night ringing up a sizable check and handed each server that attended to him a hundred-dollar bill. In addition to the 20 percent he added to the check, he put an additional $200 on it for Gabe.

As his party was getting ready to leave, Mr. Debonair heads in my direction. As he gets closer to me, I'm forced to squint, the gleam of his smile blinding, portending thanks for a triumphant dinner. The praise was effusive, and he once again reaches out to shake my hand and slips more crisp bills into my palm, gives me a hug, a kiss on the cheek, and exits. As his party headed down the gangway to, I assume, an expensive mode of transport, in my hand were two more hundred-dollar bills. This is how legends are made.

Debonair became somewhat of a regular guest, always dining with gorgeous Latina women, one of whom was recognized by a server as a former Miss Colombia. This was before Google, so I was never able to find out exactly who he was or what he did, but I had some hunches. Each time he returned he'd check his shoebox of a cell phone with me. One evening, he handed me a slip of paper with a phone number and additional numbers written below that. He asked if I wouldn't mind dialing the number at 8:00 P.M. I said of course and asked what I should say when they answered. "There won't be an answer, just a tone. Punch in the numbers, and once you hear another tone, hang up. At eight P.M., please." The requisite $200 was then placed in my palm. The next visit he asked the same of me, though I now felt comfortable enough to ask what I was doing. "You are placing a bet for me. I enjoy betting on basketball games." I was stunned. He asked if I gambled. "I do." "Take Portland this evening plus the spread." This guy had me hook, line, and sinker.

I grabbed our head valet, who always put our sports bets in. I told him the bet, he spread the word throughout the staff, and we put a sizable chunk of money on Portland. Bam. Home run. We cashed in big. Whatever the fuck Mr. Debonair did, he had major access. This was repeated the next three times he dined with us. Each time he'd hand me the phone and the slip of paper with the numbers on it. Each time he told me which game to bet on, and each time we won. After the third time I never saw him again.

To put the money in perspective, $10 then is worth $25 today, $20 is now worth $50, $50 equals $125, and $100 is a whopping $255. The typical tip then was $20. The great guests handed you $50 to $100. The legendary photographer Richard Avedon always gave me a fifty when he left. The great Wall Street guys always gave $100, never less. Johnny Carson thanked me with $100 on his way out. The $600 that Debonair handed me that night would be worth $1,542.32 today. Unfortunately, the amount handed to maîtres d'hôtel today hasn't changed in the past twenty-five years. To say that inflation has taken a bite out of our money is an understatement.

The Donald

EARLY ONE EVENING, JUST before the prime-time crush, I was at my usual spot by the podium when a gentleman I'd already seated walked up to me. I had recognized him upon his arrival. He had been in a couple of times before and each time slipped me a twenty. He introduced himself and said, "We've been watching you."

"You've what?"

"We've been watching you."

I looked over at his table and recognized the woman as the one he'd dined with at least once before, and my first thought was they were going to proposition me for a threesome.

"Well, I am not sure what to say. What exactly do you mean?"

"I represent some important people. We've had a team looking for the best maître d'hôtel in New York City, and your name keeps coming up. I've been here a few times, and we consider you the best in the city. I have an offer for you."

I'd been told so many bullshit stories, especially after someone had had a few drinks, that I'd become quite a skeptic. But he said this with such force and confidence that I was somewhat intrigued. He then hands me his business card, and he's apparently the vice president of something or other at the Plaza hotel. Continuing, he tells me that Donald Trump had recently purchased the Plaza and was making major changes.

"The Donald is going to build a private club in the hotel, and we want you to run the door." The plan was to gut Cinema 3, the movie theater below the hotel, and make it Donald's fiefdom.

Somewhat shocked, I replied, "That's very flattering, thank you, but I'm very happy here."

He was insistent, said the salary would be much more than I earned here, that this was an incredible and rare opportunity, and a position of such prestige at one of the best hotels in the world would solidify my reputation. I had absolutely zero interest.

He persisted. "Let me dangle a carrot in front of you. In six months, once we are up and running, we will give you a percentage of the club. It will be your door." I again declined. This fucker didn't stop. I almost wished it were an invitation to a threesome. I could have gotten out of it so much easier. "Ivana really wants to meet you." He said the name as though I were being summoned by royalty. Trump's wife was apparently running the hotel and leading the project. If I made it past her, I would actually get to meet the Donald, whose door I'd be guarding.

This sounded absolutely awful, though this guy was determined. "Let's set a date. I'll send a car." The last thing I needed was another limo showing up at my door in the East Village. Finally, just to shut him up, I relented, and we set a date.

The day of the appointment, a black stretch limo was waiting in front of my building. Head lowered, I emerged slowly and carefully from my apartment, checking up and down the block to make sure I wasn't spotted. Thankfully it was early and none of the junkies were in sight. I had a massive hangover from a late night at J.S. VanDam and was so not looking forward to meeting Lady Trump.

As we arrived at the hotel, I was greeted in the lobby by Mr. Vice President and led to Ivana's office, the antechamber of which I assumed a Czech brothel would look like. I sat and was served coffee in a lovely and expensive porcelain serving set. A woman sat across from me, and as she was called in to see Ivana, I realized it was the tennis star Martina Navratilova. I assumed she was not there for the same reason as me. As I sipped what was a delicious cup of coffee, my head pounding, I wondered how to address Ivana. I pondered my choices. Should I call her as Mr. Vice President did? Do I say Mrs. Trump? Madam Trump? (That might hit too close to home.) Your ladyship? Ma'am? Ivana? I had no idea.

Martina soon exited, and I was ushered into Ivana's office, which was all gold and carpet and tapestry. Upon seeing her seated behind a huge desk, I decided to forgo calling her by any name and said how pleased I was to be there, how wonderful it was to meet her, or some shit like that. She immediately started speaking in a heavy accent and I struggled to make out what she was saying. I realized she had asked me a question only when she'd suddenly stop talking and look at me, obviously waiting for a reply. I'd then say something that I thought might be in the realm of what she was asking. This went painfully on for what seemed like forever. Finally after another of her monologues, she stood, reached out to shake my hand, and dismissed me.

Get me the fuck out of here. As I tried to make my escape, Mr. Vice President appeared. He asked how it went, to which I replied that I had absolutely no idea, though my sense was that it was an absolute disaster. He then invited me back for dinner at the hotel. Apparently, some young, pretty-boy, hotshot chef was taking over the dining room, and Mr. Vice President wanted me to come and see the direction the hotel was going in. I already knew I'd never take a job here but I wasn't about to pass on a free meal.

I returned a week later, and after a mediocre meal I was presented a check. There was obviously a miscommunication. I pulled the captain aside and let him know the meal was to be on "Ivana," figuring if I used the familiar, it might lend more weight to my claim. He had absolutely no idea what I was talking about and went over to the maître d'hôtel. They huddled and were soon joined by someone who I assumed was a hotel manager. The manager walked over to the table and asked me who exactly said the meal was to be comped, since he had absolutely no record of this. Luckily, I had Mr. Vice President's card in my wallet, pulled it out, and described the situation. After another huddle, the captain returned and said the meal was on the house. I thanked him, left, and never heard from anyone at the Plaza again.

Captain Gabe comes up to tell me there's a woman on table 12 that is getting increasingly drunk, and the drunker she gets, the more obnoxious she becomes. She's been awful since she sat down; she's already sent back her appetizer and has now just sent back her lamb due to its being "too lamby." He tells me he's about to shove his cock down her throat and ask her if that's too lamby as well.

"That's probably not the best way to handle this. Go have a shot at the bar while I check on her."

She's in her late forties, dressed to kill, bejeweled, and hammered. She was dining with three, obviously prosperous, gents.

"How's your dinner?"

She glances up, looks me up and down. "Who the fuck are you?"

"I'm the maître d'." I smile.

Slurring her words, she replies, "Oh, so you're the one that wouldn't give us a fucking window table."

"Yes, that would be me. I'm very sorry but there were none available when you arrived."

She looks me over again, grabs my hand. "You're cute."

God, really? "I am so sorry you didn't care for the lamb. May I bring you something else?"

"Nah. The food sucks here. Only thing good about this place is the view. Bring us another bottle of wine."

Well, she's a fucking winner. The gents are hammered as well and thoroughly enjoying this. I pry my hand away and tell her I will send over the captain. I motion Gabe to meet me at the podium.

"She's fucking wasted. They want another bottle of wine. Ignore them for a while and let's see what happens."

Just as I say this, she stumbles up to us. "Which way to the bathroom?"

"Right this way."

As I go to take her by the elbow to guide her down the gangway, she bolts from me, gets to the end, and for some reason stops at exactly the spot where the ramp hits land, turns, and walks right into the canvas that serves as a barrier between the ramp and the river. There's a seam there, and she somehow walks straight through it and into the river. Gabe and I are momentarily stunned. We then run over and see her, arms flailing, screaming for help. As she starts to float away, one of our runners sees her, runs to grab some linen, ties a few tablecloths together, leaps in, catches up to her, hands her a tablecloth, and tows her back in. There is a God.

"Just When I Thought I Was Out, They Pull Me Back In!"

EARLY SPRING, A CHILL in the air. The restaurant is quiet on this late Monday evening. With only a few tables left in the dining room and an empty bar, it was time to sit and have dinner. The one captain left on the floor could easily handle the last guests. I was seated at my usual table, right beside the podium, which allowed me to view the entire dining room and bar, should something or someone need my attention.

The barkeep that night, who we will call J, was the longest tenured, oldest, and considered the head bartender. He was one of Buzzy's boys. Of course of Irish descent, and an early inductee in the Bartender Hall of Fame (yes, there's a hall of fame for barmen and barwomen), a lifer, and a company man. He was antisocial, generally uncongenial to guests he disliked, unfriendly to the staff, and suspicious of all new hires. In all my time there I'd never gotten a drink from him. Nor would I ask for one. When he was behind the bar, the only way of getting that needed cocktail was when he went to pee and one of the other bartenders could slip you something. Luckily, he rarely stayed late, so one could always get something once he'd gone. I don't think he spoke to me the entire first year I was there.

Our relationship took a long time to reach somewhat of a level of mutual respect, and we were eventually able to form a lukewarm bond. He recognized my talents and I his. I knew we had attained a new level of familiarity when we actually had a conversation one day and he told me he was going to the

Bartender Hall of Fame annual get-together. There would be a "new cocktail" contest, and he was going to enter. After some thought, I actually came up with the drink. I called it the Nureyev—champagne, vodka, and some other ingredient I can't remember. He liked it, entered it, and we actually won. Remember, this is the late eighties. Today that drink would be laughed out of the house.

When he returned from the event, he said, "I have good news and bad news. The good news is we won. The bad news is that the grand prize was a pair of skis. I'm keeping them. What are you gonna do with one ski?" Once a prick, always a prick.

As I sat eating my dinner, J was slowly breaking down the bar, and the last few tables were finishing up. Suddenly the valet came rushing into the dining room. "Michael, this guy just parked his car in front of the entrance. It's blocking the door, he's drunk and is cursing at me, saying he won't give me his keys. Buzzy is supposed to be coming. We have to get the car out of there!"

This presented a few problems other than the obvious, which is that a drunk and belligerent guest was out driving his car. Should Buzzy show up, as he was apparently expected to do, and see we let an inebriated guest leave his car in front, blocking the driveway and the entrance to the restaurant, we'd all be fucked. The valet would definitely get suspended for two weeks, and I would, if not suspended, get my ass ripped apart.

Just then this guy staggers past me, bulls his way to the empty bar, and asks for a drink. When there's an unruly guest, what is essential is that everyone on staff is on the same page. Even in fine-dining establishments guests get drunk, obnoxious, and sometimes violent. If a bartender says he is cutting someone off, that person gets cut off. Questions are asked later. You want to defuse the situation as quickly as possible. If I had an issue with a guest, if he was being rude, drunk, or out of line, I'd tell the bartender to cut him off. If I was unable to speak directly to the bartender, the signal we'd use was a finger or hand going rapidly back and forth across the front of the neck, a bit of a beheading gesture.

As this guy heads to the bar, I give J the cutoff sign. He sees this, glares at me. and then pours the guy a shot of Dewar's. "*What the fuck, J,*" I say to myself. J gives me a back-the-fuck-off look. Which I do. I returned to the po-dium and watched as the guy then hands his keys over to J. J then motions me to the service-bar area and in a firm, menacing voice whispers, "Do you know who the fuck that is?"

"No, J, I obviously don't know who the fuck that is or I'd have gone up to him and said hi."

"That's Fat Anthony! Just go back to your table and let me handle this."

We had the keys, and I wasn't going to make the situation worse, so I went back to my dinner.

I watched as J and Fat Anthony had an animated conversation. Fat An-thony was obviously wasted. Sensing the worst had passed, I went over to the service bar to pour myself another glass of wine. Fat Anthony spotted me and walked over. He was about five feet, six inches, at least 220 pounds, had no neck, was wearing a cheap suit, and was reeking of booze. He walks right up to me, leans his body into mine, and in a guttural, Brooklyn accent says, "I don't know who the fuck you are, what the fuck you do here, but you fucking disrespected me." I tried to not turn away and to keep as calm a face as possi-ble, even as the smell of alcohol on his rancid breath made me want to gag. He pressed his fat stomach against mine and pinned me against a shelf. "I don't know what I'm gonna do, but when I do, I'm gonna take care of you." With that he went back to the bar, downed his drink, and left. Jesus fucking Christ, I cannot believe this is happening.

J then shouts out at me, "Do you know who that is!"

"Uh, yeah, you just told me, *Fat fucking Anthony*! Did you tell him I was cutting him off?"

"The fuck yes I did. He's no fucking good. He's been coming here on and off for years. A Brooklyn wannabe. Thinks he's a tough guy and obviously connected. I am seeing him more and more, usually when you're not here. He's a fucking scumbag. You need to stay away from him."

"Great. Thanks, J."

He just fucking sold me out, the prick. "Stay away? What the fuck was I gonna do? Buzzy's coming down, his car's blocking the door, you served him a fucking drink, and now the guy wants to kill me."

This was awful. I knew well how these guys operated, knew how much they despised being disrespected. I'm now thinking Fat Anthony is going to come back, if not to kill me, at least to break my legs just to make a point. J tried, unconvincingly, to tell me it would blow over and I should just go home. I did go home, knowing certainly that this was not going to blow over.

The next day, as I arrive at the restaurant, the phone rings. It's Buzzy. "What happened last night?"

"Last night? You mean Fat Anthony?"

"Yes, Fat Anthony."

I tell him the story, and in typical Buzzy fashion he tells me to not let guys like this in the restaurant, they are trouble, and we don't want them hanging around. I say, "Sure, Buzz, I'll do my best," and hang up. Fuck, I am not getting killed because I tell some wannabe mobster that he can't drink at the bar. He already threatened me once. Does Buzzy really think the next time Fat Anthony walks in I'm going to tell him to leave? I knew this was going to be trouble.

Word soon spread throughout the restaurant. When Jimmy found out, he came running to me. "You cut off Fat Anthony!"

"God fucking dammit, Jimmy. I had no idea who he was! What was I supposed to do?" Jimmy then told me he knew Anthony and grew up in Flatbush with him. Fat Anthony was a neighborhood bully, violent, and someone to stay away from. As he got older, he became more reckless, always involved in petty crimes, and began hanging out with mobsters.

Fucking great. This made me feel so much better. Now what do I do? Wait for this guy to come kill me? A few days pass and nothing happens. I was terrified. I actually considered moving to California to get as far away from him as possible. I knew how my family dealt with these situations, and I wanted no part of it. It was one of the reasons I left Brooklyn. Especially since I'd be the victim. I couldn't even reach out to my Mob uncles since they were all dead.

My next shift was on Saturday evening, and warily I returned to work. Every Friday and Saturday evening, Buzzy had two off-duty city detectives provide security at the restaurant. Both were experienced, suave New York street kids who grew up to become legends on the force. One was Tom Nerney, a former marine, now promoted to the elite unit assigned to investigate cop killings. The NYPD paid these guys so poorly that they needed to moonlight for some extra cash.

Tom was on that evening, and when he arrived, the first thing he said was that he'd heard there'd been some trouble here. Buzzy had called him to discuss the situation. Well, at least he was somewhat looking out for me. Tom, after speaking to both J and Buzzy, thought he had a good idea of who Fat Anthony was, but it would be helpful to see him.

This Saturday was the evening before Mother's Day, and the restaurant was especially busy. Finally, at just past twelve, I sat down to have dinner, and as was usual, Tom joined me at my table. We always sat next to each other on the banquette, allowing us to keep an eye on the dining room. I glanced over at the bar and suddenly see that both bartenders had moved to the far end and were furtively gesturing to get my attention. Just then I see the back of Fat Anthony walking to the bar, followed by one of the largest humans I had ever seen. This man had obviously borrowed one of the jackets we kept for guests that were unaware of the jacket-only policy in the dining room, since it was split almost entirely down the back from his girth. Behind him, I immediately recognized the dwarf Nunzio. Nunzio was a regular at the restaurant since he was a henchman for "Stem Glass" Vinny, one of the funeral directors in the neighborhood and a regular bar guest. Vinny was reputedly connected to the Mob, and whenever he came by for a drink, he would pull me toward him, pinch my cheek, and hand me a twenty-dollar bill. His nickname arose from his always asking for his Dewar's to be poured into a stem glass. It didn't matter that we all knew he drank from a stem glass; he reminded the bartender of this each time he arrived. Nunzio would always be in tow with Stem Glass. He would run errands and was reputed to be a money collector for the bookies in the area.

The three of them head straight to the bar, order drinks, and then turn directly around and face me. "Tom," I whisper, "that's him. That's Anthony." Tom gives him a good look and pretty much confirms that he's the guy Tom thought it was. Tom whispers to me that Anthony is one of Gotti's boys, a punk who is suddenly rising in the ranks. Tom believed he'd been made a captain recently and that he was in some way connected to the Castellano killing. Paul Castellano, the head of the Gambino crime family, was gunned down outside Sparks Steak House in Manhattan. As his car pulled up to the front of the restaurant, another car pulled up alongside with four guys inside. He never got to eat that steak. He was killed right at the entrance to Sparks. It was pretty much assumed that Gotti had ordered the hit, paving the way for him to be the new head of the Gambino crime family. The police believed Fat Anthony was one of the men in the car that night.

With this, Tom excused himself and said he was going to his car to get his gun. "You're what?!" I was now about to shit my pants. Here were three mobsters, twenty feet away, glaring right at me. One of them had probably just murdered the biggest Mafia don in the country. There's no way he'd think twice about beating me to death. I was now convinced they were here to do some serious damage to my person.

As Tom got up, Jimmy came rushing over to me, furtively whispering, "Do you know who that is?!"

"Yes, I fucking know who that is."

"Do you know who's with him?"

"Nunzio and some gorilla."

"That gorilla is Furio. I grew up with him and his brother. They are fucking evil. They blew up cats with fireworks as kids, terrorized us all, and both went into the Mob. Look at his hands!"

I quickly glanced over at the three of them, still at the bar, still facing my table. Furio's left hand appeared mauled. Jimmy tells me Furio was busted, and while in jail, someone tried to kill him, setting fire to his cell. His fingers were apparently so damaged a few had to be removed.

"This guy is a killer!"

"Fucking great!"

I am now about to cry. Jimmy walks away, and as he does, Fat Anthony approaches my table. My heart is beating so fast I thought I was going to drop dead right then, denying him the opportunity to kill me. I break into a sweat as he reaches the table, leans in, places both fists on the table, and says, "How you doin'?"

It took me a few seconds to get my voice to work. "I'm okay." My voice is breaking with fear. "We had a very busy night. Tomorrow is Mother's Day." Why the fuck I said that I have no idea.

"You disrespected me. I don't know what I'm gonna do, but when I do, I'm gonna get you."

I was so terrified that I realized it was possible to cry, piss, and shit yourself at the same time. I tried to explain what had happened that night, but he wouldn't let me. He straightened up, turned, and swaggered back to the bar.

Just then Tom returns. I tell him exactly what happened. He calms me down and tells me not to worry. He's sticking with me. These guys can smell a cop, and Tom was someone not to be fucked with. They finally finish their drinks and walk out the door without looking over at us. Tom then gets up to follow them out and make sure they leave. When he returned, he told me to go home. He'd do some research and get back to me.

I went out back to the locker rooms to dress, thinking that at any moment one of them could be anywhere, behind the ice machine or the dumpster, lying in wait to kill me. I grew up with mobsters. I knew what these guys were capable of. I got into my car as quickly as possible, constantly checking for a sign of one of them. When I arrived home, I thought they might have found out where I lived and checked everywhere before unlocking the door to my apartment. I didn't feel safe till I was inside and the door locked. This was awful. I had no idea what to do. I again considered leaving the state, moving to LA to join Uncle Rob. Both of us would then be in hiding.

I wasn't due back to work till the following Thursday. The next day I get a call from Rodney, wanting to know the details. Buzzy was all over him, telling him to not let these guys in the restaurant, they were dangerous and not whom we wanted in the restaurant at all. The exact same shit Buzzy told me. Rodney agreed with me, but he wasn't about to deny them entrance. I explained what had happened the previous night and that I was afraid for my life. Rodney knew all of the connected guys who regularly dined or drank at the restaurant. He said he was going to make some inquiries, and that I should lie low and wait to hear back from him.

I spent the next few days terrified, looking over my shoulder wherever I went, always expecting someone to pop out from behind a car or a door and beat the shit out of me. Finally, on Wednesday, Rodney called. He had just spoken to Mr. T. T and his wife were some of our great guests. They dined with us weekly, would have their tiny dog in a Louis Vuitton carry bag, park it under the table, and begin with a bottle of bubbles. T owned funeral homes in Brooklyn, and we all knew he was connected. Rodney told T of my situation. T said he absolutely knew of Anthony, and though he wasn't one of T's "people," T would see what he could do. He let me know T was coming for dinner tomorrow night to talk to me. Fuck. This wasn't ever going to end.

The next evening, service began smoothly enough. T had a 7:00 P.M. reservation. I was a wreck waiting for his arrival. I was at the podium, my back to the door, when suddenly someone grabs my shoulder and I feel something against my back. I thought this was it. They were going to kill me right here. I was about to scream when I hear T's voice. I turn and he has a pistol in his hand.

"You like the way that feels?" He smiled.

"Fuck no."

"Okay. Take us to our table. Champagne is on you tonight."

He was with his lovely wife, who smiled knowingly at me as I brought the wine over. I opened it myself, my hands shaking as I poured them both a glass. "You fucked up, Mikey. This is bad. This guy's a fucking killer. He's not my people but I know of him." I am once again, for about the hundredth time this week, about to cry. As I finish pouring, T, who's facing the door, sees Stem Glass Vinny enter. "Ah, there's Vinny. I'll be right back."

He gets up and walks over to Vinny. Both of the undertakers go outside to talk. I hoped they weren't negotiating for the right of who was going to bury me. They were gone for quite some time. Both return to the restaurant. As they enter, Vinny immediately comes over, pinches my cheek, gives me a look of *You were a bad boy, Mikey*, and hands me the usual $20. T smiles at us and tells me to follow him back to the table.

"You're lucky, Mikey, Stem Glass likes you. He thinks you're a good kid. He knows Anthony very well. They know the same people. We had a little chat outside in the car."

Could my graciousness really be paying off here?

"Stem Glass," T continues, "is going to talk to Anthony. You here tomorrow?" I nod yes. "Good. If all goes well, I'll stop in tomorrow for a drink. Now, what are we eating?"

I take a deep breath for the first time in a week.

The next evening, at six thirty, T walks in the door. This time I spot him before I get the gun in my back.

"Okay. We spoke. You're fucking lucky, Mikey. I got this worked out. Anthony is going to come in again. When you see him, you need to go over to him and say, 'Mr. Anthony, I am very sorry for having disrespected you. Please accept my apology. Let me buy you a drink.' You got that? Repeat it back to me." I repeat it back verbatim. "Okay. Good, Mikey. I'll be in touch." And with that T goes to the bar, downs a shot of Johnnie Black, and leaves.

Fuck me! Fucking fuck me! I cannot believe this is actually happening. So I wait. The weekend came and went. I had a few days off before returning the following Thursday. Everyone had by now heard the story, and we were all on the lookout for Fat Anthony, especially the bartenders. The only shift J and I worked together was Monday, so I made double sure the bartenders on the other nights knew to expect Fat Anthony.

Then it happened. It's Saturday night. The restaurant is just filling up. I am returning to the door when I see both bartenders at the service area of the bar. I knew immediately what was up. It's pretty difficult to not see two bartenders standing next to each other when they would normally be standing apart making drinks. Each had a look of fear etched on his face. They nodded to the other end of the bar, where Anthony stood with a female companion, a rather unlovely woman, which I found surprising. I would think a guy who probably just killed Castellano might be able to get a more attractive date. She was heavily made up, her hair teased high above her head, and in heels that made her look like something right out of the sixties. When I finally managed the courage to walk over to them, mentally rehearsing my lines as I approached, she spoke first. She looked me up and down and in a heavy Brooklyn accent blurted out, "Is this the guy?" Jesus, am I going to be humiliated by his date as well?

Before he could speak, I sucked in my breath, greeted them both, and knowing my lines as though I were in the second year of a Broadway run, I spoke. "Mr. Anthony, I am very sorry for having disrespected you. Please accept my apology. Let me buy you a drink." I struggled to keep my hands, which were at my sides, from shaking. He listened, looked at me, stepped as close to me as possible, and said, "I don't need you to buy me nuthin'. I'm expecting a phone call. Come and get me when it comes."

He turned back to his companion, and I was dismissed. I wasn't sure how I felt. One part of me was relieved that I'd be able to return home that evening with all my limbs intact. The other part was very, very wary. What did he mean by a phone call? Was this a onetime thing? Would it continue? The only phone in the dining room was at my stand. Would he stand there talking to Furio about their next hit as I was trying to greet a guest? If Buzzy came in and saw this Neanderthal of a human standing there, phone in hand, I'd be fired on the spot.

My wariness was soon ended when the phone beeped. I picked up, and the reservationist said there was a call for an Anthony, and did I know anything about this? Fuck yes, I knew. I went over to Anthony and let him know his phone call had come. His demeanor changed completely. It was as though he'd made it, he had finally arrived. He was not only making me look like his little bitch in front of his girl, but was also getting personal phone calls at one of the most famous and beautiful restaurants in the world. He walks to the phone, picks it up, and says, "Hello? . . . Hello? . . . Hello? . . ." He looks at me. "What the fuck? Deres nobody here?"

This cretin, this Gotti captain, had no idea how to work the phone. I showed him how to press the button to take the call. I stepped away so as not to hear the conversation, prayed that Buzzy didn't walk in, that the call would be short and the end of it all.

He hung up after a minute or so and walked up to me. "What's your name?"

"Michael."

"Mikey, you know where to find me if I get anudder call."

The worst happened. Fat Anthony became a regular, coming once a week, usually for drinks and once or twice a month for dinner. Each time, those with him could have been selected from a casting call for low-rent mobsters. Bad suits, greasy hair, foulmouthed, and, what really showed how low-level they actually were, they tipped like shit. Mobsters, the ones that know how to dress and carry themselves, always want to show off, get respect, and are great tippers. Hundred-dollar bills would cross many hands throughout the night. We had a few wise guys that would come in and, instead of cash, would leave us enormous tips on their credit cards. We knew something was up when the cards were regularly being declined. This never phased them since they always had more in their pockets to use. The jig was up when the FBI showed up one day inquiring about a credit card scam and a number of charges that had come from this restaurant. We never saw those wise guys after that. Though we did have a regular guest, an FBI agent who knew J the bartender quite well. The agent was a favorite of the staff's, handing out FBI swag each time he came— T-shirts, caps, and the like. The next time we saw him, we asked about the credit card scam, but he knew nothing about it.

For some odd reason, as Anthony made us a regular stop, Buzzy backed off on our not letting him and his crew in. Anthony came regularly with Nunzio, Furio, and a few other cohorts, most of the time looking ridiculous, as they were made to wear our house sport coats over their tracksuits. They'd congregate at the bar, go out on the small deck to talk, have a few drinks, and leave. Thankfully, the phone calls were few.

One Monday, as I entered the restaurant to begin my shift, J was setting up the bar and, as soon as he spotted me, screamed out, "Did you hear? Did you see this?" He shoved the *New York Post* in front of me; the headline read, MOBSTER SHOT IN WEST SIDE CLUB. It was Fat Anthony. The story we eventually pieced together from our detectives, T, Stem Glass, and others was that Anthony was definitely involved in the Castellano hit, was a fast riser, but his temper and greed got to him. He and his crew were regularly shaking down nightclubs for Gotti. Anthony apparently put a few extra bucks in his pocket and roughed up the wrong guy. They put a hit on him and killed him in the club. I later learned the reason Buzzy never really brought up Anthony and his friends much. Our FBI agent friend was in on this, and the FBI had the place bugged. They were taking pictures of these guys and trying to get info from their conversations on the deck. Neither Buzzy nor the FBI agent would ever confirm or deny this.

Acting Proceeds Apace

It HAD BEEN FIVE years since my first meeting with Renfield. Once I'd been promoted to maître d'hôtel, he softened a bit and I'd actually grown to like him. Sadly, the year before, his AIDS had so progressed that he was no longer able to work the floor, and he eventually died of the disease. As for me, I finally felt I had made it. My time at the River Café was, at that point, the pinnacle of my restaurant career. It was my identity, my entrée to clubs and bars, and it afforded me respect in certain circles.

It was now about to come to an end. The pressure of denying guests window tables nightly was overwhelming. If another guest asked me for a window, I was about to shoot him in the face. There was also the pressure of David Burke in the kitchen. He was an incredibly volatile chef and prone to rages. Especially after a bender. He once threw a plate so hard at a woman in pastry that if it had hit her, I'm sure she would have gotten a concussion. He would continually question the seating and disliked many of the captains.

Buzzy was as crazy as ever. One evening he walked into the restaurant and immediately spotted a piece of electrical tape hanging from the ceiling above a window table. It was apparently left from a small photo shoot that was done that afternoon. He flew into a rage, called everyone off the floor, berated us all for ruining his restaurant, and was stunned that not one of his employees had spotted it. When he found out the daytime maître d'hôtel was in charge that day and responsible for not removing the tape, Buzzy suspended him for two weeks, forcing all the evening captains and maîtres d'hôtel to cover his shifts. Sadly, soon after, the daytime maître d'hôtel would also succumb to AIDS.

Finally, what precipitated the end was the stock market crash of 1987. On October 19, dubbed Black Monday, the market tanked, the Dow dropped five hundred points, and with it dropped our best customers. We went from selling thousands of dollars in wine each night to pouring glasses of house wine instead. Reservations plummeted, the door money, which had been un-stoppable, stopped. With no wine sales, the tips were minimal. Our lucrative evenings had ended overnight. We were done.

This turned out to be a blessing in disguise. With the lull in business, it was easy to give away shifts, and I spent those last two years pursuing acting. This made the banalities of the job easier. My creative life outside the restaurant made my time in the restaurant much more palatable. Having finished my training programs, I began to audition regularly, and shockingly, I began to get cast—plays, films, and commercials—all nonunion and all pretty shitty. The plays I did were mostly dreadful, performed in churches, lofts, and tiny theaters where the audiences were made up of friends, family, and other actors who were well versed in suffering fools gladly. At that time there were so many little venues where plays were performed that it afforded an actor a chance to hone his craft. The best lessons are learned from working with some pretty awful scripts and directors, and I certainly worked with awful scripts and directors. The film work I managed to get was pretty embarrassing. I was a sardine in a Season sardines commercial, replete with full sardine suit, only my face exposed. I also managed to be cast in the sci-fi epic *Robot Holocaust*, which is on most people's list as one of the worst films ever made. I eventually got my Equity and SAG cards and began to do some decent stuff, which built my confidence and finally led me to give my notice at the River Café. It was time to move on.

PART IV

Raoul's

I TOOK SOME TIME off, and after a brief stint crisscrossing the country, I returned home, unemployed and broke. This is when the universe usually steps in. I got a call from Jimmy, the legendary bartender at the French bistro Raoul's in SoHo. He let me know there was an opening for a server. I knew Raoul's well. It was considered one of the best places in the city for servers to work. The staff made bank there, generally working only three shifts a week and taking home more than enough to live comfortably while engaged in other pursuits.

Launched in 1975 by two French brothers, Serge and Guy Raoul, it opened in SoHo just as artists and galleries began moving into the many lofts and factory spaces that were being vacated as manufacturing began leaving the city. It was a mini–art world renaissance, as gallerists such as Paula Cooper, Leo Castelli, Mary Boone, and Tony Shafrazi all opened shop. As all the hip people headed downtown to see the shows, they needed a place to eat and drink. One of the only places in which to do so at the time was this sexy little French bistro on Prince Street, which had recently opened. The restaurant really took off when James Signorelli, a producer for *Saturday Night Live*, who is still a customer, brought in his gang from *SNL* and made it their little clubhouse.

The restaurant is in an amazing, old–New York space. You enter a small, narrow room with an antique bar on the left and a row of tables on the right. Halfway down the room is a fish tank; behind it, a row of small tables runs down the center of the room, with the much-sought-after booths on either side of these. It's filled with paintings and photographs, most donated by the locals and artists in the area, and in the early days many swapped a painting for a meal.

The area behind the fish tank is dominated by the now-iconic photograph of a nude woman, created by the artist Martin Schreiber, famous for his book of nudes featuring a very young Madonna. The photograph, which most think is a painting, is of a young woman, her long red hair hanging suggestively down and off the green sofa she reclines on, posed as if she were resting after having sex, her right knee slightly lifted, her left breast full and round, her left arm bent and covering her face. The rumor that surfaced years later that it was Fergie, the Duchess of York, is bullshit. The model was a young Puerto Rican girl from Alphabet City. The original was later destroyed during the filming of Martin Scorsese's *Departed*, and what hangs there now is a digital facsimile of the original photo. This extremely provocative photo anchors the dark, small, sexy, and, back then, smoke-filled space.

Entering Raoul's gives you the feeling of just having walked in off a street in Paris. Some years later, the photographer and filmmaker Larry Clark, a friend of Jimmy the bartender's, donated a photo to display in the restaurant. It's from his book *Tulsa*. The photo is of a nude young couple in the back seat of a car. The woman lies atop the man, they are embracing, kissing, and in her left hand she holds his penis. It's no wonder Raoul's has been a date spot for years.

This ambience has aroused many guests. A spiral staircase at the front of the restaurant leads to a small lounge on the second floor. There sits a tarot reader, a small banquette, a couch, and the toilets. Back then, it was the perfect place to do a few lines, finish a cocktail, and then go fuck in the bathroom. Guests complained regularly about the long waits for the toilets as the sounds of couples fucking or the slurping sounds of oral sex inside could be heard.

With Jimmy on my side and my stellar credentials and knowledge of the restaurant and its clientele, I figured I had a good chance of getting a job here. The one problem was the general manager. She was renowned for being difficult, mean-spirited, and abusive to the staff. I was told she was notoriously slow in hiring people and I should prepare to wait it out.

I needed this job. Everyone I knew who worked there said this was the last stop for waiters—once you'd worked here, you wouldn't be able to work in another restaurant again. The money was great, there was hardly any oversight, you could drink and drug and maybe get your cock sucked in the bath-room from some aroused man or woman (depending on your predilection) that was so turned on by the sexual environment that the person just couldn't resist. All this and still only work three days a week.

I pressed Jimmy to get me an interview with Miss GM. It took about a week until he finally called and let me know he'd spoken to her, and she was expecting my call. With all my experience, I was still nervous. Before calling, I rehearsed what I was going to say, took a deep breath, and dialed. I had no idea what response I'd get on the other end. Someone answered and put me on hold for what lasted at least ten minutes. Miss GM was either very busy or this was one of her power games. She finally picked up and was rela-tively cordial. She must have heard the fear in my voice and backed off, imme-diately sensing victory in this first encounter. The call was brief, and we set a date for my interview.

The Meet

THE DAY OF THE interview I prepared for the worst. My strategy was to follow the lead of Muhammad Ali—bob and weave, counter with a jab when possible, then play rope-a-dope and take her punches. Feeling seasoned enough with interviews, especially after Renfield, I thought I'd be able to deflect her best shots, give some sensible answers, and get out with only a few bruises. When I showed up at the restaurant, the bartender had me sit in the middle of the bar to wait for her. There I sat, the bartender setting up a foot away from me, servers a few feet behind doing the same, all making small talk and ignoring the elephant in the room. I had absolutely nothing to do except not look uncomfortable nor make direct eye contact with anyone. *The New Yorker* magazine I brought with me to read in case I was made to wait was useless. I'd look ridiculous sitting there reading a magazine while the staff set up. Small talk was out. I always hated when an interviewee tried to engage me in chit-chat when I was setting up, usually trying to gain information about the place. The more boorish ones attempted to see how much we servers made. I wasn't about to do this. Instead I just sat there, taking in the space, knowing I'd kill it here, if only she would give me a shot.

As I sat waiting, I remembered my many nights as a guest at Raoul's. When I first dined here, the restaurant had been run by the maître d' Rob, already a legend and known throughout the city. He regularly performed in drag, and just around midnight the restaurant lights would dim, the music would switch to Dusty Springfield, and all eyes would turn to the spiral staircase, where he would descend in full drag, his black horn-rimmed glasses the only accessory that was not Dusty. He'd lip-synch through the restaurant before ascending the bar to finish the show. He was renowned for walking the neighborhood and spray-painting in gold the dog shit that littered the sidewalk. He was one of the earliest to contract AIDS and die.

He was replaced by the "Queen Mother," Philip Saunders, the quintessential maître d'hôtel and one of the most pleasant and gracious humans to ever man a door at a restaurant. One Saturday evening my girlfriend and I popped in unannounced for dinner. The place was packed, the bar three deep. Philip was at the door and greeted us with his usual "Dahlings, my favorite couple in the world." We must have been at least the fifth favorite couple that evening, but it didn't matter. You felt like you were the only one dining in the restaurant. "Are we dining, my loves?" He scanned the room and let us know the only possible table he could give us was the large horseshoe-shaped eight top in the corner. This can actually be a private and romantic table for two. You're tucked away in a corner and mostly hidden.

"We have some riffraff there now; they've just paid and should be up in a second." This table is one of the best in the restaurant. It's where Tarantino, Travolta, his wife (Kelly Preston), Harvey Keitel, Uma Thurman, and the producer of the film, Lawrence Bender (who once waited tables here), sat the evening after the showing of *Pulp Fiction* at the New York Film Festival. It's the table where J.Lo and Marc Anthony sat for their first date after the birth of their twins, the street out front having to be closed due to the number of paparazzi that were waiting for them. It's where U2 would sit, and where Depeche Mode still sits today. As I of course said yes, those dining at the table got up to leave, and as they passed, I recognized the riffraff as Madonna and her entourage, including Sandra Bernhard, whom Madonna may or may not have been dating. I always wondered if she knew the nude hanging on the wall was by the same photographer who did her book of nudes.

They left and we were seated. We had just ordered a drink when both Madonna and Bernhard came rushing back, apologized, and began frantically searching for something they'd left at the table. We stood to let them look, and after a minute or so, finding nothing, they apologized and left. As we waited for our drinks, I reached around to put my hand on my lady's ass, and it accidentally slipped into a crevice of the booth. I felt something there, dug in, and pulled out a makeup compact. This is obviously what they were looking for. I placed it on the table, opened it, and voilà! It was stuffed full of cocaine. We turned on the whole staff that night.

In the midst of my daydream, Madame GM finally arrived, with a smile on her face that I would soon learn was completely disingenuous. She was not unattractive, thin and fit with a short, trendy haircut. What was a bit off were her hands; they were wrinkled and looked as if they belonged to a much-older woman. The interview was conducted right there in the middle of the bar, in earshot of anyone on staff that cared to listen, and you know they sure the fuck were and she wanted them to as well.

She began with the usual questions, wanting to know about the River Café, Buzzy, the chefs, et cetera. I of course gave her the whitewashed version. She then looked me directly in the eye and asked, "Aren't you burnt-out? Do you really think you can still do this? Why do you even want to do it?" It was said in such a patronizing tone that the bartender, who was about a foot away and who I could tell was listening in on every word, nearly spit out the mouthful of water he had just drunk. I sat there, remembered my objective—to bob and weave, take the punch, breathe, rope-a-dope. "No. I still love the business, the guests, the energy of this. I've taken some time off and I'm ready to get back to work." With that she gave me the same smile we started with and thanked me for my time.

Fuck, that was awful. It never fails, the most awful human beings, the power hungry, those with the least personality, kindness, and humanity, are general managers in restaurants. Their masochistic side keeps them in a business where the hours are shit, the owners are shittier, and you're continually putting out fires. Their sadistic side gets let out on the staff. I heard nothing for over a month, no follow-up, and neither Jimmy nor Philip could give me any details except to say this was how she operated. Finally, after six weeks, she called and asked if I was still interested in the position. I of course said yes and thanked her profusely, and we set a time to trail.

Another Beginning

ALL NEW SERVERS AT Raoul's are relegated to the Siberia that is the back room. A few years after opening, the restaurant was somewhat renovated. The single bathroom that was in the back of the kitchen was removed, and bathrooms were installed on the floor above, accessed by the now-infamous spiral staircase. The backyard of the restaurant was enclosed, a mural was painted on the rear wall, a few paintings and photos were hung, and the room was open for business. The problem was that no one wanted to sit there. Everyone wanted to be up front, where the action was.

Every restaurant has its share of shitty tables; this one had a shitty room full of shitty tables. The only access was to walk through the bar and front dining room—packed with the beautiful, the rich, the celebs—to then be escorted through a kitchen that looked like a Chinatown tenement. Parts of the ceiling were caving in, the stainless steel was so old it hadn't glimmered since the First World War, the floor was grimy, and the dish station was usually piled high with food scraps and dirty pots and pans, all within reach of guests walking by should one decide to assist. If the busy cooks glanced up from their tasks (in the old days a cigarette dangled from their lips), you'd get thrown a half smile or dirty look, depending on their engagement with what was being prepared. Chefs and cooks hate having anyone but themselves in the kitchen, including servers, and they regularly made the guests aware of this.

Entering the badly lit and designed room in the rear, you pass the entrance to the basement, where cooks and servers would regularly run up and down for supplies, clanging open and closing the metal gate that protected the un-knowing from tumbling down the extremely narrow and slippery staircase. Most everyone who has ever worked at Raoul's has either fallen down these fucking stairs or hit his or her head on the low-hanging pipes above. This din-ing room was for tourists and the overflow—those who either forgot to make a reservation or would walk in at prime time hoping to get a table.

The room was worse for the waiters than the guests. At least they got to eat. Servers in the back arrived with everyone else at 4:00 P.M. The kitchen opened at six. The first table usually sat at seven thirty. You'd be there three to four hours before getting a guest. As anyone who has ever waited tables knows, it's painful to be in a bad station. You watch your coworkers in the prime areas raking in the dough while you stand there counting your pennies.

At Raoul's, we who were banished to Siberia would have to go through the front dining room on our way to pick up our drinks at the bar. We'd pass tables covered with steaks and chops, bottles of expensive Bordeaux and burgundies, the big boys from California—the Ridges, Mondavis, Heitzes—bottles that sell in the high three figures. The smell of money being spent in the front room ripe, and none of it hitting our pockets. With each room pooling its own tips, if the front room made $300, we'd make $100. If they made $500, we might hit $150. I was determined to wait it out. I knew I was good enough and knew that someone would eventually get a job that allowed that person to leave the business, or someone would move or get fed up with all the shit we put up with—all the reasons waiters have to finally check out.

I was exiled to Siberia for nearly a year, occasionally picking up a shift or two in the front room when someone took a vacation, was sick, or needed a night off. Front waiters rarely wanted to come in on a night off to pick up a shift. I soon learned why. It was a moneymaking party up there, the booze flowed freely, and servers controlled their stations, sometimes telling off rude or drunk guests with no retribution. Madame GM had the cushiest job in the business. She came in the morning and left at 6:00 P.M. In charge were the maîtres d'hôtel, whom we servers tipped. They weren't about to crack the whip on us.

The servers that had a lock on the front-room shifts were the Artist, a couple of actors, and a woman who'd been there for years, all there for the quick money and trying their best to leave the business. I knew one would soon leave. The Artist was also a heroin addict. His days had to be numbered. He'd have a few cocktails, go get high, hide behind the server station for as long as possible, doodling on postcards, and do just enough to get through the night. One of the actors was Michael Massee, who'd worked there for several years and eventually went on to have a successful acting career. Sadly, he was the one who fired the gun with the cartridge that killed Brandon Lee in the film *The Crow*. There were successes and there would eventually be movement. I just needed to perform better than any of my fellow servers in the gulag, remain positive and helpful enough to those in the front to curry favor, and be the next one chosen.

One of my fellow inmates in back was fondly referred to as Girl. In fact, all the gays at the restaurant referred to one another as she. Girl trained me in the ways of Raoul's, which was actually very little: Take the order; get the food to the table; and drop the check. We hit it off immediately. We were exactly the same age, both of us had fine-dining backgrounds, and here we both were in the lower depths, in a restaurant renowned as the "last stop" for waiters. Girl is tall, extremely handsome, and, like me, an Italian American. We had plenty of time to talk while waiting for our first guests. We quickly realized that not only were we at the University of Florida in the exact same years, but we also lived in the same dorm, a floor apart, during our first year there.

Girl was perhaps the surliest waiter I have ever met. If he didn't like you, regardless of whether you were a guest or staff, he could be curt, deliberative, and at times just plain rude. His disdain for other servers was so apparent that, years later, after we had both solidified our positions, whenever new people were hired, Girl refused to acknowledge them till they'd been there for at least a year. Madame GM absolutely adored him and, despite his many indiscretions, he pretty much had a job for life. He'd make it reasonably well through the beginning of the first seating, but once he'd gotten double- or triple-seated, the shit would hit the fan. He only calmed down once the rush was over and he'd gone outside to smoke a joint. We would be a team for my entire run at Raoul's.

Harvey Keitel was in with the *Pulp Fiction* crowd just after the premiere. As I'm taking their order, he shouts to me from across the table, "What's *côte de veau*?" His pronunciation made it sound like he was saying *coat da voo*.

"It's a veal chop."

"What's the *voo* part?"

"That's the veal."

"Where's the bone?"

"It's attached to the veal. It's a chop."

"So *coat de voo* is a veal chop?"

"Yes, Harvey."

"Okay. Come back to me."

I wasn't actually with him, but how could you not love Harvey Keitel. I said of course and asked Uma Thurman what she was having.

I finally get to Harvey. "Are you ready?"

"I like a nice veal chop. The one with the bone."

"This is a nice veal chop."

"The chef cooks it?"

"Yes, Harvey," I lied, "the chef cooks it."

"It has the bone?"

I'm now about to stab him. "Yes, it has the bone. It's a veal chop!"

"Okay. I'll have the steak."

The Raoul's Brothers

SERGE RAOUL WAS THE brother who oversaw the front of the resta
brother Guy was the chef. Serge is tall, with receded gray hair and
He's not unattractive. Never much of a talker, especially with the
conversations were limited to short, crisp sentences in his French-
English. While he spoke English fluently, you were always made to fe
you couldn't speak French, you were held in lower esteem.

He was always trying to get Madame GM to hire French waiters, a
she did, those hired were your typical NYC French waiters. This lot g
despises Parisians, no matter where they themselves are from, could
about the guests' experience, and maintain a semidetached profession
safeguard their tips. They are perfunctory and have an air of Gallic sup
when tested, and when necessary, the best they can act at a table is un
Most of these waiters act as though they were all Jean-Paul Belmond
smile when not in a hurry, can be incredibly polite, and are wonderful a
ing you in the eye when speaking to you, but once they turn from the
the smile drops and they are off in their own world. They never mak
real connection with the guests, and over the years the French servers h
fewest, if any, guest requests. They are in it for the money, though they
make great tips.

When Raoul's first opened, Serge ran the door. I have never seen hi
this position, nor can I imagine him doing it. His conversations are brie
shows little interest in running the restaurant, spends little time there,

doesn't know the regulars, and has no interest in meeting them. In the seventeen years that I worked there, I don't think I had more than a five-minute conversation with him. When he enters the restaurant, he rarely says hello. Instead, he scans the few things he's interested in to see if they're in order—if the paintings and photos on the wall are straight, the music and lights at the proper level, and the orange juice is freshly squeezed. He's otherwise indifferent.

Next, he goes to his booth and expects you to tell him the specials, take his order, and serve the food. That's it. When finished, he gets up and leaves—never a goodbye. If you pick up the phone when he calls, you hear a gruff "Serge!" as though he were asking for himself. He asks for the GM first, and if she's not there, the maître d'hôtel. These are the only people he spoke to. His brother Guy was slightly more gracious but again showed little interest in the staff. He was rarely at the restaurant, having opened his own, L'Acajou, in Chelsea, and spent most of his time there.

Other than L'Acajou, which was all Guy, the Raouls had no success outside of Raoul's. These guys are not restaurateurs. They lucked out with an incredible space at the exact right time. Raoul's is failproof. If you'd read Moira Hodgson's one-star review from 1980 in *The New York Times*, you'd be shocked the restaurant didn't close that year, never mind be in the throes of a forty-five-year run. Parts of the review make you cringe: The *panaché de poisson*, "a blend of textureless bass, sole, and scallops . . . tasted as though it had been in the refrigerator for days"; the gazpacho, "thin . . . without the usual accompaniment of fresh-chopped vegetables"; the mushrooms with the crudités "on the verge of being fermented . . . Quail were so dry and withered that their legs broke off like matchsticks, and the flesh was desiccated. . . . The liver with bacon was overcooked and had the mushy texture of liver that has been frozen. . . . Striped bass with Roquefort elicited from one diner the sort of expression you'd expect to see on the face of someone who had just heard of the sudden failure of his bank. The cheese completely overwhelmed the fish, which was so overcooked that its texture was indistinguishable from that of the cheese."

There was a Raoul's in Nyack, and a Raoul's in Bali; both failed. The broth-

ers attempted a Raoul's in the Parker Méridien Hotel—they named it Seppi's, after their father, and designed it as an exact double of Raoul's in SoHo. It limped along for a few years before also failing. They had an ill-fated venture in Dumbo, an enormous space that didn't last a year. The timing was off. Dumbo wasn't even close to the renaissance it's now having. They tried a spa and hotel in Truth or Consequences, New Mexico. It was two hours from the nearest airport, and the area is pretty much a desert. The town has a few hot springs, but otherwise there's not much of a reason to go there. They tried to open a Raoul's in Turkey but called off the venture when the manager who went there to assist in the opening passed away in his hotel room.

The greatest failure may have been in 1985. Serge had the excellent idea of opening another restaurant, a high-end concept, and recruited a former chef from Raoul's, Thomas Keller. Together they opened the restaurant Rakel in TriBeCa. Keller lasted there four years before leaving and eventually opening the French Laundry in Napa, which has been named the best restaurant in the world twice and made Keller a superstar. Rakel, on the other hand, went through a few more iterations before finally closing for good in 1994, the same year Keller purchased the French Laundry. In an interview with Marian Burros in *The New York Times* in 1996, he said this about Rakel:

> I learned it didn't matter how good a cook you are. It was about organization, management. The management was not as strong as it should have been. The restaurant was undercapitalized, and we didn't capitalize on great reviews. Financially it wasn't working, and Serge Raoul wanted to run Rakel like Raoul's, like a bistro. I didn't want to compromise what I was cooking and realized I would have to make a change.

The two fundamental reasons why restaurants fail—bad management and undercapitalization. The Raouls hit a grand slam with Raoul's in SoHo. It's ridiculously sexy and has been blessed with great maîtres d'hôtel and sometimes servers, who can make the experience one of the best in NYC. It didn't matter if the steak was overcooked, the fish fishy, the escargot cold. People want to be there, be in that space, to see and be seen, to sometimes (especially in the old days) fuck and do drugs, and leave feeling like they've experienced true New York.

Table of six, typical Brooklyn, guidos and guidettes. They could have been my family. I go to take the order and ask the first woman what she'd like to eat.

She giggles, looks at her boyfriend, points to an item on the menu. "Vinny, is this what I want?"

He replies, "Yeah, give ha dat. It's a steak, right?

"Yes, sir." (Of course she ordered the steak, it's the only word she recognized.) "It's steak with pepper."

"Good, you have chicken? I want chicken."

"We have chicken."

Next woman, same routine, orders the steak. I get to the third woman, ask her what she'd like, and in her very, very thick Brooklyn accent she begins to speak.

Her boyfriend interrupts her, "Oh, oh, oh! Whoa! Hold on! When you get a dick, you could order! She's gonna have the steak medium. That is, if I don't break her jaw before."

She looks at me and says, "Dis is why I love him."

Service

COMING FROM A TEMPLE of gastronomy where I needed to know every single ingredient of a dish, all from the finest products available, plated as though slated for exhibition at MoMA, I found serving something that was not precious and to be fawned over was a great relief. All I needed to do was to be somewhat kind, get the food and drinks to the table, drop the check, and pocket the money. I wanted to spend more time on my acting career, and if I could get three days a week in the front room, I'd have enough to live well with plenty of time to pursue acting. Was all the food shit? Not really. A few dishes were actually excellent, and these are still on the menu, such as the *artichauts* vinaigrette and of course the steak au poivre, which many consider the best in the city, if not the country.

The menu is handwritten in French on small blackboards that are put on the table just before a party is seated. Servers go to the table, get a drink order, serve it, and return to take a food order. But most guests don't read or speak French and have no idea what most of the items are. Servers are supposed to translate each menu item, including ingredients, answer any questions, then take the order. While you might be able to go through the menu this way for the first few tables, it's impossible once your station was full. Raoul's has always been considered expensive, but that's not the main reason servers make a killing there. It's always been understaffed. The front room ran with two servers, one runner (who also bussed the tables), and a bartender. Each station has nine tables. Excepting diners, fast-food places, and the like, servers in more serious restaurants have four or a maximum of five tables. Most nights at Raoul's you'd be in the weeds. Once one table left, another sat.

Most who were able to get reservations were the regulars, celebrities, and locals who didn't need translating and knew what they wanted—*artichauts*, steak au poivre, and profiteroles for dessert. That's it. Drop the check and move on. Other diners, either so intimidated by the room and the French menu or too embarrassed to let on that they had no idea what most of the items on the menu were, would pick what was closest to English. This is how both the artichokes and the steak au poivre became so famous. *Artichoke* is written *artichaut* in French, a pretty simple leap in language, and the steak au poivre—well, everyone knows what a steak is. It was this or ask what we recommended. The reputation of the steak au poivre was by then so legendary that people would automatically order it. Artichoke, steak, profiteroles for dessert, drop the check. This was our service mantra. Add a big bottle of Bordeaux, and cha-ching! Cha-ching! Money in the bank. We told the guests what to order, they did, and the tips flowed.

The pace of an evening was always too much for Girl. The stations would get slammed every night, and the more guests he sat, the more the anger built. We'd regularly wait for the explosion. You knew it was coming when you could hear the menu board being slammed down on the table as the guests sat. He'd walk over, not say a word, slam the menu down, and walk away. One night I watched as he did exactly this, and as he walked away, the guest shouted, "Hey, waiter, we want drinks!" Girl turned, stared straight at the guest, and, as though channeling Dirty Harry, said, "No." Silence. Not a sound. He walked away and headed to the bar, where he needed to pick up cappuccinos for another table.

Raoul's is unique in that the bartender would make the coffees for the floor. Jimmy was bartending that night. God bless the man, he's a legend, but an incredibly bad technician in making drinks or coffee. Jimmy's bar was always packed with regulars, and when he worked, he'd hold court with all of them. His legend began when he was a roadie for the Rolling Stones and regularly scored their drugs for them. His connections spanned the globe. He began dealing in the city and soon wound up with a bad heroin habit, which he eventually kicked. He's been clean for decades and is now a renowned painter. His apartment door still has bullet holes in it from a drug buy gone bad. He knew just about everyone in the city and has countless stories to tell. One was about how he and Lou Reed would sit in the bathtub tripping from blotter acid that they had placed in their eyes. He'd make drinks between stories, picking up the ice with his hand, and as the stories went on, the ice would be melting, and he'd eventually finish, put a fistful of mostly melted ice in a glass, and serve the drink. I don't think a guest ever had a cocktail that was properly iced. It didn't matter. Everyone loved him.

Except Girl. Well, at least while working. When your station is crushed, and you need that drink, it could get pretty ugly. This night, Girl sees Jimmy in mid-story, knows he's not getting his cappuccinos, slams his fists on the bar, runs to get four coffee cups and saucers, brings them to the table of guests awaiting their cappuccinos, slams the empty cups and saucers down on the table, and says, "Here, get your own fucking coffee from Jimmy!" Girl then turns to the table that was still waiting for him to take their drink order, and the guest stands up and again shouts at him, "We want drinks!" Girl walks over, lifts the menu, and slams it down on the table. "No. Now get out."

As Girl walked away, I went rushing to the table and let them know they wouldn't be dining with us this evening. They eventually left.

Celebrity

PACINO, DE NIRO, JAGGER, Bowie, Robert Plant, Julianna Margulies, the supermodels. All came to Raoul's. Julia Roberts met Benjamin Bratt here, introduced to her by longtime maître d'hôtel Eddie Hudson. Brooke Shields lived across the street and would have romantic dinners with then Broadway star Kevin Anderson, tucked away in the back room, thankfully seeing only each other and not bothered by the awful design. Gwyneth Paltrow lived across the street for a time as well. Then unknown, she could comfortably sit by herself at the bar, being bothered only by me playfully hitting on her. She brought in the young Leonardo DiCaprio and Wes Anderson for dinner one night. DiCaprio was underage, and since we knew each other by then, Paltrow asked if I'd slip him a beer. I did, and he had a few and started to get obnoxious, enough so that I threatened to toss him out. When I saw him years later at Le Coucou, I reminded him of the story, which he had zero recollection of. He said he wasn't surprised, and that I should have thrown him out.

When Richard Gere and Cindy Crawford were together, they were great regulars. Johnny Depp came with Kate Moss. They'd sit in a booth, retreat upstairs to the bathrooms, and return so fucked up they'd have to take their dinners to go. Uma Thurman came with husband Ethan Hawke and then later with the hotelier André Balazs, their public displays of affection bordering on the X-rated. Matt Dillon was always in, regularly drinking with the staff. Naomi Campbell would come, be rude, and complain about her food almost every time. The lovely Drew Barrymore would show up with Cameron Diaz, who was dating Justin Timberlake; all three were always incredibly gracious.

The absolutely horrid Anna Wintour, who lived around the corner, would march in with no reservation and demand a table. She always ordered a steak, insisting it be very rare and served immediately. God forbid it was the least bit overcooked. She'd look at the server as though he'd just served her rat and have it sent back and redone. You'd think the raw meat would make her less sanguine. She'd then ask for the check before completing her carcass and, once done, leave.

Kate and Andy Spade were regulars. Michael Kors, Marc Jacobs, Matthew Broderick, and the always gracious Sarah Jessica Parker made it their dining room—Sarah Jessica instrumental in having a scene from *Sex and the City* shot there.

In the midst of this, Uncle Rob suddenly reappeared. He called to let me know he was miserable in his job and needed to find something else. Ever the loyalist, I got him an interview with Madame GM. They hit it off and she hired him. He was still an alcoholic mess. He trained only one night. The night he trained, Brad Pitt came in, spotted Uncle, walked over, and gave him a big hug, acting like old friends. Uncle had been the maître d'hôtel at the Los Angeles hot spot Olives when he was in California and Pitt recognized him from there. This not only gave Uncle a passing grade on his trail, but he was worked in as the maître d'hôtel since Queen Mother was leaving to open his own restaurant.

I wanted no part of the door, still shell-shocked from the River Café. Only in restaurants can the least able rise to the top. Uncle actually wasn't incompetent, but he was in the last throes of alcohol and drug dependency, and it wasn't pretty. When the Queen Mother left, Uncle was working six shifts a week, usually ten to twelve hours a shift. The only way he was getting through it was by consuming massive amounts of alcohol and drugs. He lasted about six months.

His last night was one of our busiest. One VIP after another was coming in, many without reservations and all wanting tables. As the night went on, the pressure was building, and Uncle was hitting the booze hard. Finally, at about ten, he lost it. He'd already knocked off at least a bottle of tequila. He looked at the crowd, downed another shot of tequila, looked at me, and growled, "That's it. I am fucking done." He screamed to Jimmy to give him a quarter. The scream was so loud, Jimmy actually dropped his handful of mostly melted ice, went to the register, and handed him a quarter.

Uncle slammed the shot glass down and headed to the spiral staircase. He was wasted. I followed him up the stairs, worried that he might not make it. He reached the top, wobbled to the pay phone, puts in the quarter, and dialed. I'm thinking he's calling his coke dealer, but he shouted into the receiver, "You miserable fucking cunt! I hate you, I hate this fucking job, and I quit!" He'd actually called the office downstairs and left a message for Madame GM.

A gorgeous, tall blonde walks in and asks for an order of rack of lamb to take out. We rarely, if ever, did this. We were way too busy, and the last thing the chef needed was to-go orders. I recognized her from the previous time she was in and remembered she loved the lamb. She was dripping sex and I was all over her.

"You're back."

"I absolutely loved the lamb. My girlfriend is home sick in bed, and I told her how delicious it is, and I want to bring it back to her." Her accent had to be from one of the blond countries.

"I am so sorry, but we don't do takeout."

"Oh, please, you must! I take good care of you!"

She then leaned over, gave me a huge smile and a kiss on the cheek. The woman was fucking gorgeous. How could I not do this?

"Let me check with the chef."

Hearing this, she let out a yelp, replete with accent, which immediately gave me an erection. Chef owed me, and I convinced him to make the lamb. I poured her a glass of wine while she waited, and once the lamb was ready, she paid and left me a hundred-dollar tip. The following week she returned with her girlfriend, just as tall, brunette, and equally gorgeous. I made sure they got a booth in my station. They were both pretty flirtatious. When I brought their wine, they asked me to have a glass with them, which I of course did. They soon became regulars, and each time I'd sit for a bit and have a glass with them. The conversation always turned to sex. They'd ask about my sex life, whom I was dating, what I liked sexually, the blonde usually leading the conversation, holding my hand as we talked, her girl-friend unfazed and an eager participant in the conversation. This one evening, they came in to dine and it followed the usual playbook. I joined them for a glass of wine, sitting when I could while attending to my other tables.

They had just finished their entrées, and when I went over to see how they were doing, the blonde asked, "How big is your cock?"

This stopped me cold. I blushed and didn't know how to answer her.

The blond model then pulled me close and whispered in my ear, "Hurry, get us all martinis for dessert, and come back and show us your cock."

I've been propositioned before, but this was something else. They'd both been drinking, and I thought she was fucking around. I returned with three martinis, took a sip, and had to run off and take an order. When I went back to the table, we said a few words and she then went, "So?"

"Are you serious?"

She laughed. "Yes, we want to see your cock."

I looked at both of them. They were absolutely serious. It was after ten. The manager at the time was Paolo Calamari, whom I loved and had a great relationship with. Madame GM had partially left to open her own restaurant, though she remained in charge from afar. Paolo was having dinner with some friends a few booths away. I knew the boys, all gays and all restaurant people. I went over, told them what was about to go down, and the queens basically screamed, "Bitch, go show them, then come back and show us!"

I walked over to Girl, got him to watch my station, went back to the women, leaned in, pulled my apron aside, and took it out. Before I could say a word, Model stands up, pushes me into the seat next to her, hands me my martini, puts a piece of butter in her hand, and starts jerking me off. Girlfriend leans in, elbows on the table, face in her hands, amazing green eyes staring at me, and, with a look of pure sex, says, "Does it feel good? Is she going to make you cum?" The boys at the other table are staring and giggling, girlfriend's eyes are piercing me, Model is stroking, and I cum immediately.

Drag

ABOUT SIX MONTHS BEFORE Madame GM semi-left for her own restaurant, we were all sitting around having family meal. She was in one of her better moods and making nice with the staff when she casually mentioned that she might one day leave the restaurant. The collective response was a huge "No way!" She'd already been there for years, had the cushiest GM job in the city, and was, we assumed, making bank. Why would anyone leave such a gig? She laughed that phony maniacal laugh of hers and said, "What would you do if I did?"

I was the first one to chime in. "If you leave, we'll all dress in drag."

Six months later she did leave. Well, sort of. She remained in control from afar, overseeing the books, checking the schedule, and drawing a salary. We were then committed to doing a drag night, which became the beginning of the many shows we'd do over the years. Girl ran the evening, oversaw all our costumes and makeup, created a playlist, and the party was on. The night was raucous, and as on most of the wilder nights there, someone ended up stripping on the bar. Many evenings a row of panties and bras would hang from above the bar. This night many did—men dressed as women, women dressed as men, with anyone welcome to join in. Our UPS driver walked in late and got so loaded he was soon dancing on the bar with one of our male runners, who was sexy as all fuck in a dress. We then did these nights somewhat regularly and let our guests know ahead of time so they could dress up as well. People would dance on the bar, stripping, clothes being thrown everywhere, with the mandatory trips to the bathroom for sex and coke. We had a few "straight" men get their first blow job by a man in the bathrooms upstairs. Apparently, since the person doing the fellating was dressed as a woman, it made it okay.

Harvard

MY GOAL IN GETTING hired at Raoul's was to jump-start my acting career. I had gotten a couple of regional theater jobs as well as a slew of roles in shit plays in the city, plays that only friends involved in the project go see, suffer through, and hate you ever after for. I did manage to swing a summer scholarship to the Royal National Theatre in England, which was life changing. While there, I was cast in a play that rehearsed in London and was performed at the Edinburgh International Theatre Festival. When I returned from that magical summer, I was determined to replicate that sort of training here in the States. Robert Brustein, founder of both the Yale Repertory Theatre and the American Repertory Theater (ART), at Harvard University, was running the ART program, which had an international bent. It was exactly what I was seeking. I applied, was accepted, finished, and received an MFA from Harvard in conjunction with the Moscow Art Theatre.

Newly graduated and back in the city, I got an agent and began working at Raoul's once more. I'd only been back a month when maître d'hôtel Eddie Hudson introduced me to some new regulars. I was introduced as the server who had just graduated from Harvard. They were of course shocked to hear this—one of the gents, who I later learned was a legend of Wall Street, especially so. He returned regularly, and we became friendly. On one of his visits, he asked if I did film as well, and to let him know if I was ever involved in one. At the time, one of my classmates from Harvard was writing a short film that I would be acting in. I let Wall Street know I was starting a film project and would keep him in the loop.

We completed the short, *Exceed*, and it was selected to be in the New York Film Festival. This became our calling card in the film world. I let Wall Street know of the success we were having and told him we were working on a feature. In three months we had a screenplay, which I showed to him. He told me he was interested and a few weeks later called to let me know he was coming in for dinner and wanted to talk. He shows up as usual with a beautiful date and asks me to pick out his wine. I do, we toast, and he then walks me over to the fish tank in the middle of the room, pulls a crumpled checkbook from his back pocket, and writes me a check for $100,000.

The $100,000 soon turned into a budget of $1.25 million. We completed the film, *The Brooklyn Heist*, and submitted it to film festivals. While we didn't get into Sundance, we did win a few awards. We got distribution, were screened at the Chinese Theatre in Hollywood, and had a two-week run at Theatre 80 in Manhattan. We got DVD distribution and sent hundreds of DVDs to Blockbuster Video and hundreds to Hollywood Video. This was big and I thought we were on our way. Once we shipped the videos, the housing crash of 2008 hit. Both Blockbuster and Hollywood Video went bankrupt within months of each other, digital streaming suddenly took over, and the DVD went the way of 8-tracks, cassettes, and VHS tapes. We were done. We lost everything.

I was working the door when three guests approached me for a table. One of the men was tall and bulky, the other looked a bit like Al Pacino, with the same frame and stature, and with them was an attractive woman in her thirties. It was late. Service was pretty much ending, and I had a booth available and seated them. After about fifteen minutes, Girl comes up and tells me to look at the table. The shorter guy had taken his shirt off and was obviously bothering a female couple behind him. I went over, told him to put his shirt back on and to sit down if he wanted to eat here. He was hammered. I apologized to the women, sent them over a drink, and went back to the bar.

A few minutes later the guy again takes off his shirt. This time I go back to the table and tell them they need to leave. His friend gets up and tells him they need to go. As they start to push past me, I tell the big guy he's got to pay for the drinks they had ordered. There's no way they were getting out without paying. He looks at me like I'm crazy and says, "No fucking way," and tries to push past me. I raise both my arms, gently place them on his chest, and he loses it. He tells me he's a lawyer and will sue me for assault.

"Sir," I reply, "if you think this is an assault, wait till you see what happens if you don't pay the check." He tries to barrel past me, and as I back up to block his way, the little guy reaches over and sucker punches me. I go flying back across the front room and land on a table of five women midmeal; plates and glasses go shattering.

As the trio starts to leave, the bartender leaps over the bar, a small nightstick in hand that we keep behind the bar for times like this. A few regulars are at the bar, one a former college football player, and they come running over and destroy this guy. The other two go running out, and we take this guy and throw him out onto the street. About an hour later, the woman returns, apologizes, and pays the bill.

9/11/2001

WHEN YOU START YOUR shift at four and don't get to leave till three in the morning, you tend to sleep late. But this morning something woke me up around nine, and as I lifted my head, I saw my phone answering machine blinking away like a slot machine in Vegas. The calls were from a close friend in London. He told me a plane had just hit one of the World Trade Center towers. I turned on the TV just as the other hit.

My best friend worked at the World Financial Center, just across from the World Trade towers, and she regularly passed through one of the towers to reach her job. I called her cell and couldn't get through—there was no phone service. I dressed and hopped on my bike, figuring it would be the only way to get there, and headed downtown, frantic, not knowing where she was and if she was able to get out. As I pedaled there, I saw hundreds of people walking uptown, many covered in gray ash, looking shocked, stunned, disbelief on many of their faces. I spent a few frantic hours trying to find my friend. Thankfully her building was evacuated just in time.

Later that day, I took my dog for a walk. We passed St. Vincent's Hospital, where triage tents were set up outside, the avenue lined with ambulances. It was a surreal sight, doctors and nurses were milling about the area outside the building in almost absolute silence. No ambulances were coming or going. I kept walking, went over to the Hudson River and passed Chelsea Piers, a sports facility the length of five city blocks. Lined up outside were scores of ambulances, many not from the city—volunteers from all over the tristate region had come for support. Again, there was no movement. Everything was eerily still. That's when I realized there wouldn't be many survivors.

Restaurants—at least, the successful ones that strike a chord with their city, their neighborhood—are rare and wonderful. It's the *Cheers* effect, a place where you are welcome, known, able to talk with the staff and regulars, and meet friends. Raoul's has always been one of those restaurants. While many places downtown closed in the weeks after the attack, Raoul's remained open. Despite no traffic being allowed below Fourteenth Street, each evening our regulars would trek to the restaurant, some walking all the way from uptown. That we were open lent some sort of solace and normalcy to all our lives, not just those of our guests.

Sadly we lost many regular customers that day. We had had wonderful relationships with many of the staff of the financial services company Cantor Fitzgerald. Their offices were on floors 101 to 105, and just above the impact zone. Not one of the 658 employees who showed up to work that morning survived. The atmosphere in the restaurant each evening was somber; none of us knew fully the extent of what was about to befall New York City, but to the many who came, Raoul's was safe, familiar, and a place to share our collective grief and fears. We were lucky.

The Mob Redux

WHILE AT HARVARD RESEARCHING online, I stumbled on an ad for Find People Fast. The ad promised to find just about anyone, dead or alive. It was $35 for a "live" search, and $25 for someone dead. It was one of those moments when you do something without even thinking about it. I had never known my father and decided to see what I could find. I opted to save the $10 and do the death search. From what I did know, I doubted he'd still be alive. Twenty-four hours later I get the results back, and he was apparently not dead.

Two years later, I was back in New York and decided to try again. The price was now $50. I went for it and they found him, replete with address and phone number. He was living in Queens. What's that about being careful of what you wish for? I decided to call. The phone rings and someone picks up.

"Hello!" a man said in a gruff New York accent.

I had no idea what to say. I knew his name was Fred, so my brilliant reply was "Is Fred there?"

"This is Fred."

Fuck. I wanted to hang up. "Hi, Fred, this is Michael, I was wondering if I could ask you some questions."

Unbelievably he replies, "Sure."

Now, who the fuck picks up the phone in New York City and not only talks to a stranger but agrees to answer questions? This gave me pause. This can't be the lowlife I'd heard about. If he was alive, I figured he'd be in witness protection.

I kept at it. "Did you know Connie Azzolina?" (My mother.)

"Yeah, yeah, I knew her. How is she? It's been a long time."

I tell him she's well, to which he responds, "Give her my best."

I then push it further, running the names of relatives by him that I thought he'd know, and he knew them all. I then ask the big one: "Did you have a child with her?"

He hesitates. There's about three or four seconds of silence. "Yeah, yeah, I did."

Now the tears are beginning to spill down my face. "I think you're my father."

"What did you say your name was?"

"Michael."

"Yeah, your name is tattooed on my arm."

With this we both start sobbing. He tells me he's married and hopes I'm not offended, since it's to a Black woman. I had to stop from bursting out laughing. I just found my father, a guy from the Lower East Side, Mob connected, and he's telling me he married a Black woman. That may be the only redeeming thing he's done in his lifetime, for all I know. He then lets me know I have two half-sisters. I'm getting a lot more than I bargained for.

We made plans to meet that coming Sunday for coffee. We hang up, and a minute later he calls me back and tells me that Sunday is Father's Day and his wife suggested I join them. I just found my father after forty years—meeting him was going to be weird enough, I wasn't sure I was ready for the whole family. I agreed.

We met that Sunday at his favorite restaurant, a rib joint in Harlem. This was starting to turn into a cheap screenplay. I walk into the crowded restaurant and spot him immediately. He stood out like balls on a pit bull—this little white Italian guy surrounded by three lovely Black women. I approach the table, he stands and hugs me, and we both cry. He's about five feet, five inches, close-cropped gray hair and glasses, average build, a bulbous nose, but what stands out most about him is his voice. He has that guttural, New York accent, so stereotypical of mobsters. He introduced me to his family: his wife—beautiful, tall, elegant, well-spoken—and my two half-sisters. They all couldn't be lovelier. What the fuck were they doing with this guy?

I sat next to him, and for the next hour or so he held on to me as though he were afraid I'd run away. He first showed me the tattoo on his arm, which read MIKE. I had a lot of questions that just spilled out of me, and he had no problem answering them.

My first question was about the day I was born. My mother had told me that he disappeared during her pregnancy, then showed up at the hospital and told her if she gave me his last name, they'd get married. She did and we never saw him again. He looked shocked when I told him this. He said that when she was pregnant, he'd gotten into a "jackpot." I had no idea what he was talking about. A jackpot, he explained, is when someone gets in big trouble and needs to get out of town for a while.

"You know Charlie the Chink?" I had no idea who Charlie the Chink was. "He was a guy, a big shot. Ran his own gang. One day I get a call and they tell me Charlie wants to meet me by the Con Ed plant on Fourteenth Street. I go; as I get close, I see something lying on the floor. I get closer and see it's my friend's head. I got the fuck out of town. I didn't want to be next. Had to hide out in Pennsylvania for a few months."

My father continued, "Hospital? What hospital? I had no idea you were born! And marry her? How the fuck could I marry her? She was still married to the other guy."

Now, wasn't this a kick in the fucking nuts? He seemed completely genuine, and from the way the words spilled out of him, I saw no reason not to believe him. I knew I had a half-brother and that my mother was previously married. I never thought to ask if she ever got a divorce. She hadn't. She did later marry my stepfather. I had just learned my mother was a bigamist.

"So what do you do now?" I asked.

"I'm mostly retired. I got money on the street." *Money on the street* meant he was a loan shark and perhaps a bookie. I asked why he never tried to get in touch with us or at least me. He said he tried many times, but my mother always stopped him. It went on like this for much of the meal. I kept trying to include his wife and my sisters as much as I could, but it was hard. He just wanted to hold on to me and talk. When we finished, we made plans for me to join them for dinner in a week or so.

I managed to have somewhat of a relationship with my father for the next year. Each time we'd meet, he would tell me more about himself, and the more I heard the less I liked. Was any of it true? I have no idea, but I can't imagine it was all a fiction. He was apparently a made man in the Lucchese family. "You know how I was made?" he asked one day as we sat in his living room. "We was standing outside the clubhouse, you know, in the city. Me and Tommy [Lucchese] was standing outside when I sees this car drive by, it's going slow. It's got four guys in it. I think to myself, 'This ain't good.' I wait a bit and keep my eyes on the street. Next thing, I see the car coming up the block again. I warn Tommy, and as they approach, they start to shoot. I pull my gun out, throw Tommy down on the ground, and start firing back. The scumbags took off. That's how I got made."

Every time I'd see him, he'd tell me more about his Mob life. "You know how to collect money when the cocksucker won't pay you?" He didn't wait for a reply. "You tell the scumbag, 'If you don't pay me, I'm gonna cut out your tongue and shove it up your ass. Then I'm gonna cut your cock off and put it where your tongue used to be.'" He was apparently always paid.

He grew up on the Lower East Side, on Pitt Street. The gangster Lucky Luciano was his neighbor and protector. He shined shoes as a kid—the local pool hall was a favorite and lucrative spot. One day he shined one of the pool players' shoes, the guy refused to pay, and my father left crying. As he was walking home, he ran into Lucky, who asked him why he was crying. He told him the story. Lucky took him back to the pool hall, my father pointed out the guy, and Luciano beats him with a pool stick, apparently breaking both his legs. My father never had trouble getting paid again. I guess he learned from the best.

Each time I saw him, the stories would get more violent. It was getting hard to listen to him. One Sunday, he brought the family to see me perform in a play in the Theater District. Leaving the theater, we reached the corner; he stops and looks up at a building. He's thinking, and then it hits him. "Cocksucker. I knew I knew this fucking place. The cheap fucking Jew who lived here owed us money. The cocksucker never paid. We always had to go to collect. This time he owes us a lot of money. Me and another guy go up to the apartment; he lets us in and says he doesn't have the money. I figure, 'Let's scare the fuck.' We grab him, take him to the window, and hang him out the window by his jacket. This motherfucker was so cheap, his jacket rips and the scumbag fell. Whaddya gonna do?"

My daughter had been born a year before. On her second birthday, my father was supposed to come to her party and never showed. He came up with some poor excuse, saying he had a gift for her and would bring it soon. He never came. Finally I called him. "Dad, you know, my whole life you never showed up for me. I have a child now, your grandchild. If something happened where her mother tried to take her away from me, I would do everything in my power to see her, and if that didn't work, I'd support her. You never did this for me. This is your granddaughter. You can choose to see her or not, it's your call. You know how to reach me." I never heard from him again.

Crushed

FROM WHEN I GRADUATED Harvard to the collapse of *The Brooklyn Heist*, I did my best to make it in the acting world. I was directing and acting, received an OOBR award, started teaching, eventually opened my own studio, and hoped the income would get me to finally leave the restaurant business. Once *Heist* failed, and after more than thirty years pursuing a career in acting, I was done. The failure of the film so tore me up that it took a couple of years till I was able to even watch another movie. I had closed my acting studio to make the film, and the thought of teaching again wasn't even possible.

It was time to leave Raoul's as well. Madame GM's restaurant had failed. She had returned to Raoul's and was, shortly after, opening yet another restaurant while still running Raoul's. During this time there were apparently some in-house scandals and I was approached by the Raoul brothers to be the GM of the restaurant. After waiting for at least six months for something that was never going to happen, I decided to leave.

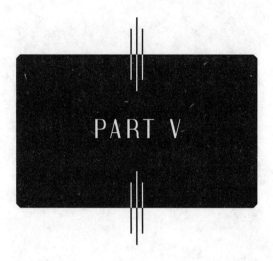

PART V

Unwanted

THE ONLY THING I'VE ever done that I actually made a living at was restaurants. Given my experience, I thought it would be a cinch to get a job. I was wrong. I sent out quite a few résumés, went to many interviews, and in many cases never made it past the twentysomething person who did the initial screening. I went to the dreaded open calls and joined scores of my fellow unemployed to wait for hours to then meet someone who's only purpose was to put our résumés in the trash bin.

I called friends to see if they knew of anything available, but there was absolutely nothing. I was no longer the young, energetic actor needing a server job to pay the rent. I now had a family I needed to feed, and I was striking out everywhere I applied.

In desperation, I thought of Buzzy. Isn't there a saying that says something to the effect that you can never go back? The River Café was still doing well, and I thought I'd be able to return. I called the Water Club, asked for Buzzy, and he actually took my call. After a brief conversation, I got a call a few hours later from the GM of the Café. He was one of the bartenders I'd worked with years ago and was still there. I'd be hired as a captain but would have to trail for two weeks as a server. I was so broke I'd have trained as a valet.

It felt strange to be back. There were a lot of ghosts in that space. Buzzy had done some renovations, and it was more beautiful than ever. Astonishingly, there were still some holdovers from my days there, and they gave me a warm welcome. The new staff was kind to me as well and were helpful during my days of training. I am not sure what they had heard about me, but I think some of the stories of my former days there had leaked down to them and perhaps made me feel less threatening.

My ill-fated return lasted only two weeks. The one issue was the maître d'hôtel. I found this tuxedoed asshole to be ingratiating, rude, and mean. I don't know if the stories he'd heard offended his sense of professionalism, but he made it known from the moment I walked down that gangway that he was in charge. We had an initial, quick meeting where he informed me "those days" were over. He'd also apparently told the staff that I was never a maître d'hôtel there and was lying to them. This fucker definitely felt threatened.

Two incidents led me to give my notice after just four days of training. First, I was scheduled to work a double on a Sunday, brunch and dinner. I arrived at 9:00 A.M. and didn't leave till almost midnight. There was no break, other than sitting for a quick bite of inferior family meal. Besides it being illegal, working a shift that long is abusive. No wonder Buzzy was sued.

At the end of the shift, every inch of my body aching, I sat and watched as the bussers counted every piece of silver before locking it all away. I called out to one of them, "Do you know why you have to do this every night?"

"So it doesn't get stolen?"

"Nope. Because years ago one of our captains was so fed up with all the shit Buzzy was giving everyone, he walked into the silver room, took all the silver onto the roof of the barge, and hurled it into the East River."

The second incident was when I was doing a running trail and the runner who was assisting me let me do something at the table instead of just watching, which was protocol. The offense was garnishing a dish of steak tartare. It's one of those typically overpriced dishes in a restaurant that achieves its hefty price tag due to the theatrics when it's served. It's designed to make a show— guests love it and are willing to overpay for the dramatics. The runner let me dole out the garnishes on the plate, and my inexperience showed. The milita- ristic, grid-like design of capers, onions, and so forth, when done correctly, is beautiful. My handiwork more resembled that of a third grader.

The maitre d' saw this, followed us into the kitchen, and dressed down the runner in front of the whole kitchen so severely that I, who'd seen just about everything involving misbehavior in a restaurant, was speechless. Husky looked like he was getting off on humiliating this person. At the end of the shift I asked to speak to him. We went into the office, and I basically told him what a piece of shit he was and gave my notice. I finished out the week and left. About four years later I received a letter informing me that I was part of a class action suit against the River Café. Workers claimed their tips were misappropriated and they weren't paid for all the hours they worked. Buzzy apparently settled for about two million dollars. Since I was employed there for the time the suit specified, I got to make a few hundred bucks for my two weeks. I was once again back among the unemployed.

I considered going back to teaching. I'd taught writing at a community college for a year when I finished my undergraduate degree, but renewing my license to enter a career that would probably pay me half of a waiter's salary wasn't appealing. I was back to scouring the Craigslist ads when I got a call from my old friend Chef Neil Kleinberg, he of the Jackie Gleason experience. He told me that Keith McNally's Minetta Tavern was looking for a manager. Neil was friendly with the GM—he let him know I was looking for work and told me to call to set up an interview.

Minetta Tavern

THE TAVERN THAT SITS on the corner of Minetta Lane and MacDougal Street had seen better days. It opened in 1937, feting such notables as e. e. cummings, Ezra Pound, and Ernest Hemingway. The walls are lined with photographs of the professional boxers who replaced the literati in the fifties and sixties and caricatures of various customers drawn by the abstract expressionist Franz Kline for whatever someone would pay him. When I was taken there for dinner in the eighties, it had lapsed into red-sauce hell, serving a rendition of Italian American cooking that would have made my mother walk out had she been with me, spitting over each shoulder as she did to ward off the evil spirits that obviously inhabited the kitchen. She wouldn't want them following her home and ruining her cooking.

Keith McNally took it over in 2008, burnished the interior, left the photos and drawings, and installed the two chefs from his hugely successful restaurant Balthazar: Riad Nasr and Lee Hanson. This trio brought the restaurant three fat stars from then *Times* food critic Frank Bruni, who called it the best steak house in NYC. The review stunned the restaurant world. Not only because McNally was never known for serving any food beyond adequate in any of his restaurants, but also because he and Bruni had a very public feud when Bruni gave McNally's Morandi one star. This led to McNally calling Bruni sexist, since the chef there was a woman. Bruni, during a book signing, said in answer to a question about the feud, "I do not go to Keith McNally restaurants anymore. I would have loved to have given Minetta Tavern a horrible review because McNally is a horrible man." McNally responded with a letter to *Eater*: "I'm not sure whether being called 'a horrible man' by the person who wrote an entire book in praise of George W. Bush (*Ambling into History*) is necessarily a bad thing. However, even though it's possible to be called a horrible restaurateur (not something I would dispute), I don't for the life of me understand how Frank Bruni—a man of limited, but undeniable intelligence—can call someone 'a horrible man' when they've never spent any time with him. This is like reviewing a restaurant without eating the food." Restaurant professionals can be so much fun.

I sat at one of Minetta's red-leather-clad booths for over an hour with the dapper, overcaffeinated general manager. I said little, while being completely enraptured by this incredibly charming man. He was unable to sit still, jumping up to greet one person or another, darting to the bar to answer the phone, directing a deliveryman to the kitchen, or greeting a server. He never stopped. With his close-cropped gray hair, ever-present smile, and jovial attitude, dressed in a sleek black suit and crisp white shirt held tight to his chest with suspenders, I felt I was being interviewed by Joel Grey and was waiting for him to burst into "Willkommen" when the next person arrived.

Either they were desperate or I was a great audience. I was unfortunately given the job. This was a seemingly perfect match. An incredibly busy, high-profile, and expensive restaurant, similar to Raoul's and with much the same clientele. It also didn't hurt that I knew McNally from his many visits to Raoul's, which he had always said was his favorite restaurant. The first time I saw him at Minetta, he again mentioned that Raoul's was his favorite restaurant and if they ever wanted to sell it, to let him know—he'd take it in a second. I assume he forgot that I was now working for him.

Suspenders was by far the best GM I have ever worked for. He was a workaholic, ever present, a perfectionist, ridiculously organized, charming (though very capable of losing it), and intent on overseeing every aspect under his domain. He ran the place beautifully, and I learned quite a bit about running a restaurant. At all the other restaurants I've worked at, including the River Café and Raoul's, they paid little or no attention to basic workplace laws, and the FOH never complained since most tipped employees lied about their income to avoid paying taxes on tips. Also, if you did complain about not getting paid for the actual hours you worked or not getting sick pay or vacation pay, you'd have your schedule cut to where you made no money or were fired. Your option would be to find another restaurant where the same shit was happening.

Old-school restaurants regularly ignored these basics and got away with all this illegal shit. But the days when restaurants could fuck over the staff were quickly coming to an end. After a spate of lawsuits, restaurateurs now had to play fair and pay for actual hours worked, account for breaks, overtime, sick days, all real-world stuff. Minetta was run legit, and we managers were there to make sure things were done properly.

There was even an HR department. No longer could I tell a chef to go fuck himself, or a server to get his ass on the floor, suspend someone for doing something stupid, or fire some incompetent piece of shit who spent most of his time trying to sneak in a phone call to his girlfriend or drug dealer. We had to make nice to the staff, and if we needed to reprimand a server, we had to have another manager in tow to act as a witness in case we were accused of some sort of workplace harassment. Staff were free to complain about anything and everyone, which they did, and in this new litigious climate where lawyers were actively soliciting restaurant workers eager to sue for theft of wages, misappropriation of tips, sexual harassment, unpaid hours, et cetera, you had to be on top of it all. These were totally new concepts to me.

Working the floor, on the other hand, was a snap. I knew the clientele: the usual smattering of the wealthy, neighbors, the elite of acting, publishing, fashion, and advertising. Once again, I was in the midst of the cream of New York City. What sucked was wrangling the staff, a group of prima donnas, many in their first three-star restaurant. The third star made many of them feel that they knew best, that they were the ones who'd earned the restaurant the stars and they could care less about the new guy. I was now the enemy and had to watch my ass or I'd get reported to HR.

As the low man on the totem pole I was required to close the restaurant, which meant I was there sometimes as late as 3:00 A.M. Closing managers are always the last person to leave a restaurant. We have the keys and we lock the place up. The bar is always the last part of the restaurant to close.

The bartender counts the till and reconciles the money. The manager checks and completes the closing paperwork, drops the money in a safe, and, after a last check of the place, locks up. Pretty simple if tedious stuff. The problem here was that all but one of the bartenders were out-and-out raving drunks. By the end of the evening, one or the other would be falling-down drunk and unable to speak clearly, let alone count money. If they hadn't reached the falling-down point, they could be obstreperous. It was like wrangling cats or drunken teenagers.

The most essential part of the closing manager's job is to make sure the money is correct. Each bar starts with a bank—the opening amount of cash you have—in several denominations so you're able to give guests change. At the end of the shift, the bartender separates the bank from the total take, and the cash remaining is what was sold that evening. If cash is missing, someone either fucked up or is stealing. When the money's off, suspicion grows, everyone's job is on the line, and those above start looking closely at the operation.

I don't think there was ever a night that the cash wasn't off. These idiots were usually too drunk to count properly, doing it over and over, two, three, four times, getting up to pee in the middle of counting, then returning and having no idea what they'd counted and having to start again. They'd drop money on the floor or leave it in the cash register or mysteriously find some in their pockets—it was a mess. I'd sometimes have to count each bill with them to ensure a correct count. My shift was long, and this sometimes made me stay at least an hour longer than necessary.

I asked the other managers what to do. They just laughed. This was no longer their problem, I'd inherited it. For a variety of reasons, the bartenders were protected. I was advised to keep my mouth shut and deal with it. I was the new guy and had to suck it up.

My other headache was the kitchen. The head chefs were great. When they were there, the place ran beautifully. The problem was that they weren't always there. Both were usually present during the day, getting specials ready, ordering, and overseeing all the prep. One or the other would stay for a bit into dinner service, then leave the kitchen in the hands of others. This group were some of the most misogynistic, rude, and hateful people I have ever witnessed in a kitchen. Servers were detested and not allowed in the kitchen unless spe-cifically instructed to enter. Any issue that arose would have to be dealt with by a manager.

The gent regularly left in charge was the worst. He lacked basic social skills, was unsmiling, dour, and basically a wretched human being. He looked upon the floor staff as pure scum. Guests were seen similarly. If there was a complaint—food sent back for being overcooked or undercooked, too salty, cold, or any of the many reasons guests have to find fault—the shit would hit the fan. Guests were seen as clueless idiots, unable to discern between medium rare and medium, how food should be properly salted, or how hot a dish should be—basically know-nothings that only came to dine to complain. If a dish was sent back as cold, the chefs would heat up the offending meal till it was burning hot and overcooked, then set it on a plate so hot that if the server touched it with her bare hand, she'd leave bits of flesh on the plate. If a dish came back as too salty, the chefs sent out another, this time completely unsalted. The guest was always wrong. We managers were the referees, and each time we entered the kitchen it was completely demoralizing.

Minetta is a gorgeous space but it's small. It's located on a strip of MacDou-gal Street, most frequented by college students getting drunk and eating at the cheap bars and fast-food restaurants that line the block. The blinds and curtains were kept tightly drawn, and a security guard was stationed at the front so our guests would not have to either see or encounter the riffraff on the street. This was not the part of society we wanted our wealthy guests to engage with while consuming their $150-per-person dinners. Spending the entire evening in that windowless space, you felt like a caged rat navigating the room, circling about, over and over and over. If you had to go to the basement for wine, you'd have to navigate a tiny, narrow wine room, where if you turned the wrong way, you'd either hit your head on the low ceiling, tear your suit, or smash an exposed part of your body against something that was inevitably in your way.

I hated almost every day I worked there. Despite the drunk bartenders, there was an absolute no-drinking policy. You had to be a Houdini to get a fucking drink to alleviate both the stress and the boredom of the redundancy of what you did each day. Cameras were everywhere. The bartenders, already treading the line with their own drinking, would be hesitant to get caught giving some of the needed anesthesia to anyone else. The only way to get a drink was to go to the service area, make sure no one was near, pour yourself a shot of wine, down it, and move on.

One evening, half on my way to numbing myself with shots of wine, I returned to the main dining room and was standing in front of the booths that served as the VIP tables. Josh Brolin, his lovely wife, Diane Lane, and some guests were at one table; at the other was Rupert Murdoch's son James and a guest. Directly in front of these booths is a four top, where two older couples were seated. These were Upper East Side, old-school New Yorkers— the women dripping diamonds, the men prosperous looking in their Brooks Brothers suits, obviously bankers or brokers. One, the older of the two men, resembled Winston Churchill.

As I was standing there, one of the servers came up behind me and whispered, "Michael, someone shit on the floor." I turned and asked her to repeat that. "Someone shit on the floor. Turn around slowly and look down." I do, and right between the four top and the banquettes holding our esteemed guests, is what looks like human turds. It took me two or three surreptitious glances before I could actually see that a pile of shit was on the floor.

The floor at Minetta is a series of black and white square tiles, and this was right in the middle of the white tile. Someone did indeed shit on the floor. As I was getting over my shock, one of the bussers who'd also seen it swooped over as though he was in special ops, motioned me to stay where I was, and in one deft motion, napkin in hand, removed the turds.

I now needed to reconnoiter and figure out where the shit came from. I looked over at the four top and saw that Winston Churchill had gotten up and was no longer seated. I then remembered either reading, or being told by someone, that you sometimes shit your pants if you're having a heart attack. While I have no idea if this is true, could it be that this was Winston's excrement that was just cleaned up? That he indeed shit his pants? That the turds made their way to the floor through the legs of his blue pin-striped Brooks Brothers suit?

He was now apparently away from the table longer than it would take to clean out his boxers. I headed straight to the men's toilet, entered, looked under one of the two stalls, and sure enough, I saw the blue pin-striped pants, crumpled around his ankles and crunched atop his brown oxfords. I detected some movement, so I knew he wasn't dead yet.

I returned to the table, excused myself, and leaned in to who I hoped would not be Winston's widow, and whispered in her ear, "Madam, I am very sorry to trouble you, but I believe your husband just shat himself, pieces of which we have just retrieved from the floor. He's in the facility now. Perhaps you may want to check on him." Without missing a blink, the doyenne turned to the other gentleman at the table and said, "James, please check on Henry in the toilet." The women then continued their conversation completely unfazed. James got up, went to check, and returned shortly with Winston in tow. He'd apparently cleaned himself up, sat down, and, without missing a beat, ordered dessert and brandy. Ah, the life of the rich.

My salvation arrived late one evening when two of my favorite Raoul's customers came to dine. We'd not seen each other since I entered the restaurant void for two years. As we caught up, they let me know they were involved in a new restaurant, and would I be interested in taking a look? An angel must have been hanging out on MacDougal Street. I of course said I'd take a peek.

There's an old ethos in the business world that states the customer is always right. Bullshit. For years, the majority of restaurants and indeed most businesses have operated under this misbegotten rubric. All this has done is create a generation of entitled, demanding, obstreperous, rude, truculent, and surly people who think they can treat servers and managers like shit and get away with it. And they do because few places have the balls to stand up to them. Not only do they get away with it, but they are usually rewarded with free drinks, free desserts, and at times completely comped dinners. The great guests, the lovely and kind ones, are those that need to be getting comped, not the assholes. It's time to stop this behavior, and when these idiots act up, owners and managers need to grow a pair of balls and throw them the fuck out. If you can't behave and treat other human beings with kindness and respect, just get the fuck out.

Hope

CARLOS SUAREZ AND I met in a coffee shop adjacent to the construction site that would soon be Rosemary's restaurant. He's relatively handsome, late thirties, tall, his brown hair expensively cut, with a welcoming smile that is undercut by a somewhat weak chin. A graduate of both Eton and Wharton, he has that warm, welcoming, yet detached air of the Brits; you can get close, but not too close, unless you're trashed. He was tieless, wearing a costly lightweight beige suit, giving off a vibe of complete nonchalance for someone about to open a restaurant. While affable, he was a bit distracted, repeatedly checking his phone as I sat there waiting for our interview to begin. I was obviously not his first priority that morning.

We had a coffee on this gorgeous early-spring morning and then went to look at the still-unfinished Rosemary's. Even though the space was still wrapped by its construction shed, I could see its potential. It sits on an incredible piece of real estate in the heart of the West Village, directly across the street from the gorgeous Jefferson Market Garden, which was once the site of a women's prison—ah, the good old days. Carlos secured the space when restaurateur Brian McNally passed on it after the local Community Board wouldn't allow him a full liquor license for the premises. Suarez obviously felt he could make do with beer and wine and locked it up. The beautiful space was in a great location, and I thought if he could nail the food and service, he'd have a winner. The concept—inexpensive Italian, large dining room, a turn-and-burn vibe, and no hard alcohol—held zero interest for me personally. I'm old-school. I want the full dining experience. Give me a cocktail, great food, a place to be comfortable, sip a martini, drink a bottle of wine, and not be rushed. I want to meet and get to know my guests. This wasn't happening here, at least not at the level I thrive in. I let him know the next day that I was passing. When I explained my reasoning, he then told me of his other restaurant—Bobo, two blocks away, which needed a manager, a spot he thought would be very much my style.

Bobo sits on the corner of Seventh Avenue and Tenth Street in the West Village. Built in 1863, this former private residence of four stories was converted into a three-level restaurant. A small staircase off the street leads into a lovely bar area, with a few tables and the kitchen in the rear. The floor above is the main dining room as well as a garden, divided in the middle by a sexy small bar. On the third floor is a small private dining room. It's a beautifully designed space.

I met Suarez there the next day, and with him was his new chef and partner, Cedric Tovar, along with the new director of operations who was going to oversee both Bobo and Rosemary's. Tovar has great experience—he had worked with the legendary chef Joël Robuchon, and had also received three stars from *The New York Times* for the restaurant Town. I liked these guys and the restaurant was beautiful and sexy, in a neighborhood I knew well. It was a place I could definitely see myself running. We made plans for me to come in for dinner to check out the food and service.

When you've worked in restaurants for as many years as I have, you can pretty much tell, once you enter a place, what the experience is going to be like. The decor, lights, the greeting you receive, the look of the staff, the clientele, all serve to give you an idea of what to expect. Bobo was a mess and a textbook example of why a restaurant is failing.

I arrived first and waited for a fellow manager from Minetta that was going to join me. I checked in with the disinterested host and then sat at the half-empty bar to have a drink and wait. The bartender was leaning against the back bar at the other end, casually chatting with a guest, and made zero movement to greet me. After a few minutes, he finally spotted me, walked over, and, instead of asking what I would like, stood in front of me and nodded, an apparent signal that I would be the first to actually use language. If I weren't here for a business dinner, I'd have walked out. I was tempted to be an asshole, but instead took a breath and asked if they had Stolichnaya vodka. He shook his head no and remained staring at me, apparently waiting for me to make the next move. This inhospitable prick just stood there, forcing me to look over his shoulder at the bar to see what vodkas they had. We were in for a challenging evening. I picked a vodka and dickhead actually made a fairly good martini before heading back to his station to lean. No manager was in sight, though I would soon learn that there was only one manager, and that person had taken a day off after fourteen straight days.

When my guest arrived, we were taken to our table upstairs in the mostly empty main dining room. Our server was pleasant enough, though it did take him three times to finally bring over the correct bottle of wine. The first bottle he brought was not the one I ordered. He apologized and returned about ten minutes later to inform me that the bottle was no longer available. Ten minutes waiting for a glass of wine is forever in restaurant speak, and I've been reamed by irate guests for taking less time. When people need a drink, they need a fucking drink. The drink order is usually your first interaction with a table, and you want to make it as smooth and expeditious as possible. After choosing another bottle, he returned, this time with the bottle I originally asked for. The saddest part is that he had no idea this was my original choice. This was going to be a very long evening.

We eventually ordered food, which was actually good. Once dinner was finished, we both agreed that absolutely nothing about the restaurant would make either of us return, and by the looks of the dining room, not many others as well. Service was undistinguished, the room had absolutely no personality, and by my experience at the bar, this place was a failure. The next day I called and politely declined the offer. I either made an impression or they were horribly desperate. The director of operations asked me to reconsider, come back, and talk to him and the chef so we could discuss the issues I had and perhaps create a plan that would work for me. Sure. Why not? Let's see what they offer. The meeting was positive. They knew the problems and felt that with me we could turn this around. So with the backing and support of the chef, I agreed to join the team. They also met my number, which didn't hurt.

"Failure Is Simply the Opportunity to Begin Again,
This Time More Intelligently"—Henry Ford

EIGHTY TO 90 PERCENT of restaurants fail in the first five years, a not-encouraging statistic. Why do they fail? Ah, "let me count the ways. . . ." Every year a slew of idiots with a few bucks who have absolutely zero knowledge of the restaurant business decide to open a place. Blackjack has better odds. Most new restaurants go under for some specific reasons: bad location, tax evasion, and lack of initial capital. Add the reasons from the existing, badly run and conceived restaurants to this, and the list enlarges. Shitty management, lousy service and/or food, lack of advertising (though this is not so true in New York City), lack of attention to the numbers (food cost and payroll being the biggest troublemakers), and absentee ownership get you to the 80–90 percent failure rate.

Bobo was a failing restaurant. On Sundays and Mondays it averaged six to ten covers an evening. Tuesdays hit twenty or so, a few more would show on Wednesdays and Thursdays. Fridays and Saturdays the bar would crush it, mostly three deep all night, and this kept the restaurant limping along. To use Minetta and Raoul's as examples since both have approximately the same number of seats, each does about 150 covers on Sundays and Mondays, about 175 on Tuesdays and Wednesdays, and over two hundred on the weekends. Had this been only a bar on the ground floor with minimal, simple food and a small staff, it would have been a success. The restaurant was taking in approximately $36,000 a week. It needed another $10,000 to $15,000 to break even, and that's with a skeleton staff. To properly staff the restaurant, build the wine list, and keep good cooks in the kitchen, we'd need at least another $20,000 to $30,000 a week. There were also the initial investors, who hadn't been paid. Things looked dismal. Frank Bruni, writing in the Diner's Journal in *The New York Times*, sounded an early warning about six months after Bobo opened:

> I've come to think of Bobo as a gorgeous blond cheerleader or lifeguard who just doesn't have to work very hard. Attention and affection come to it anyway, on account of its great looks. My companions during my meals there always began dinner pronouncing a contentment so deep and true that they didn't care what the food turned out to be like. They were besotted, and that wouldn't change. They were smitten, and that couldn't be soured. But by the end of the meal, they weren't so sure. Maybe they'd come back, maybe not. They had qualms. They had questions.

Carlos knew a lot of people, and early on they came in droves. The place was hot. With no sign outside telling you this was Bobo, it became this secret little club, with those knowing of it gaining entry, feeling as though they were among the chosen. It was a party with beautiful people, and this crowd rarely cares about the food. They also have zero loyalty, and once the next hot spot opens, they are gone. Unless you have developed a clientele that comes to actually have an experience based on the food and service to replace the chosen ones, you've failed.

Bobo is a gorgeous restaurant, inviting and warm, and once you've entered, you know it's somewhere you want to be. It has that transformative energy, similar to that of Minetta Tavern and Raoul's. Though with those, once you leave, you know you're coming back. The doubters rarely will. Suarez knew he had to fix the kitchen. After firing two chefs in less than a year, he managed to recruit Patrick Connolly, who not only received four stars from *The Boston Globe* for the restaurant Radius, in Boston, but was also the recipient of a James Beard Award, winning Best Chef in the Northeast. On paper this was quite a coup. It seemed Carlos's mantra was "If at first you don't succeed, keep firing chefs till you get one that can cook." That is, if the restaurant is still open. It was, he did, and it didn't help. Bruni returned three months later to pen an actual review. It was apparent that no one had heeded his first warning.

> Bobo was like the new kid who showed up on the first day of school in perfectly torn jeans, with a perfectly cocked hip and perfect confidence that the right pose and prettiness were all it took to get by. Bobo was aloof.... Bobo was self-impressed ... [with] food that yo-yoed between so-so and no-no.

Bruni wasn't impressed and gave the restaurant one star, pleased with neither food nor service. Not even the wine list. He encountered almost the same problem I had with wine five years later. One star is the kiss of death for most restaurants. Who wants to try out a restaurant that was just reviewed as having bad food and service? New York City has too many other restaurants. Why waste your money? Now, five years later, Bobo was about to become a casualty of the five-year-and-out rule. I must have been nuts to join the team there, but I hated Minetta so much I needed to get out. This would at least buy me some time to plan my next move. I liked Carlos, loved Chef Tovar, and figured if I could get the FOH in order in this glorious and sexy space, and if Tovar could get the kitchen in line, it would buy me some time. I might even accomplish the almost-impossible feat of resurrecting a restaurant that was about to die. I quit Minetta Tavern and was going to try to make this place work. The onetime actor who had used restaurants as a way to get quick money and party a bit, while waiting for an acting job, was now deep in the restaurant world.

The NYC Department of Health, otherwise known as the Gestapo of the NYC restaurant world, is one of the most egregious entities that has sway over a restaurant. While the intent is to protect the public from the scores of diseases potentially propagated by clueless, uninformed, and sometimes nefarious individuals that own and operate the thousands of restaurants in New York City, this, in practice, seems to be its least concern. What the department excels at is levying fines. With the advent of letter grades in 2011, to have anything less than the letter A hanging in the front window is tantamount to having to relocate your restaurant to the nether reaches of Siberia. Also, no one wants to be known as the Typhoid Mary of this century. We all want that A. Getting it is determined by a point system.

Each violation is given a certain number of points—less for minor violations, more for major ones. The more points the lower the grade: 0–13 gets you the A. More than 13, you're fucked. What the system has done is force restaurants to be on top of their game like never before. We pay millions of dollars in fines every year for infractions that range from a fruit fly in a bottle of Jack Daniel's to mouse droppings in the basement. This has led to a vigilance never before seen in the industry.

Responsibility for levying the fines falls to the hundreds of inspectors that fan out throughout the city each day searching for violations. The Byzantine rules governing the industry and enforced by these inspectors are now so drummed into the staff that everyone from busboys and dishwashers to the owners knows exactly what we do wrong each day we open our kitchens.

To prepare for the dreaded times inspectors walk through the front door and flash their badge (should they even do so), most restaurants have a protocol that goes into effect. It begins with a code word for when the inspectors arrive, since you never know when they're coming. I've used *tsunami* in two restaurants since it aptly describes the frantic, last-minute preparations we go through to avoid as many fines as possible.

The first goal of the tsunami protocol is to stall the inspector at the door and gain as much time as possible to spread the word to every person on staff to cure the many infractions that are impossible to avoid during service. However, I have had inspectors walk in the door unannounced, head straight to the kitchen, flash a badge, and begin the crucifixion. To make it all worse, the inspections are inevitably at eight o'clock at night, when the restaurant is busiest and the potential for violations is at its peak.

Once the inspector is spotted, we go into action. I've drawn up "two-minute drills," which are instructions for various servers and bartenders to follow and clear up potential violations. This includes everything from tossing all the cut fruit at the bar into the garbage, clearing bread crumbs from the bread station, cleaning the toilets, grabbing a flashlight and checking every corner and crevice for mouse poop, to dumping dairy products into the trash. Each person has two minutes to complete his or her tasks. We regularly run mock drills to keep everyone on point.

The food-temperature rule that all restaurants must abide by is 41° or below if its refrigerated, 140° and above if it's not. This is pretty much impossible to adhere to during service. For example, all dairy products used throughout the night are refrigerated, but since they are constantly being used, the refrigerator doors are continually being opened and closed, ensuring the proper temp is virtually impossible to maintain. A piece of meat or fish taken out of a refrigerator and sitting out waiting to hit the pan will inevitably be the wrong temperature. Everything suspect gets thrown out before the inspector can stick his thermometer in it and tell you to throw it out anyway since it's a violation. Bartenders toss the garnishes and unwrapped straws—all violations. Ceiling pipes in the basement and kitchen are wiped down of dripping condensation. The air vents are wiped and cleaned. Someone checks the bathrooms to make sure no trash or toilet paper is on the floors and that the EMPLOYEES MUST WASH HANDS signs are posted. Managers run to get all the licenses to show the inspector. Chefs clear out the walk-ins of any suspect food. And on it goes.

While the inspector is there, service comes to a complete stop. It's too risky to cook anything. We wind up buying most tables drinks or sending out desserts to make up for the inevitable delays. With more than 125 potential violations, the inspectors will always find something wrong. And with fines ranging from $200 to $1,000, by the time the inspector leaves, a usually hefty fine will need to be paid, even if you get an A. Each time the DOH walks in the door, it's going to cost about $2,500.

The Resurrection

THE MOMENT YOU ENTER a restaurant as a guest, if you're not immediately engaged by the staff, warmly greeted with a smile, and made to feel that, yes, we are happy you're here, the restaurant is in trouble. Those at the door need to be dripping with hospitality, warmth, graciousness, and, yes, a smile.

I quickly hired a host to alleviate this immediate concern. I had my first point of contact done. Mr. Arrogant-as-Fuck Bartender was next. Dismissing staff is difficult. The days of walking up to people and telling them they're fired are over. HR departments run the show, and you need explicit documentation to let go of an incompetent employee. Generally, three documented infractions avoids you a costly lawsuit. The files here were a mess, paperwork was spotty or nonexistent, and I couldn't rely on most anything previous management had done. When I arrived, there was one manager, overworked, unsupported, and exhausted. Carlos himself was assisting, but from what I was told, we may well have had my six-year-old daughter run the show. The glum, talentless, inhospitable guy who helmed the bar needed to go. Luckily, he was unfazed by this new regime and kept up his slovenly ways. It took just a few weeks before I had the required paperwork to fire him. God that felt good. Another bartender on staff was excellent, so I could trust at least one person.

The servers were mostly kids, students, who while sweet and eager, didn't possess the skills needed for the level of service I wanted to instill and had little interest in taking their positions any more seriously. Once they saw how the place was changing, a few decided it wasn't for them and opted to leave on their own. I did get one good thing out of my brief return to the River Café. I had immediately hit it off with two servers there. I knew they were unhappy and thinking of leaving. Once I felt I had the room somewhat in shape, I reached out, and both eventually joined the team.

I then needed a maître d'hôtel to run the door. About ten years before, we'd hired a host, Jennifer, at Raoul's. Though young at the time, she was sharp, intelligent, had the skills to converse with just about anyone, and was also beautiful. I knew she'd be perfect here. I reached out to her to run the door and she accepted. Look at me becoming the adult in the room.

I now had my professionals on the floor. Tovar was a partner and acted like one. Besides being a great chef, he was a fantastic handyman. He could do all the minor repairs we needed, and thankfully he had a second, his sous, Edwin Claflin, who could run a kitchen as if he were the chef. He could also jump in and assist with the physical repairs as well.

Built in 1836, the space was not equipped for the demands of a restaurant in the twenty-first century. A lot goes wrong in such an old space. The plumbing was a disaster. The toilets regularly overflowed, backing up into the bar, water gushing out so forcefully we sometimes had to fashion a dike out of tablecloths to block the flow till we could either fix it ourselves or get a plumber. The internet and phones were also a problem and would regularly go down. We had so many wires coming up from the basement to run the phones, computers, and the point of sale system, it looked as if NORAD was being run through the building.

The grease traps in the kitchen required continual maintenance. If it wasn't done—and this is common in many kitchens—the traps back up and the smell of old, rotting food and grease coming out of them is nauseating. Your first reaction is to puke and get as far away from the smell as possible. I have seen cooks remain at their stations as the drains backed up around their feet, standing amid rancid bits of food and grease, their noses and mouths covered with a napkin as a makeshift bandanna to stanch the wretched smell as they finished off their *côtes de boeuf* and fillets of trout, each holding steady while tossing garlic in olive oil and sautéing spinach to complete the order, then rushing out for air when complete. There's not much you can do. You bring in fans to blow the smell back into the kitchen rather than have the smell hit the dining room. Service would continue till we could get a plumber to come and charge us a fortune to snake the drain and get things back to normal.

Failing restaurants are unable to afford the maintenance necessary to keep this from happening, hence our predicament. One evening there was a leak in the basement. Edwin and I went down to inspect. We saw water dripping out of the sewage pipe, and when we touched the pipe, it collapsed at the joint, drenching both of us in sewage. Sewage lines need to be flushed out at least twice a year, otherwise all the shit that guests put in the toilet bowl—hand towels, feminine products, reams of toilet paper—clog the pipe and it backs up. We got it stopped, wiped ourselves off, and went right back to work.

If I have to come back in another life, I'm coming back as a plumber. While chatting with our plumber one day, as he was fixing a drain for the millionth time, he let me know he was planning his daughter's sixteenth birthday party. Thinking he was priming me for a discount, I asked the date and wanted to know if he was considering having it here. He replied not at all—it was costing him $50,000 to have it on the river near his house. My kid's getting dinner with her friends at the restaurant when she turns sixteen.

With the imminent collapse and flooding of the building held off for the time being, we now needed to ensure the guests who did dine with us had a stellar time and returned. It took six months to get the restaurant to a place where we felt confident that what we were doing was at a level high enough that our guests might actually want to return. I know a lot of people. For the first six months, each time I descended the stairs from the dining room and saw someone I knew at the bar or coming in for dinner, I ran and hid. I didn't want anyone I knew coming in and seeing me. You get one, maybe two chances with guests. With my reputation, if I didn't deliver on the first try, I knew I wouldn't see them again, and I wanted the customers I knew to become regulars. We needed to be ready. Tovar's food was excellent, simple and delicious. He understood the limitations of the small kitchen and created a menu that could be executed within those constraints. I was constantly on the floor overseeing service. In six months we were breaking even, in nine months turning a profit, and, after the first year, we had the most successful year since the restaurant's opening. We were back. Now the goal was to keep it that way.

The restaurant business is unforgiving. It takes constant attention. The second you look away or turn your back, something will slap you in the face. The only way to mitigate this is to be there constantly. Great owners, at least initially, are the first to open and the last to leave. They need to put their eye and imprint on everything. Not doing so is one of the biggest mistakes new owners and those new to the restaurant business make. Guests *want* to meet the owner and, if not, some proxies that can behave or act like they have a proprietary interest in the business. Raoul's succeeded because the staff made excellent money and each one of us took care of it as if it were ours, despite the absent management. We were making money and didn't want to jeopardize it. If an owner thinks he can pay a manager $60,000 a year to run the business like the owner would, he's out of his fucking mind. He will close in a year.

I was constantly in service. I'd arrive in the morning, take care of the billions of things that needed attending to—ordering wine and booze, linen, making sure the garbage was collected, that the flowers were fresh, that the outside was swept, that the restaurant was spotless, do the schedule—all the things we needed to operate. In the evening I was on the floor, overseeing service and, most important, "touching" every single table.

Touching a table refers to when a person of authority—the manager, owner, or chef—goes to every table that evening to check in on the guests, see how their meal is, the service, the food, the ambience, get to know the guests, see if they live in the neighborhood, how they came to dine here, and hopefully motivate them to come back. It's basically knowing your customers. If treated well, respectfully, given a decent meal, they will return. It's simple but it works.

Lutèce was one of the great restaurants in America. It opened in 1961 and lasted forty-one years. It was Zagat's number one restaurant in the country for six years running. The owner was the legendary chef André Soltner. I had eaten there a number of times, and each time, at the end of service, Chef Soltner would leave the kitchen in his starched, spotless kitchen whites, toque atop his head, and make the rounds through the dining room, checking on each table. It was as though the pope had come to give you his blessing. It was a spectacular part of the meal—the greatest chef in America coming to your table and checking on your experience.

Many restaurants—and corporate entities especially—are so far removed from this simple, kind, and meaningful gesture. It's reached a point that most guests take for granted the impersonal and perfunctory service. Most diners have absolutely no idea who the chef is in these places and probably don't care. These are not the restaurants I seek to dine in or care to work in. Again, it's the experience, and the best restaurants give you the complete experience. It's a pretty simple idea, showing up at your own restaurant. If you want to succeed, you need to be there. At least in smaller houses. At the factories, the large places, most people want to eat and leave, which the ownership encourages. Turning tables is the goal. In the better restaurants, the great ones, it's about the total experience. Being recognized and treated well is perhaps the most important part of this.

The great restaurateurs—Danny Meyer, Stephen Starr, Keith McNally, and many others—they know this, understand how to do it, and hire great people to run their establishments, many of whom are decently if not well paid. If you don't pay, you're left with a bunch of hacks who are out the door at the first chance for a bit more money. There is no continuity. For me, I love going to a restaurant where I will see the owner and recognize the bartenders and servers. It's familiarity, continuity, safe in a way since you know exactly what to expect. McNally and Starr succeed because they staff their restaurants with excellent people. Those at the door are attractive, pleasant, and sharp. The floor staff are well trained by talented and fairly paid managers. The kitchens are run by excellent chefs.

Tovar was putting out some wonderful French food. Money was coming in, and with the added revenue stream I was able to build a decent wine list. With Jennifer, my maître d'hôtel, and the two stellar servers I poached from my brief return to the River Café, we brought the business back. We now had a fully functioning, beautiful restaurant, replete with regulars as well as newbies, and referrals from our happy customers. Things were the best they'd ever been. Till something happens that throws that damn monkey wrench at you.

Bobo

I LIKE BEING IN control. I believe I know the best way to make a dining room work, and at Bobo I had free rein to do it. After a year and a half, I was given the title of general manager and, after my third year, became a managing partner. With the investors now paid off and the business going well, there was more money to go around.

It was always planned for Tovar to oversee the kitchen at Rosemary's. Once that opened, we saw less of him at Bobo, and once Carlos opened his third restaurant, Claudette, Tovar was mostly there. This forced us to bring in a new chef. We tried a few chefs but were never able to find someone of Tovar's talent, passion, and commitment to Bobo. While we managed to keep the food of a certain quality, it never matched his. Left without Tovar, the bulk of the work fell to me.

With three floors plus a garden, Bobo's a small, cramped, and difficult space to make work. It was a constant challenge to maintain the status quo. There was major construction outside as well that impacted our operations. To our left, a restaurant was leveled and being replaced by luxury condos (are condos ever built in Manhattan that aren't luxury?), and the street out front was being torn up for water-pipe replacement. The construction of the condos created noise that impacted our brunch business, and as the building next door rose, debris would fall on our garden roof, which ruined it. It would take more than a year to get it replaced. While this was going on, the workmen in the street putting in the new pipes neglected to seal off an old coal chute to the restaurant, allowing hundreds if not thousands of rats to enter. The infestation took months to resolve.

Carlos was attempting to create an empire, and we rarely saw him. He spent most of his time at Rosemary's trying to raise money for the next venture. He was also preoccupied with turning the restaurants into a group, branding them under one entity, which he eventually did, naming it Casa Nela. This was the beginning of the end for me.

Casa Nela was the umbrella that would oversee certain operations for each of the restaurants. This is a fantastic idea if done correctly, and with three restaurants, a necessity for a smooth, unified business, especially if you plan on growing. The departments would be Human Resources, Events, and Public Relations. These would have to be staffed and would need an office and then time to get up and running. Many capable people are out there who could do this. The thing is, the good ones are well paid and generally employed by excellent companies. To get them to leave their cushy jobs, you'd better offer some great incentives.

Money is usually the first. The problem here is that very little money was appropriated for the change. This new group was going to be started on a shoestring budget. The first hires were generally inexperienced and seemed to be because they could be had for cheap. If you're starting from scratch, you better have people that know what the fuck they're doing and aren't learning on the job. This was pretty much the case with those who were hired. The team that was assembled didn't have a chance.

Things got off to a bad start. The office that was chosen for the new group was an open space, had dicey Wi-Fi, and was to be shared by HR, Events, PR, and Reservations. Four people working simultaneously—this included the reservationist—in a small space, has the potential for disaster. The phone rang all day, and with only one person budgeted for reservations, someone else would have to drop what they were doing to assist with the calls. With the reservations phone ringing nonstop, the various departments needing to make their own calls, multiple people all talking in a cramped space, and the Wi-Fi going in and out, it was chaos.

The first sign of trouble was on the day the move to the new office was to happen. There were no arrangements made for any transportation or money to take equipment from the restaurants to the new space, and the person in charge of the move didn't have a key. In the desire to move forward, expand and create a restaurant group, the basics of operation were overlooked. Instead of giving raises and creating a positive environment for the good people already on staff, they were overworked, underpaid, and then had to deal with people less competent than many of the staff we had.

It became more and more difficult each day to sustain my commitment to the place I loved very much. It felt as if in the attempt to create a group, the product we had worked so hard on to be successful was being ruined. It was once again time to move on.

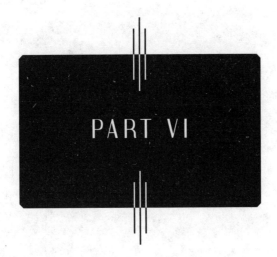

PART VI

Starr Ship Coucou

STEPHEN STARR BEGAN HIS restaurant career in Philadelphia. He's from the streets of Philly and hawked trinkets on the boardwalk of Asbury Park as a kid, then moved on to comedy clubs and the music industry. He booked many acts that would later go on to become major stars, from Jerry Seinfeld to Madonna. He then created a mini empire of restaurants, from Philly to Miami, and stunned the restaurant world in New York City with the massive Buddakan and Morimoto restaurants. The incredibly successful Upland restaurant followed.

I had never heard of him or his restaurants. I was in my little downtown-restaurant cocoon, unaware and uninterested in life above Fourteenth Street. I hate the big, trendy theme-park restaurants that are packed, loud, and serve shitty, overpriced food. All those Tao Group restaurants that are swarming with twentysomethings—the women in packs of ten, unable to walk in their too-high heels and tight skirts, screaming, giggling, and celebrating the "bitch" that just got engaged—while the guys wait at the bar in their tight pants, shiny shoes, the same untucked button-down shirt, three top buttons left open, stinking of some shit cologne, and hoping the "bitches" get drunk enough to go home with them. I'll pass.

I was sitting in my office at Bobo ruminating on my future when I got a call from Troy Weissmann, the former GM of Rosemary's. Weissmann had left Rosemary's a year or two before—having gotten fed up dealing with Carlos—and was quickly scooped up by Starr to open Upland, which got great reviews and was a fantastic success. I hadn't heard from Weissmann in over a year. He was opening a new restaurant for Starr and was calling to inquire about someone I had worked with.

Toward the end of the call, I let him know I was thinking of making a change, getting out of management and perhaps doing something else. He let me know the new restaurant he was opening was hiring and thought it would be a good fit for me. He said he'd set up an interview.

I gave it a shot. The interview was at Buddakan, with the director in charge of new restaurant openings. When I arrived at Starr's over-the-top, grandiose temple of dumplings, I was immediately greeted by one of the managers. "Good afternoon, Mr. Cecchi." Sweet. These guys had it together. It was noon, the restaurant was not open, and the place was swarming with Starr's operatives, doing whatever it is they all do. Today it seemed mostly interviewing scores of people to fill positions in many of the restaurants.

The director was professional and listened to my needs, and in retrospect I think I must have sounded like the burned-out waiter Madame GM at Raoul's assumed I was nearly twenty years before. I learned later that I was correct, and the director was adamant about not hiring me. But despite her reluctance, she put on a smile and told me I needed to meet Chef Daniel Rose, who would be helming the new restaurant. This must have been as a payback to Weissmann, who was apparently a star in the company. She was passing me off to what would end up being an obvious rejection.

Le Chef

Le Coucou was being built in the recently constructed 11 Howard hotel, right on the edges of SoHo and Chinatown, and steps from Canal Street, a thoroughfare noted more for traffic, bad smells, and dingy shops selling bizarre electronics parts than boutique hotels and fine dining. The hotel is owned by the renowned, if somewhat notorious, developer Aby Rosen. Rosen is now infamous in the restaurant world for kicking out the iconic Four Seasons restaurant from the Seagram Building, which he purchased. The restaurant had been in residence there since 1959. The Philip Johnson–designed mecca for rich, white one-percenters had lost its allure and grown stale, and Rosen deemed it time to put in new blood. Or maybe he was pissed because he couldn't get a good table. He not only kicked the restaurant out, but also removed the giant Picasso tapestry that had hung in the infamous "Picasso Alley."

Arriving at 11 Howard to meet Daniel Rose, I entered the construction site of what would soon be Le Coucou. What would eventually become one of the most beautiful restaurants in the world was a complete mess. It took forever to navigate the morass and finally locate Rose in the library of the Hotel. He's a smallish man, with curly dark hair and eyes that never stop taking in what's going on around him. Oddly, this is not disturbing, and he seemed totally engaged in our conversation. Rose is from Chicago and, as he likes to say, left for France to join the French Foreign Legion. Failing at this, he studied cooking at L'Institut Paul Bocuse in Lyon and spent the next ten years honing his craft throughout France before opening Spring, a sixteen-seat restaurant that brought him his initial success. When he moved Spring to larger quarters, it became a phenomenal success and put him at the fore as one of the top new chefs in the world. Starr found out about him, brought him back to America, and Le Coucou was born.

Daniel is easy to like, fun, playful, engaging, and smart. We hit it off immediately. We shared stories of our times in the business, discussed food and hospitality, and discovered we were simpatico. I told him how important I felt the guest experience was and shared my story of Lutèce. How Chef Soltner would go to every table at the end of service to check on his guests, and how this had greatly informed my perspective on the business. Rose had met Soltner and immediately let me know that, while having never eaten at that glorious restaurant, he knew enough of its ethos to try to re-create it in a downtown way. He wanted this to be a Lutèce reboot. When I told him the story of Jimmy the bartender and Lou Reed, we both immediately knew that Le Coucou would be a Lutèce meets Lou Reed moment. Rose, with his knowledge and experience of classical French cooking, was about to transform dining, not only in New York City, but the entire country.

He took me on a tour of the facility. As we entered the unfinished kitchen, dead center and taking up most of the space sat a partially unwrapped stove, which had recently disembarked by boat from France. He pulled aside the plastic, and underneath was the most beautiful stove I have ever seen. It was enormous. It was built for Rose by the French company Athanor. With its lovely curves, green façade, and brass railings, this sensuous piece would not only cook Rose's food but be a central design element of the kitchen. Starr was dropping some serious coin here. The only other functional, inanimate design piece I have ever equated as being so sensual was Michelangelo's staircase for the Laurentian Library in Florence. This had the same feel. I told Rose I wanted to lie down on it (I managed to refrain from saying I wanted to fuck on it), to which he replied he'd stayed so late the evening before, he had slept on it.

I knew then I was going to love this man. We ended the meeting agreeing that we wanted to work together. I was now excited. This was awakening my love of restaurants and the people who work in them that Bobo had killed in me. I let him know how excited I was and that I wanted in. But my next hurdle was to meet with the maestro himself, Stephen Starr.

Starr Man

BACK AT BUDDAKAN, I once again received a warm, professional greeting and was ushered to a seat to await my meeting. I could see Starr from where I sat, in the midst of interviews. He's apparently infamous for meeting everyone that's passed the many steps required to be hired at one of his restaurants, and now awaited his final blessing. Considering the guy has over forty restaurants, this is pretty impressive. I watched as he'd greet a candidate, have a brief chat, then send the person on his or her way. As this played out, all his current employees kept at least one eye on Starr. Each time he gestured as if needing something, two or three were at the ready to bring him whatever he might want.

My turn came, and as I walked over, he stood and gave me a warm greeting. Stephen is burly, about five-ten, with short dark hair and a big personality. He was dressed in jeans, black T-shirt, blue blazer, and glasses perched atop his head. Confident, charming, and brusque, he wastes little time, doesn't chitchat, and expects others to get to their point as quickly as possible. If not, you're dismissed. I liked him immediately. We sat and he asked for a résumé. When I laughingly replied I hadn't had a résumé in twenty years, he laughed with me and said, "Good." We talked a bit, I let him know the places I'd worked, and after about five minutes he told me I had a job. We just needed to figure out what I wanted to do and what would be best for me. I let him know I wanted to work with him and Rose at the soon-to-be Le Coucou. He said he'd discuss this with his team. We shook hands, and as I was leaving, I said, "Stephen, please don't think I'm sucking your dick here, but your organization is phe-nomenal. Everyone has been amazing. I'd love to work for you." As I walked away, he jokingly replied, "Let's not tell anyone what you just said." I laughed and told him I meant it in the biblical sense.

Weissmann soon let me know that after the meeting Stephen walked over to him and said, "This guy's great, he's gonna be the maître d'hôtel." With that, I gave my notice at Bobo.

Le Coucou

On my first day at Le Coucou, it was in utter chaos. The scene was familiar from my Water Club days, which now felt like a hundred years ago. Contractors were huddled over blueprints as workers called out to one another for this thing or that. In the open kitchen I could see a mass of cooks surrounding Rose, all involved in various steps of a recipe, awaiting his input. Starr's team was arrayed around various areas of the restaurant, pounding on their laptops and doing whatever it is the people who don't actually work in the restaurant do. In a corner was Starr himself, amid a constant huddle of his minions—contractors, designers, engineers, the chef—all frantically discussing every aspect of the restaurant. Being the last of the management staff, I knew no one and stayed to the side. They'd all been planning together for months and were deeply involved in their projects and had little time for the new guy. I'd be running the door, and we were a few weeks off from even having a door.

The army of cooks in the kitchen, all in white, were chopping, stirring, tasting, poring over notebooks, discussing recipes and sourcing products. Rose, having never worked in New York, needed to learn the purveyors, taste the products, and see what was out there, all while taking charge of a kitchen staff five times the size of that of Spring in Paris. Starr had assembled a team of all-stars to assist, including his culinary director, Alex Lee, famous for his time as Daniel Boulud's executive chef at the then-four-starred restaurant Daniel. Erik Battes, former chef de cuisine for Jean-Georges, and Gilles Chesneau,

Daniel Rose's chef de cuisine from Spring in Paris, were also there. This was way more serious than I thought.

At the front of the T-shaped restaurant sat about thirty recently hired FOH staff, waiting for talks by various members of management to fill them in on what to expect. I was blown away by the talent here. Most of the managerial staff had been general managers at major restaurants; the others all had experience working for the big boys, the Danny Meyer places, Jean-Georges, et cetera. This was going to be a killer team. Shockingly, Weissmann let me know that Starr had never had a real maître d'hôtel at any of his forty-plus restaurants and I would be the first.

It felt like no one on the team had any idea of what to do with me. It took a week for me to finally feel like I had some idea of what was going on. As the restaurant began to take shape, it became clear that it was going to be stunningly beautiful. The exterior of the restaurant is fronted by planters filled with trees and climbing vines. When you enter, the now iconic bar, considered by many the most beautiful in New York, is to the right. To the left begins a row of tables that in the daytime are bathed in light by the magnificent windows that front the entire restaurant, and in the evening by chandeliers inspired by the Hagia Sophia in Turkey. As you walk down the aisle, to the right is an entrance to the main dining area. The room is dominated by luxurious banquettes made of mohair. At the end of this is the exposed kitchen, which resembles a set piece in a film, that glorious Athanor stove in the center, rimmed by hanging copper pots, the walls tiled in green. Starr was clearly getting ready to blow New York City away, and enough money and talent was in the room to do just that. The interior was being designed by Roman and Williams—former set designers who used this experience to create what they would later describe to me as a series of "shots," each part of the restaurant having almost its own identity to create an outstanding whole.

About six months after the opening, I was standing in the front dining room, waiting for the staff to arrive. The late-afternoon light filled the restaurant. It was between services, so there were no guests. A few servers sat at the tables, quietly folding napkins; a few cooks were in the kitchen, slowly going about their finishing touches for the evening's service. I stood looking at this gorgeous scene unfolding in front of me, the light absolutely perfect, the kitchen wonderfully lit, perfectly designed, and it felt as though I were actually on a film set, waiting for the director to shout, "Action!" It was a glorious moment in a glorious space.

As we got closer to opening, Rose was still working on the menu. He was in the midst of tasting his twentieth chicken, unable to find one that he said matched the flavor and texture of those in France. He was generally disappointed in many of the products available, both protein and produce. I thought he was being a typical fickle chef, till I was with him in Paris. Coucou had been open a year, and Rose and I came up with a harebrained scheme to do a TV show together, running the idea by the wonderful Rachael Ray. Rachael took the time to hear us out, then basically told us we were nuts. She was right. Even so, we spent a couple of days in Paris shooting, but never found the time to complete the project. During one of the days' shoots, we went to the market to source meat and produce. Rose was absolutely correct. The flavors of the fruits and vegetables were more intense, more complex than what we get here in the States, especially the meat. We visited a butcher he knew and were brought behind the counter and sampled raw slices of beef the butcher had cut for us to taste. Such a different environment: no one was wearing gloves, the butchers handling the meat weren't afraid to taste it, and no one was getting sick. It was real, natural; there was a beauty in what they were all doing. These people were connected to the animals, their product. It was one, putting forth a gift for us.

At Le Coucou, throughout the day Daniel would send Starr various dishes to taste. Each time a dish was set in front of him, I'd steal a look to see what his reaction was. He'd taste, then push the plate toward his inner circle to sample and weigh in on. While they tasted the food, designers were constantly interrupting, showing various pieces of furniture or bric-a-brac they were considering. He managed the interruptions well till something, anything, would set him off, and you'd hear his voice booming throughout the restaurant: "*What are you doing! You're destroying my restaurant!*" His favorite foil was his facilities director, Michael, whom Starr screamed at regularly. We'd be in the midst of something when we'd hear, "*Michael!*"—shouted over and over till he appeared, trying to put out that moment's fire.

I soon learned that heating and cooling was one of Starr's biggest peeves.

A person could be lying dead on the floor in front of the maître d'hôtel stand, and if the restaurant wasn't the perfect temperature, was either too hot or too cold, Starr would start screaming for someone to attend to it. He wouldn't even notice the prostrate figure. *"Who's in charge! What the fuck is everyone doing! None of you know how to work the fucking thing. Get me Michael! Troy . . . !"* I'd say 95 percent of the time the system was fine. It didn't matter. Starr had an HVAC company at the ready and had to be paying this guy a small fortune to ensure Starr's restaurants were always at the appropriate temperature. If needed, a team of technicians would be at the restaurant within the hour. It could be a blizzard outside, a torrential rainstorm, Saturday, Sunday, 4:00 A.M. or 5:00 P.M., traffic could be bumper-to-bumper. It didn't matter. The technicians would arrive like a SWAT team to ensure all was working properly. Most times everything was running perfectly. In most other restaurants you could wait days for someone to come fix your AC or heat, especially on a weekend or holiday. You and your guests could either bake or freeze to death. No one was showing up. Half the time you can't get someone to answer the phone. Not Stephen. He had his guy.

We now had two weeks till opening and still no menu. Not only that, but the issue remained as to what the restaurant was going to be. Stephen told me his idea was for it to be a mix of both high and low design elements. He wanted to combine aspects of the elegant Upper East Side French restaurants, many no longer in existence, with a Canal Street, downtown sensibility. This was Daniel's and my Lou Reed meets Lutèce.

One example Stephen gave me was the ceiling. It is unfinished concrete, the HVAC ducts exposed, and this was juxtaposed with the elegance of the dining room's mohair banquettes and antique chairs covered in green velvet that hark back to 1925. The captains wore full suits with heavy black boots. The rest of the servers were in jeans and wore boots as well. Very unlike the tuxedoed staff in most elegant establishments. The goal was to give the room a somewhat more relaxed and approachable feel than you get at Jean-Georges or Le Bernardin uptown. The handmade tables are stained white oak, which cost a fortune. The debate as to whether to leave them bare or cover them with fine linen was ongoing. Tall white taper candles were going to be atop the tables. Would these sit there all evening and drip on the wood? On a tablecloth? How many people were going to get burned by the open flame? What if someone knocked one over? Would the entire place go up in flames? I thought we should go without tablecloths. The tables were beautiful and, with the eventual wear and tear, would age wonderfully. I also thought the candles would certainly set someone on fire and we were crazy to use them.

Weissmann and Rose fought tooth and nail for the linens and candles. Rose would say, "I want to throw a party; it's just that my parties have table-cloths and candles." Stephen also felt we needed the linens but was willing to try it bare. I was wrong on both counts. One evening, during friends and family, we left the tables bare, and it was a disaster. The room looked awful, the sound of everything that hit the tables was horrifying as it reverberated throughout the dining room, and we lost the incredible beauty that the white linens and taper candles gave to the room. The linens gave the room the per-fect contrast between high and low.

It also became apparent that Daniel and I are the perfect examples of this dichotomy. Daniel knows classical French cooking, excels at it, and can cook three-star Michelin food. He takes the classical recipes, throws out the ri-gidity, complements the dishes in his own style, and most of the time creates new masterpieces. He eschews the starched white jackets that many chefs don to patrol their dining rooms, instead wearing worn black pants and black T-shirts, looking more like one of the dishwashers than the chef. He regularly jumps out from behind the kitchen, copper pot in hand, filled with some sort of deliciousness that he's just cooked up, and will head to a table to scoop out what he's made onto a guest's plate.

Me, on the other hand, I am so not-your-typical maître d'hôtel of a fine-dining restaurant, French or otherwise. Walk into any of the fine-dining restaurants and the guy at the door is almost always tall, suave, good-looking, and usually surrounded by a staff of the same ilk. At Per Se, Thomas Keller's four-star restaurant, the entire team of captains looks as though they were cloned, all young, tall, handsome, and thin, in their tailored black suits, all going to a table in unison, holding only one plate, which gets set down in exact tandem with the others. If these guys were all in a lineup, you'd convict them all, they look so alike.

I'm the FOH version of Rose. Short and more Woody Allen than Jean-Paul

Belmondo. I certainly don't have French movie-star looks, nor did I have French fine-dining experience. I absolutely hate the trappings of fine dining, the sacredness of it, the bowing at the temple of fine cuisine. If it weren't for this blend of the high and low that Starr so wanted, I doubt I'd have been hired.

What I do have is that I know New York and New Yorkers. I know what they want. How they need to be treated. I don't bullshit. I know the downtown dining scene, having worked it for the past thirty years. I regularly sit with guests, drink with them, chat, and laugh. I break the rules of fine dining. In theater it's called breaking the fourth wall, throwing away all pretense and sacredness. I think this is what Starr saw in me. I doubt many French maîtres d'hôtel told their owners they weren't sucking their cocks. I think this is why he hired me over the objections of his directors, who saw the Per Se / Restaurant Daniel model and not me, the little Italian, working the door of their new gem.

Stephen is also certainly not high society. Had he been born in Bensonhurst, he would have been a mobster. He's the restaurant world's version of Tony Soprano, driven around by a chauffeur that looks more like Luca Brasi from *The Godfather* than a guy who would drive around someone that owned forty restaurants. We'd see the brand-new Maybach pull up in front of the restaurant and know Starr was there, behind tinted windows, in the back seat, always on the phone. We'd wait to see if he was coming in or if the driver would call and let us know that someone was being summoned to the car. I never knew if I was being asked to the car because Stephen needed something, or if I was about to be driven to Jersey for an execution.

One week to go and still no menu. I saw lots of dishes going back and forth, from the kitchen to Stephen's table, but while he and his consigliere got a taste, no one else did. Rose was continually trying new dishes. You could see him in the kitchen, bent over a copper pot, stirring one concoction or another that would soon be sent to Starr for his approval.

The dining room was now almost complete. One evening, we tested the candles and lighting to see how it would look. After the lights were adjusted for the eleven hundredth time, the candles finally lit, and the tables set, it was breathtaking. The bar is the star of the restaurant. It's four shelves high, soaring toward the vaulted ceiling, framed by a hand-painted landscape mural, rich with shadows, which wraps around the entire bar area, creating a dramatic effect that sets the tone for the whole dining room. The entire staff was in awe when the lights went down. This was it. We were ready.

Other than Stephen's eruptions, which were becoming commonplace, the kitchen was relatively quiet. Then it happened. The frustration of not having a menu, the constant back-and-forth of dishes being tasted, returned, retasted, had grown tiring. One afternoon, about three days before friends and family, the restaurant shook as Alex Lee, the corporate chef, bellowed, *"Enough! Everyone needs to focus and cut the shit. Everybody focus!"* There was dead silence. My shoulders, which had been up around my ears from the stress, dropped. I took in a deep breath and smiled. This was old-school and it felt good. We'd be ready in three days.

Iron Bottoms

WITH AN ARMY OF staff backed up by the Starr corporate people, who were everywhere, this was the smoothest friends and family I had ever witnessed. There were of course hiccups. Our food trolleys squeaked, drinks and dishes went to the wrong tables, and so on, but there was nothing unwarranted. We were learning a new system, a new geography, and the well-trained and ready staff rose to the occasion.

We were packed from day one. This was one of the most awaited restaurant openings of the year, and once reservations opened, we were immediately booked. Rose has a staggering following. For the first three months, nearly 80 percent of those dining were guests who had dined at Spring. I had no idea this many New Yorkers regularly dined in Paris. They all came with their Spring/Daniel stories: how incredible the food is, how Daniel did an extra this or that for them, how they arrived late and even though the kitchen was closed, he reopened and cooked them dinner, how they had to wait outside for a table and Daniel came and had a beer with them. He was loved and revered. Everyone wanted to see him, to say hello, to eat his food. Word spread quickly, even before the first reviews. Bloggers were gossiping about what he planned to cook, questioned whether he was happy in New York, if he would be going back to Paris, if his wife and family would be moving to the city. I had been unaware of this level of food fanaticism.

Foodies are nuts. They follow every move of a chef or restaurant they love, and they followed us. We were sold out every evening. Our tables were the most sought-after in New York City. All the restaurateurs wanted to come, along with cooks, chefs, waiters, the usual list of soigné guests that I was accustomed to, and others I had never met. We tapped into the world of the über-rich, the millionaires and billionaires that inhabit that small stretch of the Upper East Side, who became our regulars. They arrived in droves, limos and town cars fighting for space in front of the restaurant to drop off their suited and bejeweled clients. This was a night out when they could finally dress and dine as if it were the sixties. Old-world food and glamour were back with a modern twist. The biggest complaint I received would be how far they had to travel to eat here. You'd have thought East Sixty-eighth Street was located in Kuwait. The attention paid to every detail of the food, service, and decor was paying off. We were a hit.

Here I was, the new maître d'hôtel, ready for the onslaught. But I was currently without a door. When I'd worked the door in the past, I ran the room. It was my domain; I was in charge and I did my thing. This wasn't happening at Le Coucou, at least not for the first five months. No one ever told me this was the case, but I was quickly schooled. Starr had a director of front door operations—let's call her Iron Bottoms—who was in charge of setting up the booking system for the other restaurants. She did all of NYC and had her finger in Philly, DC, and Florida as well. This is a necessary position; it creates uniformity among the restaurants and, with similar reservation setups, makes it easier to book tables among all the Starr restaurants. We'd met a couple of times prior to friends and family and discussed how the reservation book was to be created. While she listened to my suggestions, this was clearly her baby; I was a waste of time, a potential threat to her job, and my piddling, little thoughts were annoyances.

Once friends and family began, she'd arrive each day at 4:00 P.M., station herself in front of the computer at the maître d'hôtel stand, and remain there the entire evening, leaving only to pee, and that was rare. She was there seven days a week from opening till the kitchen closed. With her there, I had no control of the book or the seating. She was in charge; my input was minimal and not wanted. She could be an ill-tempered tyrant and had a less than stellar reputation in the company. She rarely smiled, lacked grace, and could be rude to both staff and guests. Yet here she was, manning the door at Starr's most elegant restaurant and the most awaited restaurant opening of the year. But despite the negative reputation, she carried the biggest trump card in the company. She never missed a food critic. Ever.

So, what are the rules? Should you tip a maître d'hôtel? First, it's absolutely not necessary. Second, if a maître d'hôtel holds out from giving you a table or attempts to "sell" you a table in any way, if you can, leave. It's thievery and has given maîtres d'hôtel a bad rap over the years. A tip at the door should be a thank-you—a thank-you for the same warm welcome and greeting each time you see that person, a thank-you for squeezing you in, or getting you that hard-to-get reservation. Or if you want extra attention that night because it's your husband's birthday and she sees to it that the dessert has a candle. Or a complimentary round of champagne is sent over because he knows you're celebrating your anniversary.

If you don't have a reservation and absolutely need one at that particular restaurant and you're told they are booked, $100 will almost certainly get you a table. Less can be construed as insulting. Look, if the maître d'hôtel is going to rearrange her book, delay this guest or that guest, push another table along to make room for you, or use any of all the other ways the best maîtres d'hôtel know how to get someone in, you better pony up. If you don't, you're not getting a table again. One hundred dollars is the gold standard and will get you pretty much anything you want. A nice thank-you for special attention is $50. A twenty is a token and always welcome, but it's not going to put you in the pantheon of great guests. I have one guest, a billionaire, who has tipped me a twenty for almost thirty-five years. I love this person and the twenty is not necessary, but, c'mon, has he not seen how much his bank account has changed over the years? In short, if the person you see at the door each time you eat at a particular restaurant is always generous, courteous, welcoming, and indeed happy to see you, or remembers your drinks, or sends you a dessert, show your appreciation.

Soufflé

Most every restaurant has some restaurant-critic protocol. This is the procedure that's followed when a critic is spotted in the house. There's a lot at stake here. Some reviewers have the power to potentially kill a new restaurant. When they do come, you want to make sure you are on the top of your game. You don't want to blow it. The protocol begins with a code word. This is important so the word can be spread as quickly as possible to every employee in the restaurant, while not allowing the critics to know they were spotted. What you don't want are a bunch of servers and managers shouting "Critic!" throughout the dining room. Let's call our word *soufflé*.

Once a critic is spotted, someone goes through the restaurant as quickly and surreptitiously as possible, letting every staff person know that a soufflé is in the room. You want everyone on his or her A game. Staff in the best houses can at times be careless and slovenly. I once had a sommelier enter a full dining room sucking on a bottle of Evian. If not for all the HR bullshit, I'd have fired him on the spot.

The critic protocol at Le Coucou, while very similar to other restaurants, was the most intense I had ever experienced. We held a "critic's table" every evening. The table, considered the best in the house, was never seated until we were certain a critic wasn't coming that evening, and it would only be released about thirty minutes before the kitchen closed. In the event we did seat it, usually to a VIP, we always had a backup in case some critic made an eleventh-hour appearance. Besides losing the revenue that table could generate each evening, it was always the elephant in the room. When we were packed—which was every night, with waits upwards of thirty minutes, and guests glaring at you each second as they waited for a table—to see this empty beauty parked in the middle of the room made them want to kill us. Iron Bottoms sucked at hospitality, so it was left to me to schmooze the guests and politely let them know the table was being held and they would not be able to sit there. In addition to holding the table, we also kept a brand-new set of menus and a brand-new wine list to give to the celebrated guests. No smudges or wrinkles on these babies—fresh, clean, and untouched.

The best team of the evening was always put in that table's station, and only the head sommelier would do the wine service. Other than the immediate staff that attended that table, all others were instructed to stay as far away from it as possible. No staring, fawning, stealing glances—nothing. You never, ever let on that you know a critic is in the house, and you never let the critics know you know they are sitting there. They want to see you as you are and want no special attention. They want to be served exactly as every other person in the room. If the chef is not in the kitchen that evening, he better damn well get back to the restaurant as quickly as possible. You want only him at the stove, no one else. Rose wasn't getting a night off till every critic had dined with us.

Once the critic's order was put in the kitchen, the chefs would then prepare two of each dish ordered. They taste one to make sure it is exactly right and then send the other. After each course, the plates were then brought back to the kitchen for the chefs to inspect before being sent to the dishwasher. The chefs want to see what was and wasn't eaten. If something was left on the plate, that was a danger sign. Did he not like it? Was it the guest's plate or the critic's? Did she taste it and put it back? Was the critic too full?

While you aren't supposed to stare or fawn, you are required to observe the critic's every little gesture or innuendo so as to enlighten the chefs. The pressure is enormous. Bad reviews can close places down. The power of one man or woman to have the ability to either make or destroy a restaurant is immense. Stephen (like most restaurant owners) was so paranoid of bad reviews that his team did everything possible to make sure we spotted every single reviewer who entered the restaurant. Ryan Sutton's *Eater* review of Buddakan certainly put the fear of god in him. Sutton destroyed Buddakan:

In case you didn't pick up the Lonely Planet guide to Buddakan, the larger half of Stephen Starr's Vatican-sized restaurant complex in New York's Chelsea Market, here's a brief tour of what you'll witness around the Chinese-esque mess hall: four hostesses, only one of whom will take your coat, the type of inoffensive club music one might encounter at a duty-free airport shop, a red vase room (Siberia), a blue Buddha room (as inviting as a cargo plane), a chandelier room that my real estate buddy got a prime seat in after greasing the right person, a VIP library room with fake books, staircases steep enough to keep your drinking in check, cocktails average enough to make you quit drinking $16 potables forever, an odiferous ashtray inches away from the Shaq-sized entrance, and a Renaissance-style painting of a naked guy outside the men's room, whose visible penis, if you're "Tom Cruise height" like me, is at face level. . . . Mapo tofu, normally a showcase for the numbing qualities of Sichuan cuisine, sports an out-of-left-field sweetness that makes it taste like it was prepared by Chef Boyardee. Dan Dan, a classic pairing of egg noodles, pork sausage, chile oil, and scallions, smacks of bitter hand soap. What's advertised as soft-shell crab bao buns turns out to be understeamed sliders. And black-pepper beef, a stomach-warming dish from China's Guangdong Province, is a mess of overcooked rib eye in a KC Masterpiece–like sauce. The beef arrives in a stale "bird's nest," packing the taste and texture of a paper doily. If you closed your eyes and successfully identified the Chinese names of all four dishes, I'd buy you dinner at Meadowood.

Stephen wasn't about to let this happen here. Hence Iron Bottoms. She could smell a critic a block away. She knew all their faces. She could spot one in the stands at Giants Stadium. We had a critics notebook with photos of all of them. We had posters on all the walls with pictures of every food writer, editor, blogger, and critic that might possibly write something about the restaurant, and there were dozens of them. The staff was asked to look at the photos every day to help spot one. Iron Bottoms had a one-hundred-percent track record, and Starr wasn't about to let her leave the door for a second.

She was a fucking master at this. So what did I do? I wasn't going to stand there and watch. I worked the room. I touched every single table, got to know every guest, knew how many times they'd dined at Spring, where they were from, where the kids went to school, and what they did for a living. I checked on their dinners and tried to be a conduit between the door and the kitchen. I took notes on everyone and developed an incredible list of regulars who would eventually come at least once a month to have dinner with us. But mostly, I waited for the critics.

The question I am asked most often is, Where do I go when I go out to eat? I rarely know how to answer this since I seldom go out to dinner. Spending as many hours as I do in a restaurant, I prefer to be with my family and spend quiet time with them on my days off. After dealing with hundreds of guests all week, along with floor and kitchen staff, purveyors and the rest, the last thing I want to do is sit in a crowded restaurant. Also, my wife hates going out to dinner with me. I inevitably wind up knowing some of the staff and am constantly running into guests I've known over the years, and I wind up spending the meal jumping up and down greeting people. To my wife it's like my being at work.

We rarely go to new restaurants since I find them most disappointing. It's impossible to turn off the restaurateur—I'm constantly judging the operation, whether good or bad, dissecting the staff, the food; it's like being at work again. I am usually disappointed in the food and the generally exorbitant prices for a mediocre meal. When we do go out, it's usually to a rotation of two or three small restaurants in the neighborhood where we've come to know the staff and they treat us well but leave us alone and I rarely run into guests I know. After being in the restaurant business for so long, you develop a radar that lets you know immediately if a place is going to be good or bad. When we travel, I usually walk into a handful of restaurants, then walk right back out till I find a spot where I think we could get a good if not great meal.

The Arrival

THE WAIT WAS INTERMINABLE. Days and then weeks went by with no crit-ics. Table 34 sat empty night after night. Finally, our first critic of note, Steve Cuozzo of the *New York Post*, made a reservation. Cuozzo is a lifer at the *Post*. He began his career as a copyboy and eventually became an editor in various departments. He's a grizzled New Yorker, grew up in Brooklyn, and knows the city as well as anyone. He's not a bullshitter nor does he take it. He's a newspaperman first and tells it like it is. The *Post* no longer does regular food reviews, but Cuozzo will stray out on occasion. This was such an occasion.

Cuozzo actually called to make the reservation since he was well-known in Starr quarters. He's gruff, knows what he wants, and if he doesn't, he'll ask a question. He's not going to chitchat. When he's finished his meal, he's done, wants a check, and leaves. There's rarely time for a goodbye, and again, no chit-chat, no bullshit. The night he came, I seated him and let him be for most of the evening, only checking in after entrées were served. That was it. You can't read him at all, and once he dashed out of the restaurant, we had absolutely no idea what he thought of us.

The review came out a week later. The headline read THIS NEW YORK CITY BISTRO IS ONE OF THE BEST RESTAURANTS OF THE CENTURY. We were stunned. We were blown away. According to Cuozzo, we were also one of this century's four or five best restaurants of any kind. This was an incredible first review. I was happiest for Starr and Rose. Stephen took the risk, poured in the money, and Daniel received an incredible homecoming. The entire staff was psyched. This was the first validation for all the work each and every one of us had put into making this restaurant happen. If reservations were already hard to get, this made it impossible. One down. We still needed the big three.

Adam Platt was the next to arrive. He's easily spotted. It's hard to miss the bald pate atop an over-six-foot frame. Iron Bottoms saw him immediately and he went right to table 34. In his party was his young daughter, a gourmand herself, who proclaimed to the captain that Daniel's Spring was her favorite restaurant in the world. Hopefully this would bode well for us. Platt's pretty amiable and writes a lot of food reviews. Maybe too many. He's been doing it numerous years, and perhaps that's the reason he dined with us only once, returning a second time to squeeze in with some friends who were already here and having some nibbles from their plates. Not something you usually do when writing a review of the hottest restaurant in New York City. The review was lukewarm; he liked us but didn't love us and gave us three out of five stars.

We all found this disappointing, me especially, since nearly everyone I spoke to was absolutely blown away by the food, service, and ambience. While a disappointment, it did nothing to alleviate the crush of guests wanting to dine with us. One down, two to go. Again we waited. It had been three months since we opened. Where the hell were Sutton and Wells? I probably wanted it to happen faster than anyone else so as to be finally rid of Iron Bottoms. She was good, though. Very, very good. Whatever Stephen was paying her was worth it. She spotted every single one of the lesser critics as well as all the food editors and their lackeys.

On a Thursday evening her biggest spot yet finally arrived—the dreaded Ryan Sutton of *Eater*. He tried to sneak in on a crowded evening. The door was packed with guests, and as Iron Bottoms was checking them in and our hosts scampered about trying to get people seated, her radar went off. She looked up just as he was trying to slip in through the crowd and head to the bar. She was prepared for this. She was always alerting us that he loved to eat at the bar, and this is what he would probably do. But the bar at Le Coucou is the size of a VW Beetle, about eight feet wide, with no stools and barely anywhere to stand. And we absolutely did not serve any food there. I had never encountered Sutton, but most of the staff had, and not one had a good word for him. He is reputed to be rude to servers and bartenders and impatient, and he can be cruel in his reviews. To wit, the Buddakan piece.

A target was on his head, and Starr wanted him spotted. Iron Bottoms didn't fail. The bartender recognized him as well and came to tell us he was here—and pissed because we didn't serve food at the bar. Then Iron Bottoms did something unexpected. She approached and offered him a table that she pulled out of her ass, since we were totally booked. We couldn't sit him at table 34 since it was a four top and he was only two, which would have raised red flags, so she switched some things around and got him seated. Once he was down, we put the soufflé protocol into action. His behavior eventually softened and the service went flawlessly. Each time he came back he was spotted, and each time our team was on point. The review that came out in *Eater* was good: we received three out of four stars. He liked most everything except for one dish, the *oeuf norvégien*. Writes Sutton:

> So let's talk about a certain pre–El Bulli spherification: *oeuf norvégien*, a soft-boiled egg wrapped in chive cream and artichoke and covered by a sphere of smoked salmon. Call it brunch in a ball, a pescatarian Scotch egg designed to make a 1970s *Better Homes & Gardens* editor swoon. Let me describe how it tastes in four words: do not order it.

It was immediately removed from the menu. The power of one man. Yet this wasn't the one man we really wanted. As the opening weeks dragged into months, there was still no sign of Wells. We would come up with reasons why he hadn't shown. Our reservation book was completely filled every night, and if there were openings, they were usually at five thirty or eleven, so perhaps he wasn't able to get a reservation at a decent time and was holding out till he did. Or he was waiting for all the other reviews to come out—the king waiting for the minions. We came up with dozens of reasons, but for whichever one, he wasn't showing. As this dragged on, I had to still be under the insufferable tutelage of Iron Bottoms. God bless her though, she showed up every day, not taking a day off till each and every reviewer was present and accounted for.

It took till fucking November for Wells to finally show. Five long months we waited. The reservation popped up on OpenTable late on a Monday evening. Iron Bottoms saw it come in around 9:00 P.M. and knew there was something fishy about it. Whatever her method was, we all trusted her and were put on high alert. The reservation was for 10:30 P.M. We had pretty much completed our second seating, the room was three-quarters full, and we knew that by ten thirty half of these guests would be gone. We didn't want him sitting in a half-empty restaurant. The Starr machine quickly jumped into action. Iron Bottoms got the word out and the team called as many people as they possible could to come and fill up the dining room. No small feat for lesser mortals, but the Starr machine went to work, and by 10:00 P.M. we had most of the room filled. We were ready.

After all this it would have been really fucked-up if it wasn't him. Iron Bottoms had a reputation to uphold. Wells has a habit well-known in restaurant circles. He arrives neither with nor ahead of his party. The guests come first, get seated, and then he shows up late and surreptitiously slides himself in, hopefully unknown to the staff. He's been the food critic for the *Times* for so long now, his picture so widely circulated among restaurants, you'd have to be dim-witted to miss him, hence the sneaking in. True to form, an incomplete party showed up under a well-known Wells alias. We sat them. Approximately ten minutes later, he appeared in the doorway, head down, walked to the maître d'hôtel stand making no eye contact, and gave the name of the alias. Bam! Iron Bottoms did it again. Our biggest soufflé had finally arrived.

Fortuitously, two lovely women were in from Paris, one who'd worked for Daniel at Spring and her friend. We'd seated them right next to the table we assumed was going to be Wells, hoping a bit of Gallic eye candy might add a bit of flavor to the experience. I walked Wells to the table, and our biggest soufflé protocol was launched. The group he was with was fun and were all in good spirits. When he went outside for a cigarette, I made my move to the table, checking in, asking how everything was. This great group was willing to talk, and we had some fun chatting about the restaurant and also Raoul's, since one of the guests recognized me from there. When Wells returned, he had apparently shared a smoke outside with the French gals, who were already out there, and the next thing you know, when the next course arrived, the two tables were sharing dishes. I knew things were going well when I spotted Wells licking the sauce from the bottom of the pan that held the sweetbreads. The room was lively with friends and employees from the other restaurants. This was a good start. We felt we nailed his first visit.

He returned twice more and was spotted each time. Again we waited. We knew the review was imminent when someone from the *Times* called to fact-check the review. Each menu item the caller asked about was then parsed by the entire team. Which items did the person ask about? What was left out? Did the fact-checker ask about a lot of the dishes? We sought any inkling as to what was forthcoming, a common, futile practice in any restaurant that awaits a review.

Finally on November 1 the review came out. It was spectacular. We received three of four stars, which is exactly what we wanted. Four stars is way too difficult to maintain, and two stars would have been seen as a failure. The lovely review praised most everything about the restaurant. Our two women even got a mention:

> One night, I sat next to two Parisian women who said they were regulars at Spring. A French-speaking waiter appeared and engaged them in a long deliberation about the cheese course. They sent over their cheese, we shared our desserts, and then I slipped outside with them while they lit up their Gauloises. "This is very different from Spring," one said. "But it makes sense in New York."

Touché.

Gone at Last

AND WITH THAT SHE was gone. Five long months and the wait was over. I was now able to run the door as I saw fit. The reviews were all in—we were a smash and the hottest table in New York City. Guests from all over the world wanted in, though with only twenty-six tables and a three-hour turn time, most were not getting in. I had to turn down Danny Meyer one evening. It killed me but we were overbooked, and I knew I'd have to keep him waiting for at least an hour, and I wouldn't do that to him.

The phone rang incessantly, so much so that I wasn't able to take phone calls or I'd be on the phone all day and night. Every request went through email. It was the only way to handle the volume. We booked one month in advance, and OpenTable would release the available tables at midnight. In two minutes everything would be booked solid. The press was nonstop—not only the food zines but *Architectural Digest, W, Vanity Fair*. All chimed in on the wonders of Le Coucou. His eminence himself, the irascible Graydon Carter, along with his beautiful and elegant wife, Anna, were regulars.

Carter is the éminence grise of the NYC dining world. Besides being the editor of *Vanity Fair*, he was also a restaurateur, and arguably one of the most influential people in New York City and, for that matter, the entire country. Starr loved him and let me know in no uncertain terms that he *always* got a reservation. Stephen rarely says this about anyone. It's the rare guest that can intimidate me. Carter was one.

One particular night he was due in at eight. The restaurant was, as usual, packed. He obviously had to get one of the four VIP banquettes. Getting a table to turn at the allotted hour is a combination of detailed planning, a bit of artistry, prompt and efficient service, and luck. Some nights I'd have to ride the team hard to keep service flowing so I could get a table back in time. Some nights I gambled, and depending on who was due to arrive, if the wait would be ten or fifteen minutes I'd buy the guests a drink at the bar and could usually seat them with no ill will.

This didn't work for everyone. The problem with having someone wait for a table at Le Coucou is that there really isn't a bar to wait at. The bar area only fits about five or six guests, there are almost no seats, and the actual bar has no stools. This makes the area quite inhospitable. Starr, whose mantra is hospitality, missed it on this one. When we were crowded, guests in the bar area were continually jostled—by servers, bussers, other guests, hosts—it was the proverbial clusterfuck. Most guests were unable to reach the bar to order a drink, which added to their irritability. If I had celebrities, I could not make them wait. There was always some idiot at the bar ready to harass them.

I always try to have one table I think will definitely turn, and another that might possibly turn as backup. But this evening was the perfect storm and both these tables weren't budging, despite my being up the ass of the captains to keep them moving. Carter was due at eight, and at seven thirty I started pushing the teams to get the tables up and out. To make it worse, Starr was in the restaurant and planned on staying to say hello to Carter. If I didn't seat him at the best table at exactly eight, Starr would lose it and I'd get my ass handed to me.

As the arrival time approached, Starr came to the door and asked which table I was going to sit Carter at. When I told him, he scowled, "That table is never getting up at eight."

"Stephen, I got this."

"He better sit on time." A stern warning from the boss. Starr is always either getting calls or texts, or someone in the restaurant wants his attention, and this was the case. He got distracted and moved on. At quarter to eight I'm pacing the dining room and realize it's going to take a miracle to get Carter his table on time. I then went into my "I'm fucked" mode. This mode has three parts:

1. An immediate stiff shot of vodka to numb the pain.

2. Tell the captain to drop the check and hover by the table
    till a credit card comes out.

3. The time-honored tactic of every great maître d'hôtel
    around the world—hide.

Sadly, the bar was packed, and I wouldn't be able to get a shot without having to stop and talk to the guests who were already waiting for tables. I headed straight to the computer, printed the check for the table I needed, handed it to the captain, and told him to drop it immediately. I then went to hide. My hiding spot was at the complete opposite end of the restaurant, next to the kitchen and concealed by a wall where I could still see the dining room, but guests couldn't see me. I left Victoria, my lead host, in charge. She was quite capable of parrying with guests in my absence and knew where I'd be hiding.

Once concealed, I channeled my inner altar boy and prayed. I prayed for the table to get up. I prayed for traffic. We were so far downtown and near the arteries to the tunnel and the bridges that guests were always late because of the traffic. Especially at prime dining times. "Please, God, let Graydon be stuck in traffic."

I spotted Starr pacing the room as I prayed, staring at the table I wanted for Carter, knowing that these fuckers weren't budging. From where I stood, I could see the front door, and at seven fifty-five I saw Carter enter. I'm fucked.

I glanced at the table with the check and suddenly . . . a miracle. The credit card goes down. They are paying. I sprint from my hiding spot to the table, grabbed the credit card, and handed it to the captain to process with the admonition that if he doesn't do it immediately, I'll cut his balls off. I then grabbed a busser to clear the table of whatever was not being used, an affront to our points of service, which would, in a normal service, get him reprimanded, so I actually had to push him to do it.

I then took a deep breath and headed toward the door. Carter was in the midst of a crowd, so thick with waiting guests he couldn't move, but as soon as he spotted me, he raised his arm, pulled his sleeve up to expose his watch, pointed at the time, and gave me the death scowl, which read, *Where the fuck is my table?* At the same time, Starr turned the corner, saw Carter, looked at me, and gave me the exact same scowl. I'm fucked.

I rushed over to Carter, told him how nice it was to see him early, and how glad I was to see he hadn't gotten stuck in traffic. As I say this, I spot Starr bull-rushing toward us, and directly behind him the table I need is getting up. Starr greets Carter and they do kissy-kissy, which buys me some time. I rush back to the dining room, oversee the reset of the table, rush back to where Starr and Carter's retinue are standing, and once the kissy-kissy was over, I was there, ready, smiling away. "Your table is ready."

Our guest list ran the gamut from António Guterres, the secretary-general of the UN, to Kanye West, George and Amal, Sonia Sotomayor, Brad Pitt, Robert De Niro, and on and on. Every great chef came to see Rose—Éric Ripert, Michael White, Thomas Keller, Daniel Boulud, Joël Robuchon just prior to his passing, the wonderful Jean-Georges, a regular—all were beyond gracious and welcomed Rose into their fold. The great Jacques Pépin came one evening, and the first thing he did was enter the kitchen, in full view of our guests, and greet every single cook and chef there.

André Soltner, the legendary chef and owner of Lutèce, arrived unannounced one afternoon, the reservation under the name of his guest. This was a huge deal. When I seated them, his guest remarked how difficult it was to get a reservation. I responded somewhat bewildered, "Chef, all you had to do was call and you would get a table in a second." Soltner sat there, looked me up and down, and with a scowl said, "Michel, I do not take someone else's reservation. If you have the table, you have the table. That is it. I expect no special treatment." This came from one of the greatest chefs of his generation, and he saw the look of disbelief on my face. He said, "I will tell you a story."

One afternoon at Lutèce, Soltner's wife, who always answered the phone and ran the reservation book as though she were booking appointments for the pope, said, "André, it is the ambassador on the phone, he wants a table tonight. I tell him no. He insists on talking to you." She was referring to the French ambassador to the United States.

"I pick up the phone," said Soltner. "The ambassador continues, 'André, I need a table tonight, it is for a very special person.' Before he says another word, I say I am booked, I have nothing, and hang up."

The ambassador called back, Soltner's wife again answers, turns to André, and says, "André, the ambassador again." Soltner takes the phone. "He tells me the important guest is Giscard d'Estaing! I tell him, 'I do not care who it is. I do not have the table!'"

With so many guests wanting in, I had to curate the room accordingly. Stephen always had one or two guests that needed a table, but of all those in the company that needed tables, Stephen was the only one who almost never forced me to take a reservation. There were exceptions, but not many. Carter was one, Woody Allen was another. One night Allen was coming in on my night off, and Stephen absolutely wanted me there to greet him. Coming from the Upper East Side, he was of course late to arrive, as most of our guests from that toniest of areas always are. He was also the last to join his party. When he arrived, I walked him to his table and we chatted for a minute. I sat him, and then I went to alert the kitchen.

As I got closer to the kitchen, I saw that all the cooks were staring at me, a look of disbelief on their faces. Most of them were young and obviously didn't know Allen, since the first thing they shouted to me was "Is that your father?" Thankfully they didn't say brother. My whole life, as I approached a table, guests would ask if I knew whom I looked like. "My mother" was the standard retort. When they almost always said, "Woody Allen," I'd reply, "Thank God women find him sexy or I'd still be a virgin."

One afternoon, our head reservationist called over to let me know she had a woman on the phone insisting on a reservation for two, at a private table. When told we had no private tables, the woman was insistent, stating that she was bringing in royalty and only a private table would do. This royal escort was both irate and rude to our reservationist, who asked me to take the call.

It's always amazing how when irate guests are passed on to someone in authority, especially a male, their attitude changes 100 percent. At least initially. She was at first as kind as could be, until I was adamant in letting her know that we had no private tables nor a private room, that this was a public restaurant and every table was next to another table. She then asked to be seated between two tables and for me to leave the adjacent tables empty. Really? I told her the best I could do would be a corner table with only one table beside them. She eventually acquiesced and I made the reservation. I still had no idea who the "royal" was, nor did I care.

On the evening of the reservation they of course arrive twenty minutes early. When I informed them the table would be ready at the time of the reservation, and they were welcome to have a drink at the bar, the escort became incensed. "Are you aware my guest is dating Prince Harry and about to be a duchess? Don't you have a private area for us to wait? We absolutely cannot be amongst a crowd of people." My first impulse was to laugh. I could give two shits about Prince Harry's date, and by the attention the escort was drawing from the crowd at the bar, nor did anyone else. "I am very sorry, but as both I and my reservationist have already told you, this is a public restaurant with no private areas. If you'd like, you can wait outside, or the hotel has a lovely library on the second floor."

The escort looked at me as though ruing the day the peasantry were given any positions of authority. But she turned and went to the bar. At precisely eight o'clock I escorted them to their table. When the escort saw where they were sitting, she stopped. "You're not sitting us here?"

"Actually I am. I told you I would give you a table that is next to only one other. It's a lovely table. I am very sorry, but I have held this especially for you and your guest. I have nothing else." She scans the room, sees every table is full, and, with a huff, sits. The duchess-to-be never uttered a sound.

The only time I was actually threatened by someone was when Iron Bottoms was still running the door. We had a guest who was sent to us from hotel owner Aby Rosen. The guest was supposed to get one of the VIP booths, but Iron Bottoms fucked up and seated him at the only table that was available, which was the worst table in the house—adjacent to the front door and right in front of the maître d'hôtel stand. Obviously pissed, this Master of the Universe gets up, walks the short distance back to the maître d'hôtel stand, and rips her a new asshole.

As this is happening, the host seats another VIP, higher in the pecking order, in a booth that was just vacated. He sees this and goes ballistic. He's some billionaire hedge-fund guy and is used to getting his cock sucked by probably everyone except his wife. It's certainly not going in anyone's mouth here. Iron Bottoms is shaken up by this, so it's left to me, the junior Woody Allen, to make nice.

I have to say, I am usually 99 percent successful at this. But as soon as I get to the table, he goes off on me, screaming that I'm a fucking liar, a piece of shit, do I know who he is, blah-blah-blah, and that he's calling Aby right now to have me fired. Aby is our landlord and has nothing to do with the restaurant. He can't fire me. He could call Stephen and tell him to fire me, which is doubtful, but still a possibility. If the three of them have some deal going and I fuck it up, I might be gone.

I'm in a bind here. I am ready to lose it on this scumbag, but age and experience tell me to breathe, I'm still new here, and this guy is not worth losing my job over. Though he's not stopping. His dinner guest is a retired All-Pro football player, and it seems to me this has to be about whose cock is bigger, since the man can't be given a shit table in front of Mr. Macho football guy.

As he's screaming at me, a table right next to the kitchen becomes available. These tables are polarizing. Some guests love them, especially the foodies, and we consider them chef's tables, since guests are right up there with the action. I let this guy know we have the chef's table available in the main dining area, and I'd be pleased to move his party there if he'd like. This gets his attention, though I know he's not going to like this table much better than the one's he's at. I thought that throwing in the "chef's table" might make it seem like he's won, and he'd be able to save face in front of Mr. All-Pro.

As I walk them over, I see how big Mr. Football is and think they all hate me so much right now, that this guy might just crush me. We get to the table, and of course Master of the Fucking Hedge-Fund Universe doesn't like this one either, though since it's in the main room he's somewhat placated. As they sit, he's still trying to get Aby on the phone to have me fired. Being unable to reach Aby only pisses him off more. They sit and I see the veins bulging in the man's neck, and I'm thinking if he doesn't kill me first, he's going to have a stroke and drop dead right here. Sadly, neither his date nor his guests have the balls to speak up and tell him to chill. He kept acting like I had just killed his firstborn. Obviously mommy and daddy didn't meet this jerk's needs, and he's one angry little boy. It's not my fault that mama didn't give him any titty.

The rest of the evening I tried to avoid the table as much as possible, though the one time I went near it, he was still pissed. He spotted me, stood up, and shouted, "You're a fucking liar." He obviously did get through to Aby because a few minutes later I got a call from Starr, asking what the fuck I did. I let him know I didn't do a damn thing; this was Iron Bottoms's mess and I got sucked into dealing with it. Apparently the jerk and Aby were working on some deal together. Starr told me to make nice and send the jerk something. I didn't. Fuck him. He never came back.

So why do you sometimes have to wait fifteen, thirty, even forty-five minutes for a table when you have a reservation? Is it the incompetence of the reservation team? Is the evening overbooked because the owner is trying to milk every penny possible so he can actually meet that month's exorbitant rent? Did the maître d'hôtel or host forget you are here? Maybe. It does happen. But I am here to tell you the one most egregious thing that guests will do that will absolutely fuck up the entire timing of the evening and create those fifteen-, thirty-, and forty-five-minute delays. Cell phones.

We all do our best to get parties seated on time, despite the litany of things that can go wrong—a missed order, guests arriving late, food arriving late, it all happens and is somewhat expected, and we do our best to mitigate this. What we can't do anything about are the fucking cell phones. I cannot tell you how many times, on a busy night, the restaurant packed, guests have arrived and are waiting at the bar for their tables, we've done our job, seated the earlier tables on time, took the orders and gotten the food to the table in a timely manner, served coffee and dessert, the meal is now over, and we drop the check. The table is cleared of everything. It's now time to leave. Inevitably, someone pulls out a cell phone and the games begin. Who needs to get an Uber? Do we take one or split up? Then someone decides to start showing pictures of the kids, their vacation, or the last fucking meal in the other fine restaurant they have dined at this week. It goes on ad nauseam and can last for ten or fifteen minutes. What do we do? We clear every possible thing off the table to let you know it's finished. We have a server or host stare at you to make you somewhat uncomfortable and finally realize it's time to leave. We try everything short of throwing you out. Yet the phones remain. Please, when it's time to go, realize that and go because, one day, you will most certainly be one of those people standing at the bar and getting pissed because you're table is not ready at the appointed hour.

The Shah

FEW GUESTS ARE DESPISED by both FOH and BOH at the same time. The Shah was one. His first visit was on an extremely cold January evening. A guest complained to the captain that the dining room was freezing, so I went to the table to do damage control. Seated were a young couple, late twenties, and a debonair balding gent, impeccably dressed, mid-fifties or so. I could see they were pissed.

The woman spoke first. "Who are you? Why is it so cold in here? What's going on? It's freezing. Do you know how hard it is to get a reservation here? It's impossible! Then to finally get one and have to sit in subzero temperatures is ridiculous. You need to move us to where it's warmer." I did actually know how hard it was to get a reservation. Also, we were packed and there was nowhere else to move them. "I am so sorry. I am the maître d'hôtel of the restaurant. I just raised the temperature. It will warm up in a minute."

The young guy just scowled and said nothing. The Shah gave me the death stare, a look that I was sure he'd practiced hundreds of times on his employees and wives. He then said, "Why don't you have chicken? Every great restaurant has chicken. Can the chef not cook chicken?"

Yes, he can cook a fucking chicken. "Funny you should ask that. Actually, when Daniel first arrived, he went through about twenty or so different types of birds, but couldn't find one he liked and that matched what he was preparing in France. He decided to not put chicken on the menu."

"He can't fly in a chicken from Paris? My brother brings in raw Iranian caviar and he can't fly in a chicken?"

This wasn't going to go well.

"What's good here?"

I can't stand that question. Nothing's good here, you fucking twerp. All the cooks wake up in the morning and the first thing they think about is how to fuck up the entire menu when they arrive.

"So much of what we serve is wonderful. The lamb is particularly good."

"I love lamb. I eat it at the best restaurants all over the world. It must be perfectly seasoned and exactly medium rare. Can the chef do that? Is he capable?"

Now I want to punch this guy in the face. "He's very capable. I am sure you will love it."

With this, I left the captain to take the order and headed straight to Justin Bogle, our chef de cuisine. Daniel was in Paris, and Bogle was running the kitchen. Bogle is about five feet, seven inches, bald, tattooed, and built like a fireplug. Not someone you want to fuck with.

"Chef, we have a complete asshole with his asshole friends on fourteen. They've already complained about the temperature in the room. We need to take care of them. He's a world-class diner and wants the lamb to be a perfect medium rare. Please don't fuck this up."

"Fuck him. Just throw him out."

"I'm sure Stephen would love that. Please make sure everything on that table is perfect."

Bogle is a great chef, and I knew it would be perfect.

About a half hour later the captain came to me. "Table fourteen wants to talk to you. They are awful, awful people. He hates his lamb."

Jesus fucking Christ. "Okay. I'm coming." I went straight to the bar, poured myself a shot of vodka, and headed over to the Shah.

In my charming we-may-have-fucked-up maître d'hôtel voice and concerned look, I said, "Uh-oh, is there a problem?"

"Look at this lamb. Is this medium rare? I asked for medium rare. Can the chef cook? This is awful."

The Shah pushes the plate toward me. It is a perfect medium rare. "It does seem a bit over. I am so, so sorry! Please know this never happens. Let me have him cook you another."

"You freeze your guests and then serve them badly prepared meat? This is the best restaurant in the country? This is a joke."

"I am so sorry. Please let me get you another."

Death stare.

I take the lamb back to Bogle. "Chef, he said it's over."

"Fuck you, Cecchi. It's not over. Tell him to fuck himself. That's a perfect medium rare. Throw him out."

"He said it's over. Please cook him another one. He's fucking horrible."

Bogle throws the dish in the garbage. "Fuck him." He shouts to a cook, "Give me a lamb. Rare!"

This is not going to go well. "Send a runner over to me when it's ready. I'll deliver it."

I was going to take this one for the team. About ten minutes later the lamb is ready, I pick it up, Bogle gives me the fuck-you look, and I head over to the Shah. "Here you are, sir. The chef apologizes. Please enjoy."

Again the death stare. I stay. He picks up the knife and cuts the medallion right down the middle. It oozes blood. He looks at me, throws down the knife and fork. "Take it away. It's too rare. Can the chef not cook? Did he go to school? Can he not cook a piece of meat?"

Fuck me. I apologize. "Can I get you something else? Fish, perhaps?"

"No. The check. We are finished."

Okay. I grab the captain; we pull up the check on the computer, and I comp the entire dinner. "Here. Give this to scumbag."

I walk back to the maître d'hôtel stand and wait for the exit. They soon stand to leave, and as they walk to the podium, I step out, apologize once again, and hand the Shah my card. "Again, I am so sorry. If you should ever care to return to the restaurant, please email me directly and I will guarantee you a table."

He takes my card, looks me up and down, and they leave.

Exactly one month later I get an email from him. He lives in London, will be in town in two weeks, and wants a table at 8:00 P.M. I'm booked. The guy's a total ass, and all I have to do is apologize, say we're booked, and move on.

But for some stupid reason I take the reservation. Two weeks later I am going through the book at pre-shift and I get to him. "Ladies and gentlemen, I regret to inform you that the Shah is coming to dine tonight."

A collective groan emanates from the staff. I then hear shouting from the kitchen pass. Bogle: "What the fuck, Cecchi! You gave this asshole a reservation!"

"Yes, sir, I did. Let's all take the high road here. I'm sure we can win him over."

All bullshit. The thing is, I still have no idea why I took his reservation. This guy is awful, he certainly won't tip me, he's a pompous ass, and any other customer that acted like this, I wouldn't serve.

The Shah arrives at eight with an elegant woman in tow. I greet him as though he actually were a Shah and take them to a great table. I tell the captain to show me the order before he puts it in. The captain does, and of course this scumbag orders the lamb again. I walk over to Bogle. "He ordered the lamb again."

"Fuck you, Cecchi."

I then go over to the Shah and try some humor. "I guess you're feeling lucky tonight."

He actually smiles. "Let's see if the chef went for some cooking lessons."

I force a laugh. What a fucking dick. I tell the captain to call me when the food is about to be dropped. Five minutes later, the captain beelines over to me. "He wants to see you. He hates his wine." We both say "Fucking asshole" at the same time.

I go to the table. The Shah shoves his glass at me. "This is awful. You charge two hundred dollars for this?"

The wine is actually a decent white burgundy. I am about to throw the glass in his face when the great Guy Sussini, my first maître d'hôtel at the Water Club, rises from the dead to whisper in my ear, "Zee beeg blow job!" So instead of dousing the Shah with expensive burgundy I apologize, take the wine back, and send over our head sommelier to fix the situation. I retreat back to my podium and prepare myself for round two. I hate this motherfucker.

It's busy and I forget about him, till I see the captain heading toward me. He tells me entrées are being served. I head to the table, get close enough to see the reaction, but out of view of the Shah. The plate is set down. He picks up his knife and fork and cuts into the lamb. He looks at it as though a rat just jumped out from it. Pushes the plate away and with a look of utter disgust scans the room, obviously looking for me.

That's it. I'm going over, picking up the Laguiole steak knife, and running it through his heart. I arrive at the table and he's so apoplectic he can barely speak. I look at him, look at the knife, get ready to pick it up, then I hear it again: "Beeg blow job, beeg blow job!" Instead of picking up the knife and before he can get a word out, I say, "Do you like Dover sole?"

This stops him cold. He nods.

"Two minutes." I whisk up the lamb, head to Bogle, who sees me approaching, lamb in hand, and before he can speak, I put my hand up. "Don't say it! I need a Dover sole."

This time *I* throw the lamb in the garbage and head back to the podium.

For some reason this worked. The Shah loved the fish and left happy, shaking my hand on the way out. He returned three or four times more without incident. When he emailed me one of these times for a reservation, he asked if I liked caviar. I love caviar. His next visit, when he entered he handed me a sixty-ounce tin of raw Iranian caviar. I shared it at the end of the night with the team that served him.

Even though the bar area at Le Coucou was tiny, we had quite a few guests who wanted to be in this glorious space. They would arrive later in the evening to avoid the rush, get a seat at one of the two couches at the bar, and sip some wine or cocktails. Though none as much as the young blonde who started coming in almost every night.

Anna Delvey, aka Anna Sorokin, was living upstairs at the 11 Howard hotel. She'd arrive, saunter to the bar, get a glass of wine, and take a seat on the couch. She'd spend hours there, sipping wine, and on many nights being joined by one or two employees of the hotel. She always paid.

I found her way too chummy. I don't generally gravitate to those who, when after having met me one or two times, act as though they'd known me their whole life. I did my best to keep my distance. Many of our staff didn't and became familiar with her, some joining her in her room upstairs after work.

She always tried to make nice. She'd invite me to train with her and her celebrity trainer in the early mornings or ask me to sit with her so she could show me photos of the multimillion-dollar apartment she was going to buy a few blocks away. She'd talk of Aby Rosen, the owner of the hotel, and the building they were purchasing together in Nolita. She would be creating the space—an environment for the arts and artists. I had no reason to doubt her. She was living upstairs (which was not cheap), paid for everyone, and would many times have dinner with us.

Each time, when asking for a reservation she'd let me know how important the dinner was going to be. That she was being joined by investors, publicists, and so forth. She always wanted a special table. She once asked me what I liked to drink. A few days later, a case of vodka arrived. She'd apparently asked other members of the staff the same thing. Along with the vodka came Dom Pérignon and expensive Scotches and wines, all for various members of the staff. I'd apparently shot too low. While it's not uncommon for guests to send gifts, this felt forced to me, as though she was trying to buy our favor and attention. But she was more of a mild annoyance and seemed relatively harmless.

One evening she came up to me and asked for a reservation the following week, again saying how important this was and that she needed a special table. I made it happen and thought little of it, until I came to work the day after her dinner and was told her various credit cards had been declined. She left, unable to pay her $500 tab, and told one of our managers that she was going up to her room to figure out what the problem was. That was the last we saw of her.

The next day we found out that she had been tossed out of the hotel for not paying her bill and, as we soon learned, she'd done the same thing at other restaurants. About a month later the story broke on how many people she had bilked. She was eventually arrested and served four years in prison. I kept the vodka.

Fashionistas

FASHION WEEK IS ONE of the dreaded hells of the restaurant world. For about two weeks in both the spring and fall, the city is invaded by fashionistas from all over the world. This group generally acts entitled, rude, and unpleasant and at times enters the realm of the loathsome, repellent, and odious. They tend to come in bunches, like grapes and monkeys. If the reservation is for two, it's a guarantee that four or more will show up. If it's for four, you can expect eight to ten. They come dressed to make a statement, and sadly, most times, the statement is a testament to Wilde's dictum that "fashion is a form of ugliness so intolerable that we have to alter it every six months."

They rarely eat and never sit still, continually popping up and down to air-kiss someone from another bunch, who also just happens to be at the same hottest place in New York. They continually ignore the server no matter how many times she approaches the table, till they realize they've been there for thirty minutes with nary a drop of booze or mineral water to lubricate their dry lips, now parched from the cool breeze stirred from the jumping up and down and misplaced kisses, and then complain about the service. They never arrive as a complete party. They arrive with models in tow, who dart about making the rounds, and they will insist that chairs be brought for whomever may appear, so they can kowtow to that publicist or influencer du jour. The table originally reserved for four now has ten people spilling into the nearby guests' laps.

The "host" will continually demand things for the droppers-by and insist they be brought immediately, since one or the other of the group will be *walk-*

ing in a show that's going to begin any minute. Many times, once an item is brought to the table, the intended recipient is already gone, and when it comes time to pay, the myrmidons left are forced to divide the check. This takes forever, and once accomplished, they leave a gratuity proportional to their rank in the fashion hierarchy, which is tantamount to shit.

The abhorrent ones are never the designers themselves. Of all the designers I've served over the years, to a person they are gracious, kind, good tippers, and generally wonderful to have in the dining room. It's the press agents, handlers, influencers, and the like that are appalling. This group *must* be seen at the place of the moment, which was Le Coucou. Compounding the disaster was that the 11 Howard hotel was full of fashionistas and they all wanted to dine at Le Coucou, which was impossible. A few did manage to snag a table through the auspices of Aby, or via connections made through our regular guests.

I, as usual, bicycled to work on this Monday of fashion week and, with a deep sense of foreboding, observed the beau monde darting through the streets of SoHo. As I entered the restaurant, my host, Victoria, was already at the podium. She immediately let me know that one of our top clients was on the phone and was requesting a reservation for this evening. There are a handful of guests whose call I will take when I first arrive (I prefer to get a sense of what the book looks like before I start fielding favors), and this was one of them. He needed a table of four at eight thirty for some fashion personage that was in town. This was one of our biggest clients and I acquiesced.

When he gave me the guest's name, I had to stifle a groan. This person, whoever it was, had tried at least ten times the week before to get a table, having various people call for her, and each time she was denied. We were just too busy, and I needed to keep our held tables for super-VIPs only, which she certainly wasn't. I took the reservation but knew there would be trouble. I hadn't even met this person and I already hated her.

At seven thirty, two guests approached the podium and let us know they were here for the Adams party. Bam. This was them. The one I had to take. I politely let them know the reservation was for eight thirty.

"No, it's not. I booked it for seven thirty." Lie.

"I'm so sorry, Ms. Adams, but I took the reservation myself and it's for eight thirty."

"I'm not Ms. Adams."

"I see. Why don't we wait for her and I am sure she will be able to clarify."

"We can't eat at eight thirty. We have a show."

"I'm so sorry, but the reservation is for eight thirty. Why don't you have a drink at the bar, and we can discuss this when she arrives."

The woman gives me the how-fucking-dare-you, you-piece-of-shit-restaurant-person look. She and her companion take a few steps back to the front door and stand there and stare at me. At seven fifty, the apparently real Ms. Adams arrives. She speaks to her guests, then marches over to me.

"We have a seven-thirty reservation. We'd like the table."

"I am so sorry, but your reservation is for eight thirty."

"Well, can't you seat us now? We have a show to go to."

Of course you fucking do. The restaurant is packed, and I know there's no way I'm getting them seated by eight thirty. It probably won't be till nine.

Her male companion then chimes in. "Do you know who this is?"

"I assume this is Ms. Adams."

"Do you know how many Instagram followers she has?"

"I actually don't."

"She has hundreds of thousands. We want the table."

"Well, hopefully they're not all joining her. I'm very sorry, but as I have already noted, I made the reservation myself and it is for eight thirty. If you can't make it, I am happy to cancel it."

He gives me a you're-a-useless-piece-of-fucking-shit look. They powwow, and the real Adams then says, "We are going up to the Blond for a drink. We are friends of Aby's. We will be back at eight thirty."

They leave. This is going to be a disaster. At eight fifteen two other people show and ask for the Adams party. I tell them they are upstairs in the Blond, that the table is for four, there are already four in the party, and were they planning to dine with the Adams party? The man rudely lets me know that he is positive the reservation is for six. "Perhaps you should go upstairs and speak to Ms. Adams." They leave, and at exactly eight thirty, Adams returns with her entourage of five others.

"We're back."

"Wonderful. Sadly, we are a bit delayed, please give me a few minutes. Also the reservation is for four. It seems you are six."

"Yes, we are six. I made the reservation for six."

"I'm very sorry, but as I told you, I took the reservation myself from Mr. Z. It is for four at eight thirty."

"It is eight thirty. Are you going to seat us?"

"I am very sorry. I squeezed you in as a favor to Mr. Z. We are very booked this evening. I will have your table of four as soon as possible." I am now hating my life and am about to lose it on her.

"I told you we are six. Can't we squeeze?"

"I am so sorry, but the table only seats four. We have guests sitting on either side of you."

The gent speaks again. "Do you know who this is! She has hundreds of thousands of followers. If you don't seat the six of us now, she will close this restaurant down. No one will come."

"Sir, she is welcome to do what she wants. Your reservation is at eight thirty for four. We are delayed. You can wait or leave."

The extra couple says not to worry, they aren't hungry and will wait upstairs at the Blond. They all look at me as though I were Richard Speck. We seat the table at nine. A few minutes later the captain comes up and tells me there are now six at the table. These motherfuckers. I go to the table, and sure enough, the extra couple snuck back in and seated themselves. By the time the captain got to me, he had already served them drinks. I am so fucking busy that I just let them stay.

The captain, a Black gentleman, was one of our best. He once again comes up to me and tells me only two of them are eating. That's it. I have fucking had it. I tell him to print the check. I take it, go over to the table, drop the check, and tell them they need to pay and leave. This is when all hell breaks loose. They start screaming they will close us down, the restaurant is shit, who the fuck do we think we are, et cetera.

"You're done here," I snarl sotto voce to Adams's boyfriend. "Pay the check and get out." She screams how she will have me fired, how the restaurant will go out of business once she posts about us, and some other bullshit, as boyfriend pulls out his card and pays. As they start to exit, they turn to the captain and scream, *"Black lives don't matter."*

I am buzzed at the podium by Eve, our head reservationist. I pick up the phone and she tells me that someone from Valentino is on the line and he wants to come in for dinner.

"Is this for Valentino or someone from the company?"

"He said it's for Valentino."

I get so many calls from the offices of various designers saying that so-and-so wants to come in, and it's inevitably some minion just trying to get a reservation. Not that we don't want minions dining at the restaurant, but when you have a wait-list of over a hundred guests and many are VIPs, one needs to be selective. I pick up the phone.

"Michel, Valentino is dying to come dine with you. Could you accommodate a group of six?" I could tell by the voice and the way he asked that it was going to be the actual Valentino. We almost never take parties of six, but I thought I could make it work.

"Of course. We'd love to have you at the restaurant."

An hour or so later I saw a black SUV pull up, and out came five beautifully dressed men with the frail and elderly Valentino in tow. They enter, Valentino walks over to me, he grabs my hand, and I escort him to the table. We briefly chitchat, and when we arrive at the table, he sees that I have a banquette prepared for him. He leans over and whispers in my ear, "Michel, a pillow, *por favor.*"

"Of course."

I run to get one of the pillows we keep for such requests since the banquettes are plush and some guests need a pillow for their backs. When I return, as I go to place it behind his back, he shakes me off, lifts himself up, and says, "For my *culo.*"

I laugh, and as I place the pillow under him, he immediately sits on my hands, which are still on the pillow. He looks at me and with a huge grin says, "*Merci,* Michel!" We all burst into laughter.

Mr. James Beard

THE START OF A new year. The accolades kept coming. Wells was so impressed that in his end-of-year rankings of the top new restaurants in New York City, he listed us as number one. It was nearly impossible to keep up with the demand for reservations as it was. This made it pretty much impossible to secure a table without some connection to the restaurant. We had to increase our reservations staff from one person to three and I spent my mornings responding to reservation requests. Once I was at the restaurant, this continued, and by 8:00 P.M. I would be just about caught up.

As if this weren't enough, we were nominated for the James Beard Award for Best New Restaurant in America. Stephen Starr also received his seventh nomination for Restaurateur of the Year. Many of our guests had Beard affiliations. There were board members, award winners, and nominees, and we were one of the must-go destinations when chefs brought their teams in from out of town to cook at the Beard House. The Beard Awards are the Academy Awards of the food world. Winning this would solidify our place at the top of the dining world. After all the years I'd worked in restaurants, to be acknowledged at this level was pretty fucking cool. I asked Weissmann who from Coucou would be going to the awards, and he said only him and the chef. This was crushing. I needed to be a part of this. I wanted to be there. I wanted us to win. There's no way I wasn't going. Daniel and I were the faces of the restaurant. Rose was of course the king, but I played my part and wanted to be there, especially if we won.

Beard Award winners are selected by a committee of food writers and critics. God knows we had our share in for dinner, and most seemed to like what we did, though it's not as if they'd say anything if they didn't. I'd not heard of the other nominees except for Olmstead restaurant, a cool small spot in Brooklyn whose chef had worked at the heavyweights: Alinea, Per Se, and Blue Hill at Stone Barns. Sutton had given them three stars, Wells two. They had a cool and eclectic menu, with entrées under $20, great reviews, and a working farm in the backyard with crayfish, quail, and veggies. They were the hip upstarts. I thought they'd win. Perhaps there would be a backlash against our elegance, against the expat chef, famous in Paris, returning to cook in the Big Apple, and against the millions of dollars the perpetual Beard Award loser Stephen Starr had pumped into the restaurant.

I decided to pay my own way and take myself to the awards. Except when I saw that the price of a ticket was $500, that idea went out the window. Instead, I decided to work on Stephen. Every chance I'd get, I'd bring up the awards. "Stephen, you need support this year, Coucou has to have a contingency, you need some of us there if we win. It's going to be incredible. You don't want to be there alone." I kept up the pressure, albeit gently. Weissmann had been working on Stephen as well. He told Stephen it wouldn't be right for me not to be there considering how much a part of the culture I had become. Apparently Stephen agreed. Finally, as the day of the awards was closing in, he pulled me aside and told me I was in, but I had to keep it quiet. He didn't want to piss off the other managers and chefs. Are you kidding? I wasn't saying a word. This was going to be a blast.

The Awards

WE WENT TO OUR seats and waited. The evening is long—four-plus hours. The tension was building as we watched awards being handed out in a seemingly endless array of categories. I had no idea when ours would be called. This was taking forever. Weissmann was sitting next to me. We were wrecks, sharing the last of my bourbon, and as I was about to tell him I was heading to the toilet once again, I heard the announcement that Best New Restaurant was up. Finally. Here we go.

The presenters were two guys from some refrigeration company. Couldn't we get an owner or chef to present, or at least someone who worked in a restaurant? Nope. We got two refrigeration guys pushing freezers. Now I'm in a knot, heart pumping, while they talk about the refrigeration business. We were all warned at the beginning of the ceremony that the only ones to accept if we won were Stephen and Daniel. Copy that. Stephen had thirty people there that worked hard and long for him. We all couldn't get on the stage, but, man, wouldn't that be fun? I would be so happy to give my boys a standing ovation if we took the award.

The envelope is opened, the refrigerator man stumbles over the name, and I couldn't tell at first what he said, but then realized he had called out an awful pronunciation of *Le Coucou*. We won. I just about fucking died I was so happy. The whole Starr group screams, as well as the apparently thousands of supporters we had in the audience. It was loud. I jump to my feet, applauding Stephen and Daniel as they stood.

Starr made his way to the stage, got to the first step, and shouted, "Troy!," waving him toward him. Then, as Weissmann headed over, Stephen turned and shouted, "Get Cecchi."

As sappy and stupid and pedestrian and simpleton and egotistical as this sounds, hearing that, I welled up. After thirty-five long years in the business, to be recognized like this blew me away. I stood onstage with Stephen, Rose, and Troy, trying my best not to look like a ridiculous pissant fool. Rose gave a great speech. Then Stephen took the mic. Stephen is a great public speaker, and he didn't disappoint. At the end of his speech, he turned to thank Rose, and then thanked Troy. And then he thanked me, calling me the best maître d'hôtel in New York.

That's it. I was done. After all the years of stress, the pain, the abuse, the long hours, the blown-out knees, the feet that have given out a dozen times, the sadists, the screamers, the owners, the managers, the awful guests—this felt really, really good. We did it.

Starr was up next. His seventh time nominated. Would the award to Coucou impact his chances? Would they give two awards to the same restaurant, or would one be enough? Stephen at least got a restaurant guy to present—Ken Friedman of the Spotted Pig stood at the podium, envelope in hand. As he opened it, there was not a movement, not a sound, from the Starr retinue. Many had their heads down. They'd been here six times before, and each time the name they wanted was never called.

Friedman opened the envelope, looked directly at Starr, sitting in the audience, and said, "Stephen Starr." This was wonderful.

Epilogue

I'm sitting in a restaurant in the East Village with my daughter Olivia, who is now eighteen. We are two years into the pandemic. It's my first time in a restaurant since it began. No one knows me here. I've been out of the game for over two years. It's nice to be able to just sit and watch. This must be our server's first job. He's obviously green, doesn't know the menu, and looked quizzically at me when I asked for a Stoli martini. He doesn't know what Stoli is. He's also apparently forgotten our first course since it's been about twenty minutes, and I see a runner approaching the table with what is obviously our entrees. I was him once, a lifetime ago, when I walked into La Rousse, green, scared, cocky, with zero experience and just enough balls to think I could do it. For me it became a show. My first New York City theater job. I got to play a waiter. What I didn't know was that I'd spend most of my life doing it.

Our young server approaches to see if we're okay. I don't say a word about our appetizers, nod, and tell him everything is fine. He's obviously not an actor and it doesn't seem the other servers are either. This is not their stage. He and the others all seem uninterested in their jobs—college kids looking to make a buck. But I've worked with all of them, or some incarnation of them, a long time ago. We were all looking to make some quick money till the next thing happened. For most of us, the next thing never came. A job born of necessity became a career.

Except many of those I've worked with are gone. Some left the city, defeated, beaten down by the pressure of making it. Others took "real" jobs, ones with health insurance, paid vacations, and all the benefits taken for granted when you're not slinging hash in a restaurant. They left disillusioned with an industry that has historically been brutal to its workers. Left because of the stress of constantly having to be "on" every single night. Left because of the abusive customers, the long hours, never having holidays off. They left because they didn't want to keep standing for hours on end with no breaks, waiting eight to ten hours to finally get to eat, knees and feet slowly giving out. They left because they got sick of having to deal with scurrilous and psychotic owners, belligerent cooks, chefs, and managers. It all takes its toll. And some are gone because they died, victims of a disease that's easily treatable today but which was a frightening death sentence when it first appeared. Though the ones here now, the servers, the bartenders, the runners, they don't know any of this. Not yet. I hope that they have their eyes set on something tangible, not in the business, something they can make a living at that's fair, that they are treated well, and maybe, if they choose to, can support a family with.

The martini is delicious. The bartender knows what he's doing. My daughter is talkative, and I am half listening as I scan the room. I watch the host ignore the person standing right in front of her. She's too engrossed in her phone. I want another martini, but our server is nowhere to be seen. Yes, I stayed in the business and fell into the lifestyle. Living for many years like a vampire. I came alive at night—worked late and went out to play even later—slept sometimes till two or three in the afternoon, then went back to work at four. That can only last so long. I grew up, became somewhat of an adult, got married, had kids.

But the demands of the business never change. The temptations get harder and harder to indulge. The lifestyle wreaks havoc on relationships. It takes a special person to be a partner of someone who works in hospitality. You do your best to make the relationship work, but for many it doesn't. The stress of not being home for dinner five or six nights a week, or coming home after midnight while your partner spends most of the week home alone or taking care of the kids and putting them to bed. What many wind up doing is cycling through partners. And the cycle can be endless, till you wake up one day and you're older and alone.

My daughter asks if I'm okay. "I am," I tell her. She knows I can't help checking out the place, how it's run, who the people working here are, how they operate, where the manager is. She has spent most of her life with a father in the business. She smiles, sees the waiter, beckons him over, and asks him to bring her father another.

I miss many of the ones I've worked with. I can see them standing here as if we were still doing it. The ex-Mormon, Rick the bartender, the comedian. I have no idea where they are or what they are doing, even if they are still alive. Of those I kept in touch with: Uncle Rob is still waiting tables. Arnold, the great GM at Minetta, is still at it, working the floor every night, one hip already replaced, the other about to go as well. Claire has finally quit after two hip replacements and apparently has some new knees in the offing. Chef Neil Kleinberg is still at it—his Clinton Street Bakery as well as his other ventures are a huge success. Al left the business many years ago. The Singer, Rick McKay, is dead. Boyd is dead. The Jock is dead. Of the Three Sisters, one died, one is a bitchy butler, and the other a teacher. The Queen Mother has settled into the life of an estate manager. Girl finally left the business a couple of years ago, thankfully before murdering a guest.

Most of the others I've lost contact with. I sometimes run into a few of the old faces, but this happens less and less often. Every few years I watch a new generation enter the business, and when they try to get me to join them for a few drinks after work, I politely decline and go home to my wife and daughters. I know where that leads, and this body is too beaten up to do it anymore.

Young server drops off dessert menus. Olivia loves dessert. We order Liv's favorite, the panna cotta. She looks at me.

"Dad you're lost in thought. What's going on?"

"Just remembering. We haven't been in a restaurant in a very long time." She smiles.

After Le Coucou I was poached by the Standard Hotel and reopened the Standard Grill with Rocco DiSpirito. The restaurant eventually failed. I then returned to Raoul's as the general manager. They were looking; I needed a job and thought a going "home" of sorts would be good. It's a place I still liked and knew very, very well. But exactly five months later the restaurant closed due to the COVID pandemic. And just like that, it ended. Thirty-five years of working nights and holidays, missing dinner with my family five nights a week, having a schedule opposite to most everyone else's—it just stopped. I've used the time to be with my wife and kids, write a book, and reflect on the business. I've been living a "normal" life—up at 6:00 A.M., in bed at 10:00 P.M. I take my daughter to school every morning, prepare her lunch, then cook dinner and spend the evening watching TV with my wife. All during a pandemic that has destroyed lives and businesses and put an entire planet in turmoil.

But it's also opened the eyes of many in this industry. We've had a chance to rethink the business—who we are, what we do, what we need to do, what we want to do. So many people have refused to go back to their shitty and abusive restaurant jobs that restaurants are desperate for help. Those who choose to stay are now able to ask for more: better pay and benefits. Who knows, a restaurant job may actually become a "real" job.

"Dad, the pandemic is finally coming to an end. What are you going to do now?"

I look around the room. While I will never forget the bad, what I most remember is what I loved. There's nothing like the camaraderie of going into battle each evening with your entire team and seeing how it all unfolds. Like theater, the script rarely changes, but it's a different performance each night. I'd put on my costume, a suit and tie in the late afternoon, and head to the restaurant. I'd check the book to see who was coming in that evening. Plot the seating. See who needed their regular tables, which divorced husband is coming in, and do I have to call the ex and tell her it's best she not stop by tonight. I'd field calls from various PPXs—the UN secretary-general's office wants to see if I am able to squeeze in the secretary that evening; Amal and George want in because they are bringing Justice Sotomayor to dinner; Common absolutely needs to come back and he's only in town tonight. And on it goes.

I miss it. I miss heading to the kitchen to go over the book with the chef, while inhaling the glorious aroma of food being prepped for that night's service. I miss watching and listening to the servers banter while setting up the dining room. I miss the sound of silverware being pulled in heaps from the stations to be set on the tables, the clinking of glasses being polished and set. I miss sitting with the staff and having family meal, listening to what they did last night or where they'll go tonight, the jokes and ribald stories we all shared. I miss the pre-service meeting, listening to the chef talk about that night's specials, going through the list of who of note will be joining us for dinner, announcing the birthdays and anniversaries, hearing the affirmations when I read off the name of a great guest or the moans and groans when I let the staff know a difficult one is coming. I miss opening the front door, letting in the first guests, getting the early seating down, ensuring as best I can that we make the turn for the second seating, greeting the regulars, catching up with them, the hugs, the kisses, the smiles. I miss schmoozing the room, sitting at this table, sharing a bit of wine with that table, checking to see who's at the bar, chatting with those I know, making friends with those I don't.

Even the bad gets better with time. The stress of needing to turn tables, getting the late guests down before the kitchen closes, pushing the servers to drop a check, getting screamed at because a table isn't ready, hiding when I am so deep in the weeds that I want to kill myself and have to head to the bar for a quick shot to kill a bit of the pain before a quick return and jump back into the fray. It's been my life. I suppose this makes me an addict.

"I don't know, Liv." She watches me looking around the room. "Dad, there's only one thing you can do. It's time you opened 'Cecchi's.'" She's right, of course. I've talked many times of opening my own place but there was always a reason not to. Rents were too high, possible investors moved on to other things, not being sure if it's what I really wanted to do—always a reason not to do it. But the pandemic has left opportunities. So many restaurants have closed. So many spaces are available. I pass them on my bike waiting for the right one to speak to me. To say, "This is it. Come and get it." And then one day I found it. It called out to me, and I answered. I've decided to cross the proverbial Rubicon. I've taken a space, signed a lease, and reached out to those still in the business. I'm putting together a team. A team of my own. And this time it'll be all on me as to whether I end up in that 90 percent of restaurants that fail or the 10 percent that succeed.

It's a crazy business. But I can't help loving it. So it's time to come back. It's time to feed the addiction. It's time to let my guests know—their table is ready.

Author's Note

THIS BOOK IS MEANT to both entertain, as well as shed a light on the restaurant world as I experienced it. As an actor I was trained to tell stories. My interactions with guests and fellow employees in the restaurant world allowed me a forum for not only telling stories, but also gave fodder to most of the ones I've written here. Some of these, after years of telling, have at times taken on a life of their own. They are enhanced, having been added to by those who were there and remembered things I'd forgotten or saw things in a different way, and sometimes because memory is a fickle thing. Through necessity, some names and details have been changed.

Additionally, the abuses inherent in the restaurant industry are well documented. For years I was a part of this culture and reaped its rewards, as well as being victimized by it. It is not my intent to demonize certain individuals named or alluded to here, but to the best of my ability document things as I remember them.

Acknowledgments

I MUST FIRST THANK all the amazing guests, friends, family, coworkers, and employees who have listened to these stories over the years. To those who didn't tune me out and said something to the effect of "You have a book here. You should write this shit down," thank you. I did.

I am indebted to Alan Richman, who gave it the first read, took me to school, and tried to show me how to write. Bruce Gibney, whose notes, support, and wisdom of the publishing industry kept me going. To Daniel Rose, one of the first readers, who told me how the book should begin. Chris Patterson, Joe and Tim King, and Troy Weissmann, all who helped me to remember. To my wife, Nina Azzolina, who helped edit. To Judy and Eric Vatne, whose support during the pandemic allowed me to keep writing. Galil Gertner, who read the whole damn thing and gave wonderful notes. Jeff Gordon of Writer's Bootcamp, whose scholarship got me writing again. This book would not be finished without him. Julian Kheel, the best editor and friend anyone could ever have. Doug Davis, who took all of five minutes to help me find an agent. To my agent, Robert Guinsler, I thank you for believing in me. And to my editor, Elizabeth Beier, this would not exist without you.

And of course, to my wife and two daughters, who I love more than anything in the world.

And last, to all those whom I worked alongside who succumbed to AIDS:

Charles Wheatland, Brian Wish, Dolph Hood, "Shirts," George, Rob Jones, Paolo Calamari, Marty DiLorenzo, Richard Thomas, Chip Butler, David Kendig, Brian Straub, Rodney Garbato, John Collison, Aiden Quinn, and Mika Stone. You were all loved.